"Here, Our Culture Is Hard"

BOOK TWO

Louann Atkins Temple Women & Culture Series

Books about women and families, and their changing role in society

"*Here, Our Culture Is Hard*"

Stories of Domestic Violence
from a Mayan Community in Belize

LAURA J. MCCLUSKY

University of Texas Press, Austin

Publication of this book was made possible in part by support from Allison, Doug, Taylor, and Andy Bacon; Margaret, Lawrence, Will, John, and Annie Temple; Larry Temple; the Temple-Inland Foundation; and the National Endowment for the Humanities.

LIBRARY OF CONGRESS CATALOGING-IN-PUBLICATION DATA

McClusky, Laura J., 1963–
Here, our culture is hard : stories of domestic violence from a Mayan community in Belize / Laura J. McClusky.— 1st ed.
        p.   cm. — (Louann Atkins Temple women & culture series)
    Includes bibliographical references and index.
    ISBN 0-292-75248-2 (cloth : alk. paper) — ISBN 0-292-75249-0 (pbk. : alk. paper)
        1. Maya women—Belize—San Antonio—Social conditions.   2. Maya women—Crimes against—Belize—San Antonio.   3. Maya women—Belize—San Antonio—Psychology.   4. Abused wives—Belize—San Antonio.   5. Family violence—Belize—San Antonio.   6. San Antonio (Belize)—Social conditions.   7. San Antonio (Belize)   I. Title.   II. Series.
F1434.2.W65 M33   2001
362.82′92′097282—dc21
                                                    00-048846

This book is dedicated to
the women in southern Belize
who helped me learn about their lives.
I hope it helps them and their daughters
to face the challenges ahead.

It is also dedicated to
the memory of my father, "Pappa Joe."
I miss him greatly.

Contents

Acknowledgments

It is time to birth this project, to send it out into the world on its own. It has had many fathers and influences. Most important are the women whose lives this book is about. The women and men who appear in these pages befriended me, helped me to understand their lives, and openly told me their stories. I am greatly indebted to them, and I hope they find this work as respectful and as helpful as it is meant to be.

Also important are those who helped me to think and write about these stories. The list here is long, including academics, friends, and family. Please excuse me for only mentioning a few. Most important among these people is Robert K. Dentan. He has been my friend and mentor for many years and has spent long hours going over various drafts of this work. His help has been invaluable. Michael Niman has spent many days and nights listening to me talk through some of my fears and worries about writing this book. His support has been long-standing. My mother, Phylis McClusky, has been an inspiration and a model of endurance throughout my life. Her ready sense of humor, easy wit, and emotional support made this project possible.

Christine Eber and Lynn Stephen reviewed the manuscript for the University of Texas Press. Both provided useful suggestions and accurate criticisms that made this a better book. Besides providing these helpful suggestions, Christine has been a supportive and critical friend. Her work and style of being an anthropologist have been inspirational. Susan K. Topa, my sister, provided the illustrations that are scattered throughout this book. Her talents are many, and her work has enhanced this book greatly.

Others who have influenced and fathered this work are Rachel Marcus, Grant Ingram, Deb Crooks, Phillips Stevens, John Mohawk, Charlie Keil, Tom Lechner, Evelyn and Hank Niman, and Elliot Niman. I am indebted to them all.

I am also indebted to the University of Texas Press, especially Theresa May and Rachel Chance. They have both expressed great enthusiasm for and patience with this exceptionally unwieldy text. Thanks also to Carolyn Russ for her careful editing and helpful suggestions.

Introduction

1: The Topic

Why Focus on Domestic Violence? The Haunting

> *You don't choose to write the books you write, any more than you choose your mother, your father, your brother, your children, or your comadre.* (Behar 1993:xi)

> *So-called participant observation has a way of drawing the ethnographer into spaces of human life where she or he might really not prefer to go . . . .* (Scheper-Hughes 1992:xii)

I was sitting on the veranda of the hotel. My companions, two other anthropology graduate students, had left earlier that morning. They went north looking for a field site. I stayed behind, to think. I was enjoying time alone, swinging back and forth in a big colorful hammock. The comfort I felt was important. It was the comfort that let me know that this village would be my field site.

A woman, maybe thirty years old, wearing a bright yellow dress and carrying a multicolored plastic woven handbag, appeared at the top of the steps. I smiled at her, dismissively, and tried to ignore her. I knew she would try to sell me some baskets or embroidery, and I didn't feel like buying just then. I was busy planning my future. I was trying to think about what sort of project I could do here. In my graduate training I was interested in a wide variety of subjects. I had written my master's thesis on dream theory, but I also had interests in midwifery, health and healing, and concepts of self and gender. I was all over the place, really.

The woman smiling at the top of the stairs, I later found out, was named Antonia. On that day, when we first met, she sat down on a bench along the railing and ignored my attempts to ignore her. She giggled and smiled. Her top incisors were missing, making her canines look like fangs. Still giggling, Antonia pulled samples of baskets and embroidery from her handbag, as I knew she would, and carefully placed each one on the bench next to her.

"I'm not interested in baskets or embroidery, thanks." I forced a sweet little smile across my face. I faced her so she could see my smile, so she could see I wasn't rude. I didn't look at her, though. Eye contact gets me into trouble with vendors. It traps me into buying, and I didn't want to buy. I already had enough. Deb, one of my companions, was already saying I had too many and was reminding me of the time we spent together in Guatemala, when I hauled a backpack full of textiles and jade and wood carvings all over the country due to my inability to say no to vendors.

Antonia giggled.

"REALLY," a little sterner, my smile a little more taut, "I don't WANT any."

That's when she began to stare at me. I could feel her gaze on the side of my face. She was trying to trap me, a big fish in her net. But I was holding my ground. I was stubborn. I just kept swinging, back and forth, back and forth, silently. If she looked away for just a moment I would escape from this standoff. I would get out of the hammock and go to my room where she couldn't follow. So I waited, silent, swinging. She'd have to give up and look away.

When, finally, she did look away, it surprised me. I could tell she wasn't packing up her wares. She wasn't giving up. She wanted my attention. Without her gaze on the side of my face, I didn't know what she was doing. I became intrigued. I looked at her. She had her hands in her lap, and her head was bowed. Her soft whispery voice, barely audible, asked, "Do you like men?"

What kind of a question was that? "Do you like men?"! Did I hear her right? Was this some kind of proposition?

"Excuse me?"

"Do you like men?" She spoke a little louder, shifted her gaze from her hands to the mountain view. "I don't." She glanced at me. I expected a giggle but none came. "My husband, he lash me too much."

I stopped swinging. I couldn't respond. Emotionally, I was frozen. I couldn't speak, I couldn't move. I was blank. Not only was emotion blocking me, but I didn't know what to say if I could speak. In the States, I would tell the woman to get help, to contact a women's shelter, to leave her abusive husband. Here, I didn't know what to say. I didn't know what options she had; I didn't know who she was or if what she said was true. I was upset that she would pull me into such a mess when I wasn't even part of the village yet. All the warnings I had heard about upsetting a field site, being careful not to ally oneself with any particular faction, being careful not to make waves, all of that flashed through my mind. I said nothing. I stood up and went into my room as I had planned.

Writing this today, I still feel the chill in my spine, my inability to move, my inability to speak. I still ask myself, How could I have been so cold? So selfish?

I know women in the States who have left abusive partners. We rarely talk about it, though. The knowledge just hovers between us; only occasionally do we let it affect our emotions or our time together. We never talk about it without some sort of preparation, without some sort of warning, never spontaneously, never out of the blue as Antonia did. Nor have I ever been approached by a stranger in the States who told me her partner beat her. Of all the topics strangers have confided in me during "bus experiences," long encounters with strangers wanting to tell other strangers their woes, domestic violence has never been raised.

When I returned to the States, Antonia's desire to talk and my inability to listen haunted me. When a man I was dating confronted me, saying that he didn't like the way my anger tended to be violent, Antonia's stare hit me across the face again. When the *Buffalo News* Sunday magazine ran a cover story about spousal abuse, complete with color photos of a battered woman in a blood-stained powder blue housecoat (Deed 1991), I remembered the way I blocked Antonia's attempts to talk.

So, I Started Studying the Topic

When I found almost no anthropological discussion of wife-beating or battering, I called Judy Brown for help. Because of her long interest and considerable expertise in women's issues, I knew that if anyone would be familiar with the anthropological literature on wife-beating and battering it would be Judy. Intrigued with the problem, Judy did her own search of the literature. Her research results were similar to mine; clearly anthropologists had ignored or had glossed over with throw-away one-liners a topic of serious dimensions and great importance to women.   (Counts 1992:xi)

I found hundreds of articles and books by sociologists, psychologists, and political activists presenting theories, case histories, and statistics on domestic violence in the United States and England. Surprisingly, my own discipline had little to offer. There were only a few articles and just one monograph written specifically about domestic violence from an anthropological perspective (Levinson 1989). All, at the time, rested on cross-cultural analysis using the Human Relations Area File (HRAF).

I didn't know that Dorothy Counts, Judith Brown, and Jacquelyn Campbell had organized a session for the 1987 American Anthropological Association, and three sessions and a symposium for the Association for Social Anthropology in Oceania between 1986 and 1988, on the topic of domestic violence. These were the first organized attempts anthropologists had made to discuss the topic seriously. I was excited when, in 1992, two years after my first visit to Belize, their book, a collection of papers presented during those sessions, appeared (Counts, Brown, and Campbell 1992). The book is the first anthropological collection of ethnographic articles focusing on domestic violence. Finally, eight years after Gerald Erchack (1984) called on anthropologists to take domestic violence seriously and contribute to our understanding of the problem, the topic had been broached.

While I am happy my discipline is beginning to discuss domestic violence, I am reminded of a phrase my Belizean friends would use when I thought I was being generous by offering a small gift: Only this? The number of anthropologists who focus on domestic violence is few.

It is true anthropologists haven't completely ignored the issue. Indeed, rereading Mayan ethnographies, I found a scattering of anecdotal information, enough to know that Antonia was not unique (Wisdom 1940, Wagley 1949, Bunzel 1967, Danziger 1991). Bunzel even proposes a theory to explain the high prevalence of wife abuse in Chichicastenango. She suggests that men are frustrated by social requirements to remain monogamous and to gain sexual satisfaction from wives chosen by parents for reasons other than sexual attractiveness. Bunzel proposes an alternative theory as well, suggesting that men need to beat their wives in order to feel they control their own lives, to build a sense of manhood.

Other Mayanists have discussed spouse abuse in the context of their work on alcohol use (Eber 1995) or gender dynamics (Rosenbaum 1993). Scholars of domestic violence would classify their data as supporting the status-inconsistency theory. Status-inconsistency theory suggests that in societies maintaining a gender hierarchy, men are likely to beat their wives if their wives reach a status higher than their own. Husbands beat wives in order to maintain a status consistent with the requirements of the gender hierarchy. Eber and Rosenbaum (1993) say essentially the same when discussing increases in "marital tension" resulting from women benefitting from the global market for Mayan women's weavings.

Scholars of women's movements and social revolutions in Latin America have also raised the topic of domestic violence (Alvarez 1990, 1994, Jaquette 1994, Stephen 1997, Hernández Castillo 1997). Many Latin American women's movements have organized around the issue of domestic violence, trying to decrease its rate and ensure support for victims of abuse. Most scholars, however, rarely look at the violence itself, rather, they focus on the organizing.

Some scholars have also pointed to the fact that men sometimes violently punish their wives for participating in women's marches and other activities associated with women's movements (Hernández Castillo 1997, Stephen 1997). Such scholars tend to place their understanding of domestic violence within patriarchal theory, emphasizing the ways men use many types of violence, including rape, to control women politically, economically, and sexually. Few scholars coming from this framework recognize domestic violence as a unique form of violence against women.

In general, anthropologists who discuss domestic violence have treated it as a symptom of patriarchy, or as an issue women organize around to gain rights, rather than seeing it as a social phenomenon within a specific cultural context. Few have taken domestic violence as a primary topic. Why?

Problems with Studying Domestic Violence: "It's a Closed Topic"

The problems I least expected about doing research on domestic violence were financial. My first hint came when a faculty member warned me that I would never get grant money if I were to submit proposals to study domestic violence. "It's a closed topic," she said. Her discomfort, she stressed, came from her belief that the topic would never get funded, and she felt getting funding was an important part of building a good curriculum vitae. She never expressed concern about the topic itself.

Gerald Erchack, with whom I was in contact before I went to Belize, agreed that the topic would never get funded. He had tried to study spousal abuse in Micronesia in the early 1980s but faced a wall of harsh reviews, causing him to reroute to the United States. Later, he published his thoughts on why anthropologists have avoided the topic (Erchack 1994). Anthropologists, he says, are uninvited guests of the people they study. As a result, they tend to turn a blind eye to the less savory elements of native cultures. For many, it isn't polite or ethical to focus on certain topics. While this practice is understandable, he suggests, it harms our understanding of domestic violence as a social phenomenon.

Anthropologists do turn a blind eye to less savory elements of native cultures for ethical reasons; likewise, granting agencies will not fund projects on domestic violence out of ethical concerns. Anthropologists should first and foremost be advocates of the people they write about. They shouldn't focus on topics that make their subjects' lives difficult. That concern is reflected in our professional code, *Professional Ethics: Statements and Procedures of the American Anthropological Association,* under "Principles of Professional Responsibility, Section 1."

> In research, an anthropologist's paramount responsibility is to those he studies. When there is a conflict of interest, these individuals must come first. The anthropologist must do everything within his power to protect their physical, social and psychological welfare and to honor their dignity and privacy.   (AAA 1973:1)

The problem in determining whether a study of domestic violence CAN be ethical comes from how one defines those who are being studied. The people I am "studying" are women. It is these women I put first. By telling the stories of their lives and their experiences with domestic violence, I hope to protect their physical, social, and psychological welfare. By showing their strength in dealing with the violence they face, I honor their dignity; by keeping them anonymous, I honor their privacy.

Counts (1992:xi) experienced numerous negative responses to her attempts to make domestic violence an anthropological topic.[1] The one she discusses is the idea that, by studying domestic violence, we would be imposing a political agenda, inappropriately and possibly harmfully, on the host society. I agree with her response. Anthropologists are frequently "caught between our own ethnocentrism on the one hand and the sterile aloofness of extreme relativism on the other" (Counts 1992: xii). She reminds us that, yes, it is important to keep our sense of values and sensibilities in check when doing our work. However, many people where anthropologists work see domestic violence as a problem and are interested in addressing the problem. Our work can assist their efforts.

I find anthropologists' treatment of domestic violence as a "closed topic" bizarre. We have regularly dealt with unsavory topics: cannibalism, infanticide, ritual warfare, suttee, genital mutilation, the spread of AIDS, foot binding, colonization, witchcraft, and genocide, to name a few. Wrestling with unsavory topics is really what we do best.

We are comfortable talking about the injustice and violence indigenous populations have suffered at the hands of white European peoples. We are less comfortable talking about the injustices and violence that indigenous peoples have suffered at the hands of their own, thereby perpetuating a kind of paternalistic sentimentality (Dentan 1995:229, Iyer 1989:13). Topics in this second category, especially domestic violence, are unspeakable. Why?

Perhaps domestic violence is not exotic enough. Unlike foot binding, unlike suttee, unlike cannibalism, we ourselves perform this ugliness, just like "exotic" cultures. Perhaps studying an ugliness that we share causes categorical confusion and therefore aversion (Douglas 1966). Anthropology is part of a Western tradition that places native Others into one of two categories. We "represent" the "Other" as Noble Savages, whose lifeways hold the key for our own salvation from our own destructive cultural norms. We also "represent" the "Other" as somehow less than human, practicing barbaric rites that we, as members of an enlightened world, must come to understand. In order for differing peoples to inhabit the world, we must come to understand why others do the things they do and what function their actions have within their society. Domestic violence disrupts this binary legacy in anthropology. It crosses the line, blurring us and them. Perhaps that is why it is taboo.

Or perhaps it is taboo because it is just too ugly. That is how I felt in the field, especially when I met Antonia a second time. This time she came to visit my neighbor's house while I was there. We were stripping dried corn from cobs and talking when she arrived. I stared at her face, unable to speak. I listened to her tell how her husband hit her with a big piece of firewood the night before. I was disgusted as the swollen, deep purple bruise across her face contorted when she laughed. She was laughing at me because I was so amazed. She laughed because my reaction strengthened her belief that women in the United States never experience battery. I couldn't convince her otherwise, even though I tried.

Women in the United States do experience spousal abuse. In fact, the U.S. statistics are overwhelming. Battery is the single major cause of injury to women, more than car accidents, muggings, and rapes combined (Stark and Flitcraft 1988:301). According to the U.S. Department of Justice, there were 4.1 million cases of family violence between 1973 and 1981. The Justice Department estimates that 450,000 cases of abuse develop annually (U.S. Department of Justice 1984). Recently, in my own part of the world, western New York, six men killed their female partners in a six-month period (Warner 1998). In Erie County, New York, an average of 20 percent of the homicides reported are the result of domestic violence (Warner 1998). Furthermore, as in other parts of the United States, women in western New York are far more commonly the victims of such physical abuse than are men (Browne 1987, Kurz 1989). Women in the United States also suffer far more injuries from spousal abuse than do men (Berk et al. 1983, Kurz 1987, McLeer and Anwar 1989, Stark et al. 1979).

The physical effects of being beaten by one's male partner in the States vary: minor contusions, missing teeth, fractures, severe burns, and spontaneous abortions. Further dangers to a battered woman's health take the form of drug and alcohol abuse (Gelles and Straus 1988:136, Stark and Flitcraft 1988:302). Drug use among battered women increases both from self-medication and from physicians' attempts to relieve their overanxious, apparently overstressed patients.

Psychological problems are also common. Battered women tend to suffer from low self-esteem, feelings of helplessness, worthlessness, and powerlessness (Davidson 1978, Gelles and Straus 1988, Dobash and Dobash 1979). Many are ashamed of being beaten and feel responsible for the beatings (Gelles and Straus 1988, Dobash and Dobash 1979). Abused women think about and actually commit suicide more often than nonabused women (Gelles and Straus 1988, Stark and Flitcraft 1988:304). Women respond to continual physical abuse with emotional numbness, sexual dysfunction, and general desperation (Davidson 1978, Dobash and Dobash 1979). Physicians are also more likely to refer battered women for emergency psychiatric treatment, labeling them hysteric, neurotic, and hypochondriacal (Stark and Flitcraft 1988:303). Finally, abused women in the United States say that they express their anger violently (Gelles and Straus 1988). Violence therefore begets violence.

Most social-science research on wife battery in the United States and England has taken place since the 1970s, after the women's movement brought the topic to light. The women's movement led scholars to examine the problem, and the women's movement in turn has benefitted from social scientists' efforts to understand domestic violence. Research has helped the women's movement to coax the issue out of the closet and has sparked anti-abuse advertising campaigns, the establishment of shelters, and the development of group therapies for both batterers and their victims. Battery in the United States is becoming recognized as a serious health care issue. The tendency for doctors to treat the symptoms of wife battery without dealing with the abusive situation or without even questioning the patient about her home situation is currently under challenge (Chez 1988, Chez and Jones 1995, Sheridan 1993, Sheridan and Campbell 1989, Kurz 1987, Greany 1984).

Yet anthropologists have done little to contribute to American efforts to understand domestic violence. Keeping domestic violence a closed topic protects it both in the places we do fieldwork and in the United States. We could do a lot better than we are doing.

A Problem with the Literature: Where Have All the People Gone?

Our very idea of what a human being is, how a family thrives or fails, and how love and fear shape our lives are all given over to experts in white coats and translated into cold, quantified studies.

(Moore 1996:28–29)

For a while we were able to keep our distance. We handed out surveys to college students. Later we ventured out into the community to interview people in their homes. Still, we were insulated by the scientific approach and the numbers. Always the numbers enabled us to remain detached.

(Gelles and Straus 1988:12)

We base this conclusion on a cost-benefit ratio, which we calculated for each of the eight strategies used by victims of

> *violence. The ratio was computed by dividing the percent of*
> *women who said a strategy was effective by the percent who said*
> *the approach made things worse.*   (Gelles and Straus 1988:155)

That day on the veranda, I realized I was frightened by domestic violence. Confronted with the reality, I wanted to flee. Domestic violence made me feel helpless, and I didn't like that feeling.

Back in the States I could read about domestic violence at a safe distance, far from people's suffering, far from that woman with her baskets. But how strange that is. After the initial comfort, I became amazed by the realization that many of the books and articles I was reading had no people in them. Their pages were filled with statistics and analyses. Among these peopleless pages one might find a short chapter or paragraph describing the types of women abused and the types of men who abused them, but that is all. I got no feel for their lives when they weren't being beaten, when they were shopping, eating dinner, fixing their cars, or playing with their children. The descriptions were cartoonish. It was as if the people were not important. Only the systems, cycles, and numbers counted.

This eerie depopulation is common to social-science depictions of violence and may contribute to our acceptance of atrocities (Dentan 1999, 1997a). To dehumanize violence and to depopulate our depictions of violence is to take the bite out of the offense. If violence occurs and we obscure the victim, does that violence have significance? Can we come to understand the sometimes violent responses of the "victims" (Dentan 1999)? Can we understand "resistance" in any form (Ortner 1995)?

The peopleless books and articles I read about domestic violence reminded me of some ethnographies I have read, especially those influenced by anthropology's struggle to be a science. These ethnographies give the feeling that culture and social systems exist on their own, devoid of people. They provide no clue that people, moving, thinking, emotional people, are a necessary ingredient for cultures and social systems to exist. It is important to say that anthropology has been moving in many directions, and such ethnographies are becoming rare. However, it is ironic how often in the past, and into the present, that the study of people has been so depopulated. It is only recently, with the idea of reflexivity, that the ethnographer has even included herself in her text.

The opposite extreme is also typical of literature on domestic violence. There are books filled with case histories. The author presents us with people, specific women suffering pain. But again the emphasis is on the abuse they suffer. They themselves are faceless women carrying pseudonyms. The author may tell us something of their background, usually to show that domestic violence happens in all kinds of homes. The author does not portray women's experiences, wants, or desires outside of their experiences with violence. Often they fail to discuss women's efforts to change their lives.

Certainly case histories have done much to highlight domestic violence in the United States. It is undeniable that they have provided a useful method for understanding and theorizing about the problem. They have also allowed many women to speak out about the experiences they have tried to hide so hard for so long. Case histories have provided inspiration for others to seek help. However, they often leave us feeling pity; a patronizing sympathy that separates (healthy, strong) unbeaten us from (sick, weak) beaten them.

Indeed, some scholars of domestic violence and advocates working to help women to leave abusive relationships have emphasized the fact that abused women are "survivors," not "victims" (Dobash and Dobash 1992, Hoff 1990, Gondolf 1988, Bowker 1983). They question the degree to which "learned helplessness" characterizes battered women. Indeed, their studies show that battered women are not passive, nor do they enjoy being beaten. Women continually try to enlist help from friends, family members, and authorities, to little or no avail. They emphasize women's attempts to change their lives.

Likewise, feminist theorists have recognized and criticized anthropologists' tendency to portray Third World women as passive victims unable or, worse, unwilling to affect their destiny (Mohanty 1988, Hernández Castillo 1997). Both groups of critics, those who criticize "learned helplessness" and those who criticize anthropology, reflect the current feminist focus on women's activism in women's terms (Harding 1986:31, DuBois et al. 1985). They emphasize women's "activity" and reject the tendency to portray women as passive victims of complex and pervasive structures of domination like "patriarchy" or "capitalism."

This book is within this emerging tradition. Like Hernández Castillo's (1997) work on Mayan women who are trying to include issues of women's rights in the Zapatista rebellion in Chiapas, this work focuses on women's attempts to change their lives. It also discusses the social forces that facilitate and frustrate their efforts. Unlike Hernández Castillo's (1997) work, however, it does not deal with women's collective resistance. Instead, it deals with individuals working within specific life situations. My emphasis is on variation among women rather than on how women find similarities in their lives.

Anthropology, influenced by hermeneutics and following a linguistic model for understanding culture, has also become interested in "agency": how people affect the world around them, using, manipulating, challenging, and creating "culture" (Marcus and Fischer 1986: 27–30, Stewart 1988:1–13, Ortner 1995:183–187, DuBois et al. 1985:40–48). In this way, anthropological theory suggests that people create culture through a dialectic process of understanding and giving meaning to their actions and the events that happen around them, rather than following static rules of behavior. In other words, anthropologists are now thinking about culture as a repertoire, a system of possible understandings and actions, rather than a code, a limited and prescribed way of being.

This book is meant to fit within the "repertoire" trend of anthropology. However, rather than argue the ways Maya give meaning to domestic violence or the ways Maya create the concept of abuse, it demonstrates them. Within these stories of women's experiences with, or reactions to, wife abuse are examples of the ways Maya legitimize wife abuse and of the ways young women are beginning to redefine gender in efforts to curb future abuse. This work emphasizes repertoire over code, actions over passivity.

As an anthropologist, I try to place Mayan domestic violence in the context of Mayan lifeways. My purpose is to establish an understanding of Mayan women, not to use them as a metaphor for ourselves or to "colonialize" their experiences (Mohanty 1988). This goal is also in line with current feminist theory, which has begun to complicate and deconstruct the category "woman," rather than assume women all over have similar lives and experiences (Behar and Gordon 1995, Alcoff 1988, Moore 1988, Flax 1987). Therefore, I spend little time in this work comparing Mayans' experiences with those of women from other culture groups. Nor do I assume Mayan women are some primitive form of Western middle-class white women. Instead, I have tried to represent a specific linguisic and cultural group of Maya, Mopan, in a specific geographic location, southern Belize, in as complete detail as I can.

I should note, however, that I assume Mopan women in Belize share certain life experiences and sensibilities with women from other Mayan groups. I have surveyed the works written by Mayanists to place the experiences of the women I met into a larger Mayan context. I do this even though few Maya recognize or espouse pan-Mayanism. Maya tend to identify and understand themselves on much more local terms, often through village of birth. My assumption may be wrong, or at least limited; it is, however, common among anthropologists. Certainly, as my relationship with Mopan women develops, I will come to know these limits better. Until then, the reader should be aware that my tendency to understand Mopan lives through a pan-Mayanism may result more from "looking to the literature" or following the traditions of my discipline, than from asking the right questions when I was in the field.

Due to the conditions of my field experience, this study is "woman-centered" (Scheper-Hughes 1992, Eber 1995). Women talked often and openly about abuse. Unprompted, they told me stories of the abuse they, their daughters, and their friends had suffered. Women often included me in discussions about marriage and violence, sometimes imagining scenarios in which my husband beats me. One woman enlisted my help in her efforts to leave her abusive partner.

Mayan men and women live in separate spheres. Although a complementary project of understanding domestic violence from a man's point of view, examining men's roles as perpetrators and as victims of domestic violence, would be interesting,[2] I never felt comfortable in the men's world. I had trouble developing an easy rapport with men, even though some of them are good friends of mine. As a result, I never talked to men about wife abuse and none ever raised the topic with me. Because I have little information about men's thoughts on abuse, few men appear in these pages. Most appear as batterers. I have tried to convey, especially within the narratives, the complicated feelings and understandings I developed about these men.

2: Style

Narrative Ethnography

> *Indeed, it is difficult to classify these portraits. They are neither fiction nor conventional anthropology.* (Lewis 1959:18)

> *Products of the "imagination," such as novels, can be especially useful tools for understanding how things work in societies far removed from our own experience. Through the telling of a story,*

a sound ethnographic novel conveys more than information. It involves the reader in the dynamics of life in places where the rules for action are very different from the rules the reader makes his own decisions by.   (Wilson 1974:1)

The style of this ethnography differs from previous studies of Maya in Belize. This style has various names. Oscar Lewis calls it "ethnographic realism" (Lewis 1959:18).[3] Carter Wilson (1974) uses the term "ethnographic novel"; Clifford Geertz (1988:141) uses the term "faction." I prefer the term "narrative ethnography," because the goal is to tell a story.[4] In fact, I want to tell several stories of several women.

Narrative ethnography is not new to Mesoamerican studies. Ricardo Pozas, a Mexican anthropologist, published *Juan the Chamula,* an "ethnological re-creation of the life of a Mexican Indian," in Mexico in 1952. Ten years later, the University of California Press published an English translation. The translator of the 1962 version said that, "Although the author's primary purpose was not literary, his book has come to be considered one of the most effective treatments of Indian themes in contemporary Mexican literature." Refreshingly, Pozas gives no justification for using the narrative form; he just writes it. He is concerned, however, that a fictional autobiography in the first person might not provide the cultural and historical background readers need. Therefore, he gives a brief account of Tzotzil culture in the introduction.

Like Pozas, Oscar Lewis does not spend time justifying his use of narrative in *Five Families* (1959). He is more concerned with promoting peasant studies. However, he does link his justification for using the day as a unit of analysis with a brief explanation of the narrative form. In a sense, he conflates the two. There is really nothing intrinsic to the analysis of a day that makes it "an excellent medium for combining the scientific and humanistic aspects of anthropology" (Lewis 1959:18). It is his use of narrative ethnography that does this.

For Carter Wilson (1974), narrative ethnography, like his *Crazy February: Death and Life in the Mayan Highlands of Mexico,* can "convey more than information" and can be "'true to the spirit' of the place" that it tries to describe (Wilson 1974:2). Indeed, it is this spirit, missing in traditional ethnographies, that is narrative ethnography's strength.

Wilson addresses the criticism that ethnographic novels are like field notes, unanalyzed statements of field experiences. Playing on the title of Lévi-Strauss' (1969) famous work, he suggests ethnographic novels are "cooked" rather than "raw." Authors of ethnographic novels process and analyze their raw data, or field notes. They choose to include certain things, in certain ways, and they choose to exclude other things altogether. Information in ethnographic novels is therefore not raw data, but rather is carefully chosen and presented.

Wilson's defense of ethnographic novels as processed (and therefore analyzed) data is echoed in later suggestions that all ethnographies are "fictions," since the Latin root *fingere* glosses as constructed or fashioned (Clifford and Marcus 1986:6). We often think of fiction as untrue, contrived statements with a limited base in reality. However, the degree to which fictive events are based on lived experience is up to the author. Wilson, for instance, tells us that he made every effort to base his work on "actuality," a mix of real experiences and projected possibilities in the flavor of the place and time about which he writes (Wilson 1974:2).

Indeed, no representation can be true in the sense of being complete, free from the constraints of linear text or the imposition of the cultural conventions of any given epistemology. At best, a representation can be a partial truth (Clifford 1986:6), based on a certain perspective or particular understanding. It is impossible to convey a complete reality through a single text, because reality is a complex understanding of that which is around us. Much of reality cannot be accurately described, just as the telling of a dream never feels true to the dream itself. But this philosophical approach to defending narrative forms wasn't part of Wilson's thinking, at least not as he represents it in the introduction to his narrative ethnography. It is only within the past ten to fifteen years, during an "experimental moment," that anthropology has taken up questions of representation.

The Crisis of Representation

While ethnography has taken various forms in the past, such as Oscar Lewis' narrative representations of Mexican peasants, it is only recently that anthropologists have begun problematizing and theorizing about the nature of ethnographic representations. Anthropology is not alone. Those interested in this aspect of anthropology are finding allies in "law, art, architecture, philosophy, literature, and even the natural sciences" (Marcus and Fischer 1986:7). Indeed, anthropology's "crisis of representation" can be situated within the "postmodern condition" of Lyotard (1988), the "crisis of legitimation" of Habermas (1975), and, perhaps, within Thomas Kuhn's (1962) discussion of paradigmatic shifts within the sciences.

For anthropology, the crisis of representation is a problematizing of the ways and means by which anthropologists represent "Others." Basically, the movement has taken ethnography to be a literary phenomenon with accepted styles and rules, guided by the spoken and unspoken rules of Western intellectual traditions. That is, ethnographies are cultural artifacts. They are complicated representations, which can be examined in their own right and should not be confused as simple translations of culture (Hastrup 1990:55).

Likewise, the crisis of representation is a problematizing of cultural anthropology's primary research method: participant observation or fieldwork. Rather than calling the method into question as unscientific, anthropologists are investigating its messy, complicated, dialogic nature. Some anthropologists have shifted from thinking that a good fieldworker can eventually obtain "truth," to stressing the idea that there are many truths, or ways of understanding a given phenomenon within a culture. Furthermore, the translation of those truths is much more complicated than standard forms of ethnography can convey.

This crisis of representation is not unique to what has come to be called postmodern or poststructuralist anthropology. Feminist scholars have also been interested in these issues. Indeed, feminist scholars have emphasized the power relations behind who gets to make truth claims and who does not. This has led many feminist anthropologists into collaborative projects with women from Third World nations, across disciplines and within the field of anthropology, to produce works about women's lives (Stephen 1994, Behar 1993, Eber and Rosenbaum 1993). Scholars vary in their willingness to recognize the role of feminist theories in recognizing and dealing with the crisis of representation (Behar and Gordon 1995, Clifford and Marcus 1986).

The Experimental Moment

> *So what will come of this? Some of our colleagues will not notice that "an experimental moment in the human sciences" (Marcus and Fischer 1986) has come and gone; others have already dismissed it; some of us will find ourselves more self-conscious about what we do in the field and how we write about what we did when we return home; some of us will not be aware*

of how much we have changed until some fearless graduate
student draws it to our attention in a term paper; some of us will
gradually drift off into writing fiction.   (Wolf 1992:138–139)

As Wolf suggests, the crisis of representation affects anthropologists differently. The movement may not be important to many. Indeed, it probably shouldn't create the paranoia, hatred, and confusion that it does. In these competitive times, however, the so-called "postmodern" or "post-structural" movement has led to many harsh words in writing, at professional meetings, and certainly, with perhaps its greatest ferocity, in graduate-student lounges.

Those sympathetic to the movement are affected in different ways. Some have taken on the role of literary critics, evaluating the anthropologist as author and focusing on the genre of ethnography as a written text rather than as an unproblematic representation of another lifeway (Geertz 1988, Clifford 1988, Clifford and Marcus 1986, van Maanen 1988).

Others, continuing with the basic anthropological task of describing lifeways, have included some of the topics highlighted by the crisis. For example, Behar (1993) frames her work as a border crossing, investigating, among other things, the relationship between a Cubana ethnographer (herself) and a Mexicana street vendor (her key informant). The relationship between subjects and author has become a common topic in this experimental moment (see Rabinow 1977, Dumont 1978, Crapanzano 1980).

Still others are experimenting with form, diverging from the ethnographic realism of traditional ethnographies. For example, Tedlock (1991) presents an ethnographic novel which makes use of juxtaposition to compare Zuni and white American understandings of the world. Dentan (1998, 1997b) explores Semai relationships to the violence of slavery by describing ritual possessions through the eyes of the possessing spirits. He also uses the literary device of juxtaposition to develop a theory of violation, which helps to understand the effects of violence both among African American youth and among Semai.

It is within this climate of exciting experimentation and worrisome divisions within the discipline that I present this work: a narrative ethnography, of sorts; a standard ethnography, of sorts. My approach is not unique, nor is it especially innovative. Others have done the same or something similar (Eber 1995, Stephen 1997, Scheper-Hughes 1992,

Wolf 1992). This book is, however, part of a growing trend of experiments, a trend that makes room for newly legitimate ways of knowing and many ways of understanding.

Why Narratives? Reasons for This Experiment

*Until anthropologists can deal rigorously with the "subjective
factors" in the lives of "primitives" their work will be flat and
insubstantial. Unless they can learn to delineate the emotional
structure of societies, serious persons who wish to learn about the
life of human beings in groups will properly continue to turn to
literature rather than science for enlightenment.*
                          (Kluckhohn, quoted in Stewart 1988:4)[5]

*The fictional form of presentation devised by the editor
[Elsie Clews Parsons] has definite merit. It allows a freedom in
depicting or suggesting the thoughts and feelings of the Indian,
such as is impossible in a formal, scientific report.*
                          (Kroeber 1922:13)

In Mama Lola, *I am most interested in telling rich, textured
stories that bring Alourdes and her religion alive . . . [M]y aim is
to create an intimate portrait of three-dimensional people who are
not stand-ins for an abstraction such as "the Haitian people" but
rather are deeply religious individuals with particular histories
and rich interior lives . . . [I]n other words my aim is to create a
portrait of Vodou embedded in the vicissitudes of particular lives.*
                          (Brown 1991:14–15)

*Anthropologists need to try out different styles of representation,
in the Taoist tradition that doing something beats talking about it.*
                          (Dentan 1997a:4)

I choose to write narratives about domestic violence for several reasons. First, I feel narrative ethnography is particularly appropriate for this culture group. Pozas' concern that readers may lack the historical or cultural knowledge to understand a narrative ethnography is softened by the fact that several anthropologists have worked with Mopan Maya in southern Belize. Their ethnographies provide the background for a greater understanding of the characters and their stories. Reciprocally, this ethnography provides greater understanding of previous ethnographies by presenting the "spirit" Wilson talks about. My characters are people living in particular life situations that make up the culture, society, and language of those earlier works, albeit somewhat changed with the passage of time.

Even when their discipline required them to be as "scientific" as possible (Stewart 1988:1–3), anthropologists have suggested that literary forms can provide an understanding of humanity that standard ethnographies cannot. What Kroeber identifies as thoughts and feelings, Kluckhohn (1945:79–163) groups together with motivations, emotions, and personality as "subjective factors." These aspects of humanity are absent in standard ethnographies, making them somewhat peopleless. Perhaps narrative ethnography, with its promise to focus on people rather than social structures (Stewart 1988:13) and its ability to represent subjective factors, can rehumanize anthropological research.

As previously stated, students of violence have suggested that it is important to avoid representing violence in ways that dehumanize the issue since doing so obfuscates the danger violence presents and thereby makes it more acceptable (Dentan 1999, 1997a, 1995; Brass 1997; Daniel 1996). Likewise, scholars of domestic violence have warned that certain depictions of abused women leave the impression that such women are passive victims rather than active survivors struggling to escape or prevent the abuses they suffer. Furthermore, critics of anthropology have suggested that ethnographers too often portray Third World women as passive, almost pathetic beings. All of these problems are based, at least to some extent, on the dehumanizing form social-science research takes. Perhaps narrative ethnography's promise to rehumanize research, to create rich textured portraits of three-dimensional peoples, as Brown states, will alleviate some of these problems.

Indeed, narrative ethnography may have even more to offer. It is ironic that anthropologists, who take holism as a basic tenet, break up their works into chapters titled "Religion," "Kinship," and "Economy." The narrative form can allow ethnographers greater room to describe the holistic nature of social systems by demonstrating how culture works. Focusing on people within a social system as participants within a cultural understanding facilitates an ethnographer's representation of how individuals affect these systems as well as how these systems limit people's lives. This is the kind of holism Ortner (1995:173–174) suggests is integral to the ethnographic method and unique to ethnographic understandings. Narrative ethnography may be better suited for presenting living culture (Stewart 1988:13). As Dentan suggests in the above epigraph, I am willing to give it a try.

3: Structure

Writing the Narratives

I describe my field methods in the following chapter. Here, I will discuss my methods of writing. The characters in the narratives are all based on real people. The Michael who appears here is my real-life life-mate, and Rachel is the real name of a dear friend. Both have agreed to allow their names to appear here. All other names are pseudonyms.

Occasionally, I have blended people together to make conglomerate characters. For the most part these are minor characters. Their conglomeration is to prevent the reader from being bombarded with too many characters. Having one stand in for the other doesn't change the impact of the events in narratives.

I have chosen to portray myself as a character in this ethnography. Doing so is part of a trend in anthropology to demystify the construction of "anthropological facts." As Scheper-Hughes (1992:25) states:

> By showing, as I go along, the ways that I work in the field, offering glimpses behind the scenes, I hope to give the reader a deeper appreciation of the way in which ethnographic "facts" are built up in the course of everyday participation in the life of the community.

I also feel that this practice helps to rehumanize the social sciences. Describing how social scientists create knowledge places the emphasis on people rather than the sometimes vague phrases and descriptions that make up theory.

The events within the narrative are, for the most part, exactly how I remember them. I spent long hours taking notes in the field. I have recreated some events in the narratives from events my friends witnessed and later related to me. When recreating these events, I have tried to maintain what Wilson calls "actuality" (Wilson 1974:2). That is, I have tried to keep descriptions of events close in spirit to the way things happen among Mopan Maya in southern Belize, and close to the descriptions given to me.

I have occasionally played with the sequence of events that happen within a chapter in order to maintain a linear story line. Also, the reader may notice that events sometimes overlap between chapters. These inconsistencies are the result of my grouping stories and events according to the themes raised in each chapter. Everything I report happened, just sometimes not in the exact sequence in which I present it. I feel, however, that I have maintained respect for the "sacred" (Dentan 1995:230), that is, the data I have collected. I also feel I have maintained people's anonymity, disguising everyone enough so that someone visiting the village after reading this will not be able to identify anyone's real identity. Not revealing the name of the village, I feel, further protects anonymity.

Language

Throughout the narratives the reader will find words and phrases in italics. Some of these are Mopan, the language villagers use to talk amongst themselves. Readers may recognize some of these as Spanish. Mopan have a history that includes a long relationship with Spanish invaders and colonizers. They have taken many Spanish words as their own. Some quotations are in Belizean Creole; others are Mopan speakers' attempts at Belizean Creole. A few are my attempts to speak the Mayan version of Belizean Creole. Language is complex in Belize. Code switching is common and people have learned to assess a person's level of comprehension in different languages quickly, in order to hide or reveal knowledge. This is especially true of Creole speakers. Belizean Creole can resemble Belizean English, or can be incomprehensible to an English speaker. The Belizean Creole that appears here should be easy for an English speaker to comprehend and therefore is not set off by a specialized font.

Belizean Creole shares a lexicon with English. However, the meaning of the words is often slightly different, and the grammar, especially the conjugation of verbs, differs. Unfortunately, when English speakers hear Creole, they may think that the speaker is erring in his or her attempts to use English. In reality, the speaker may be trying to assess the listener's ability to use and understand Creole. While appearing uneducated, unsophisticated, or unintelligent, the speaker is actually undertaking a complex task which requires great skill.

The complexity of this phenomenon is much more easily misunderstood in written form where the "speaker" can't assess the ability of the "listener" to comprehend. Written words are inanimate letters on pieces of dead processed tree pulp, and "speakers" are simply representations of real people. The dialectic of meaning and language is lost, leaving more room for misunderstandings in content and in the significance of what language is used to communicate.

Creole, therefore, means something different in this text than it might in person. Here, Maya speaking Creole can indicate three things: The speaker has attended Belizean school and has therefore been educated by Creole teachers; the speaker has had great experience dealing with people outside the village; or the speaker is a young "hip" kid trying to portray herself as sophisticated or "worldly." Young people in the village use Creole to express their hipness, just as suburban white kids in the United States may use Black English. Among Creole characters, speaking Creole simply means they are Creole.

The Creole I write here does not conform to the standardized written Creole many Belizeans advocate. Instead, I have tried to write Creole the way the people in this work speak it. Few Maya speak Creole as Creoles do. Furthermore, the Creole and Garifuna who speak Creole with Maya and people from the United States sometimes use a form that is easy to understand. The purpose of speaking is to communicate, not to adhere to linguistic rules. Language in Belize is flexible; I have tried to reflect flexibility here.

Furthermore, I have tried to translate Mopan and Creole words and phrases within the text. A glossary at the end of this work provides translation and guidance for pronunciation. The glossary also indicates whether a word or phrase is Mopan, Creole, Garifuna, or from some other source.

Some words in the text, and occasionally parts of words, appear in capital letters. This is to indicate the speaker's emphasis on certain words or parts of words. It is meant to provide the reader with a sense of how the speaker speaks.

Structure

This work consists of six chapters, plus an introduction, a summary, an epilogue, and an appendix. Chapter 1 provides a general overview of the village, describes husband-and-wife relationships among Maya in general and Mopan specifically, and presents the conditions of my fieldwork. It provides a context for understanding the events in the narrative.

Chapters 2 through 6 consist of a narrative or a set of narratives that deal with specific themes important to understanding women's experiences and responses to domestic violence in the village. An analysis section follows each set of narratives. Each section provides additional knowledge related to that theme, to help the reader gain a deeper understanding of Mayan domestic violence. The juxtaposition of narrative and analysis in each section may disrupt the narrative flow for some readers. Some readers may want to read the analysis sections after they have finished all the narratives.

The conclusion summarizes the patterns of domestic violence among Mopan Maya in southern Belize, occasionally drawing on information about domestic violence elsewhere. The epilogue reflects on the research and writing process.

Many characters appear and reappear throughout the book. The appendix provides a list of the main characters, with basic descriptions. The glossary of Mopan, Spanish, and Creole words and phrases used throughout the text follows, as well as the list of references cited.

CHAPTER ONE

The Field Site and Fieldwork

This chapter is in three parts: (1) a brief description of life in the village; (2) a sketch of husband-wife relationships among Maya in general and Mopan specifically; and (3) an outline of the conditions of my fieldwork. My aim is to describe the village and my relationship to it in traditional ethnographic style. This description sets the stage for the subsequent narratives. Part 1 also presents issues other than domestic violence that villagers feel are important.

1: Mopan in Toledo, Belize

Belize, formerly British Honduras, is just under 9,000 square miles, located east of Guatemala and south of Mexico's territory on the Yucatan peninsula. It lies across the Honduran Bay from Honduras. Belize has a decidedly Caribbean feel, sharing many aspects of pan-Caribbean culture with the islands, like reggae and Soca music. It has also built strong economic ties with Caribbean nations through the Caribbean Community and Common Market (CARICOM).

Belize's diverse population is just under 200,000. Creole (39.7%), Mestizo (33.1%), Garifuna (7.6%), Mopan Maya (7%), white (4.2%), Kekchi Maya (2.7%), East Indian (2.1%), and a growing Chinese population (0.1%) all share Belize, in relative harmony (Central Statistics Office 1990). This is not to say there are no tensions between ethnic groups in Belize. Most tensions arise around issues of economic resources and national identity (Wilk 1991, Medina 1997, Ch'oc 1996).

Conflicts are relatively minor, however, partially due to the low population density, 7.8/square mile (SPEAR 1990). Each ethnic group lives relatively apart from the others.

Nearly all Mopan live in Toledo, the poorest and southernmost district. Belizeans say Toledo is the most "backward" and "primitive" district of all (Wilk 1991:xi). The tendency of the British colonial powers and the newly formed Belizean government to overlook Toledo's needs has led to its nickname of "the forgotten district." Maya, both Mopan and Kekchi, make up 56.9% of Toledo's population; most live in rural areas. Garifuna and Creole make up another 24.6%, most of whom live in the district capital, Punta Gorda (Central Statistics Office 1990).

The village in which I did my work is one of the two larger Mayan villages in southern Belize. Population figures for the village are hard to estimate since many people "job out," taking jobs in more urban areas where jobs are more plentiful. Many who job out return to the village with their savings, build houses, and marry. Others never return. The length of time people spend away varies from a few months to several years.

The village is "lone Maya," with no Mestizo, Garifuna, or Creole families except for the regional police constable, a Creole who lives with his family in the police station on the highest point in the village; a Mennonite missionary family from Pennsylvania; and the nurse, a Garifuna woman, and her son. During the school months non-Mopan teachers live in three collective barracks near the Catholic church. A few non-Belizeans occasionally sojourn in the village as missionaries, Peace Corps Volunteers, or anthropologists.

In Belize, "Maya" often refers only to Mopan, excluding Kekchi in the south and Yucatec Maya in the northwest. When the villagers say their village is "lone Maya," they are making such an exclusion. Mopan, like other Belizeans, often suggest Kekchi are unsophisticated country folk. There is little sense of pan-Mayanism.

Making A Living: Farming

Unlike Maya peoples in Mexico or Guatemala, many Belizean Maya have land rights. These rights are tenuous, but allow most people access to land (more on this later in this chapter). Most people grow food for themselves, and many sell produce at the market in Punta Gorda. Some grow rice for the national market, and some grow cacao, mainly for a British organic chocolate company. Farming techniques vary accordingly, from slash-and-burn horticulture for personal-consumption goods, like corn and beans, to mechanized farming for rice.

Generally, men plant and harvest agricultural crops, and women process foods. While work is gendered, men assist women and women assist men without stigma, especially if a particular harvest requires a lot of work.

Women play much less of a role in mechanized farming, where processing is unnecessary, and more of a role in subsistence farming. Both men and women gather rain forest edibles.

Men sometimes hunt peccary, deer, and *gibnut* (paca). Occasionally, men trap ground moles and other small animals, especially if the pests are plaguing their crops. To the best of my knowledge, women never hunt.

Every family raises some sort of livestock, usually chickens, turkey, or pigs. In the past, several men made a great deal of money raising pigs, trucking them to Belize City and selling them on the national market (Gregory 1984). Today, however, it doesn't pay to raise pigs. Feed and transport are expensive and the market value is low. Cacao and rice are now relatively big-money crops.

Women usually tend poultry. Current government development projects often take the form of "chicken projects," aimed at women. Government development officers instruct women on the proper care and feeding of specially bred "Mennonite" chickens: layers and broilers. Women also raise "local" chickens, which are less susceptible to disease and can eat dried corn, tortillas, and various things they find in the dirt.

Making A Living: Professionals

Not everyone in the village is a farmer; many are professionals. The number of shops is growing. Three shops opened during my ten-month stay in 1994–1995, and one expanded considerably. Shops vary in size. Indeed, almost anyone who has the money to buy a refrigerator and pay the electric bill sells soft drinks, beer, and *ideals* (flavored sugar water frozen in a bag). The larger shops sell a great variety of things: bicycles, toiletries, notebooks, nails, cloth, bicycle parts, soap, food, candy, and liquor, much like general stores in rural areas of the United States. Men own all the shops, but their wives tend them when their husbands are busy on their farms. Shop owners say they consult their wives about important business decisions.

Construction work usually consists of laying cinder blocks and cementing over them. Such jobs are scarce. Men usually get them through traditional means, kin and fictive-kin ties. The network is, however, somewhat expanded, since relatively few men can do construction work. Unlike traditional workers, construction workers demand cash; normally, however, they work for less than the minimum wage. Jobs outside of the village are more formal, and, therefore, workers usually make at least minimum wage.

Many young men and women attend high school in hopes of becoming schoolteachers. Several teachers hail from the village. Half the staff (including the principal) at the local Catholic primary school grew up in the village. Other teachers from the village live wherever the Department of Education assigns them. Some return during summer recess.

Many young men join the Belize Defense Force (BDF). Although the BDF accepts women, I knew only one girl from the village who thought of joining. BDF soldiers make relatively a lot of money and often contribute to a household's finances, making it possible for brothers and sisters to attend high school.

While some professionals augment their income with farming, especially shopkeepers and construction workers, others do not. Those that don't farm themselves help family members, especially parents, raise, harvest, and process various crops. They get food or baby-sitting in return. Several teachers I talked with said that they always work on their parents' and brothers' farms when school is in recess. It helps them, and others, they said, to remember that they are "still Maya."

Land Rights and Poverty

The Belizean reservation system allots each village several hectares of land. The Reserve associated with the village is approximately 22,000 acres. The exact amount is difficult to determine because the Belizean government has not maintained accurate or up-to-date records, and frequently produces contradictory reports (Berkley 1994:28–29). The village holds communal rights to these 22,000 acres. However, the government can change reservation boundaries or revoke reservation land at any time (Wilk and Chapin 1989, Berkley 1994).

Under the present system, individuals can lease, and eventually own, land inside and outside of the reservation. One government report estimates that forty people now lease 7.5 percent of the 20,785 acres of the land reserved for this particular village (Medows and Matola 1990, in Mohrmann and Nelson 1993).

Leasing land, however, does not ensure private ownership. To buy land, the lessee must make improvements to the land for five years, and then pay for an expensive survey. Until the actual purchase and survey, the government continues to own the property and can cancel the lease at any time without compensation to the lessee for improvements made.

People say that the government rarely denies purchase. However, many fear that local officials can delay or deny purchase if the lessee supports the political opposition to the government (Sutherland 1998:63). Tenuous land rights contribute to growing factionalism in the village. Generally, however, villagers' fear of landlessness focuses on the fact that people can lease and own communal reservation land, and simultaneously hold traditional communal rights. The result is that those with money have more land rights than others, and less and less reservation land is available for a growing population. Many fear that eventually there will be no land left for future generations or those without the funds to lease or buy.

Anxieties are compounded by the fact that some people use owned land, again both within and outside of the reservation, as collateral for bank loans. If the owner, for whatever reason, cannot pay the loan back, the bank forecloses and gains rights to the land. Sometimes the bank sells the land to non-Maya, further reducing reservation lands (IWGIA 1986:18).

Toledo's Maya increasingly worry that the government will eliminate the reservation system entirely. The government's land reforms are changing forest reserve land use policies. The government wants to secure its resources and is therefore implementing a conservation system of "use zones" (Sutherland 1998:137). After extensively mapping Belize, the Forestry Department will designate areas for logging, farming, and hunting, and areas protected from these activities. These changes will affect Mayan land use, restricting hunting, gathering, and farming. As of the last day of my fieldwork, the government has shown little interest in listening to the many Maya who reject their plan.

In response to Belizean land policies, Mopan and Kekchi came together in 1985 as the Toledo Maya Cultural Council (TMCC) to secure a Mayan homeland: communally held land reserved solely for Maya (IWGIA 1986:17–20). The TMCC recently requested twenty-five acres of land for each Maya in Toledo, to be reserved as a Mayan homeland. That amounts to 500,000 acres, nearly the whole of the Toledo District (Mohrmann and Nelson 1993:9). The government is unlikely to grant this concession. In lieu of this, the TMCC has requested a more secure land rights policy which ensures Mayan rights, whether or not the Maya have the cash to buy land.

In 1994, the Belizean government, with the help of USAID, published its first comprehensive report on Belizean poverty (Lewis 1994). With 41 percent of the population in poverty, Toledo District is the poorest in Belize. Rural Toledo, almost exclusively Maya, suffers the worst poverty in depth (how far below the poverty line a population is) and severity (how far a population is below the poverty line in relation to other Belizean populations) (Lewis 1994:19).

The report's calculations of poverty do not consider people's relationship to land or their ability to grow food. For this reason, rural Toledo poverty figures are somewhat inflated. This point was continually raised in newspaper editorials and in private discussions when the government first released the poverty report. However, with the growing threats to land rights, and as the reservation shrinks, Toledo's poverty will surely increase.

Ethnic resentment may also rise as Belize's diverse peoples begin to clamor for resources. Indeed, many feel the depiction of Belize as a peacefully diverse nation is already a falsity.

Housing

Families tend to live in household clusters: several houses built close to each other, each with its own kitchen, living room, and sleeping spaces. These clusters usually consist of several generations living close by but not in the same house, and are, by a narrow majority, patrilocal. A few household clusters are matrilocal, especially if a woman's family has an exceptionally good location.

As you leave the village, household clusters become more sparse and more often patrilocal. There are fewer and fewer household clusters until you reach small off-shoots of the village, or *aquillos*. People say that those living here are living *pach kut,* literally "beyond the fence," a phrase most translate as "in the bush."

Professionals are less likely than farmers to live in the bush, since the village center is more convenient for communication and travel. They are also more likely to live in cement houses than in thatch.

Thatch houses usually consist of two rooms, a living room and a kitchen. Both are spacious, dark and cool. The inhabitants can transform them into whatever sort of space is needed. Men can instantly construct benches and chairs out of boards and plastic five-gallon buckets if a meeting space is necessary; or, after killing a pig outside, they can clear away the furniture and cover the floor with banana leaves to make a place to finish butchering the animal.

Both rooms are similar, with hammocks slung into the rafters waiting to be pulled down for a midday nap or for a full six hours of sleep at night. Upturned buckets, stools, or *bancos* (small seats carved from wood) await weary visitors or women and children shelling corn or sewing.

Kitchens, of course, house hearths, low cement structures of cinder blocks and sifted moistened ashes. Metal slats cross one side of the hearth, where women cook soup and boil corn in large pots. The other half molds around a grill or *comal* where women bake tortillas and roast coffee and hot peppers. Kitchens usually contain a table where women grind corn and prepare food. In older homes, you may find a stone *mano* and *metate,* a horizontal mortar and pestle of sorts, which women use to grind cacao and occasionally small amounts of corn necessary for various ceremonies. Plastic five-gallon buckets usually line one wall of the kitchen. One is filled with corn soaking in water, which the women will later boil and grind to make tortillas. The rest are filled with water that someone has hauled from a nearby pump, water vat, or, in the dry season, from the river.

Women usually sleep in hammocks hung from the kitchen rafters. Men sleep in the living room. Either room may contain a small wooden bed. Here young children or nursing mothers and their babies sleep. Sometimes a family has partitioned off a section of either the living room or the kitchen to make a separate, more private bedroom, usually for the senior couple of the household.

Somewhere inside the house is a neatly stacked wall of dried corn. Sometimes people make a cross within the wall using ears that have dried darker than the others. People decorate other walls with pictures cut out of magazines, plaster-of-paris depictions of Christ or the Virgin Mary, political posters, or murals of ancient Mayan figures a family member has copied from a book.

On my first visit to the village in 1990, a generator supplied the village with two hours of electricity each night. Just before my return visit in 1994–1995, the government strung high-tension wires from Punta Gorda into the village. While electricity is now available twenty-four hours a day, fewer people can afford the new-style grounded hookups.

As I left the village, the government was working on a water system that had been proposed a few years earlier. Like anything in the village, the water system generates disagreements. One man said it was simply preparing the village for pollution. He argued that defecating in the bush makes for a cleaner watershed than defecating in a flush toilet. Some women expressed concern that they might lose the opportunity to socialize with their friends while doing their laundry at the river every day. Many were confused about why someone would want to pay for something that is already free. Like electrical hookups, access to the water system will probably be expensive. I expect the water system will contribute to the fledgling class division within the village.

Religion

Most people in the village are Roman Catholics. The Catholic church holds novenas on many saints' days and other Catholic holidays. Two Mopan men act as catechists, caring for the church building and occasionally performing Mass when the Toledo District priests can't come to the village. *Compadrazgo* (co-parenting), common throughout Latin America, remains strong in the village and centers around the same Christian rites of passage, such as baptism, confirmation, and marriage, that Catholics feel important.

The Catholic church is also the focus of education in the village, providing the largest school.

The Mennonites seem to have the fewest converts. Only one Mayan family regularly attends services.

The Nazarenes and Church of Christ both have a growing membership. Church of Christ missionaries from the United States donated a fax machine to the village. The machine is indispensable during the annual health drives, when U.S. health professionals and other volunteers set up shop and provide free medical care and health supplies, such as toothbrushes and plastic basins for washing hands.

A few Jehovah's Witnesses living in the village and an American expatriate couple living in Punta Gorda make house calls, much as Jehovah's Witnesses do in the States.

Danziger (1991) reports that Mopan Maya in Belize continue to pray to the mountains, the morning star, and the sun, as ancient Maya did. While I never heard such prayers, I have no reason to believe the tradition doesn't continue. Traditional healing is popular and continues to rest on indigenous religious beliefs. The discussions I had with people about souls and spirits fit with those reported by anthropologists working with Maya elsewhere.

Politics

Those who have identified with the national parties—the People's United Party (PUP) and the United Democratic Party (UDP)—often quarrel with one another. The red (UDP) and the blue (PUP) each feel the other is "against" them. On some levels this might be true (Sutherland 1998:62–65). One's role in development projects and ability to obtain land are sometimes determined by one's relationship to the party in power.

Toledo has over the years elected several Mopan from southern Belize to national office. Maya from this area are still, however, greatly underrepresented in the national government.

The local government system is twofold, with an *alcalde* and a village council. The *alcalde* system may have roots in Post-Classic Mayan civilization (Shoman 1994:160, Bolland 1988:126). Spanish colonial powers, however, transformed the position as it existed throughout Latin America, as did the British in Belize (Bolland 1988:126–128). While traditional *alcaldes* served as military leaders, under British colonial powers they moderated minor disputes and allocated parcels of land. The *alcalde* system may be the only non–Anglo-Saxon political system that the British maintained (Bolland 1988:131).

Today the role of *alcalde* is more like that of his colonial predecessor than his ancient ancestor. He settles minor disputes, levying small fines for crimes against property, organizing his deputies or police force to bury the dead, and organizing *fahinas*. *Fahinas* (or *pahinas*) occur every three months and are a means to organize all the adult men in the village to clean up public areas, such as around the church or along the roads. A man who does not attend the *fahina* must pay a fine to the *alcalde*.

Alcaldes serve for two years. Before 1960, a group of *pasados*, those who served in that position in the past, elected the next *alcalde*. In 1960, young men took over the position, claiming they didn't want the old men to run the village anymore. Since then the *alcalde* has been elected by all the men from the village who attend the election meeting (Gregory 1984:111). Women can attend and vote but usually do not for fear of rumors that they are "looking for another man" (Danziger 1991).

The British instituted the village council system in 1965 (Gregory 1984:112–113). Councils have no independent powers. They mostly deal with development issues that require interaction with the village and national government officials. The council petitions for Peace Corps workers, organizes development projects with the Toledo Development Officer, and plays an active part in the Village Health Committee (Crooks 1992:75).

Factionalism pervades local as well as national government. Much of the factionalism may be rooted in the "young men's revolt" of 1960, when economically advantaged young men insisted that their newly developed skills qualified them to hold positions of authority, like that of *alcalde* (Gregory 1984:112). Their success in taking over the traditional legal system weakened the traditional civic-religious system and inflamed preexisting factionalism (Gregory 1984:112).

Education

Education is free and compulsory for Belizean children under fourteen. The British government began public education by subsidizing denominational schools. Today, most primary schools continue under Roman Catholic, Anglican, or Methodist administration (Barry 1989:33).

The village centers on a large Catholic church. Most schoolchildren attend the attached primary school. During the 1990–1991 school year, 80 to 90 percent of the child population of the school district attended this Catholic school (Crooks 1992:88). There are no Anglican or Methodist schools in the village.

Attendance is less regular than the teaching staff would like. Parents sometimes need their children at home to help harvest or process certain foods.

Small children and children with a number of same-sex siblings about the same age usually have uninterrupted education. If a child shows a particular talent for school, and has same-sex siblings who can help their parents at home, the parents may encourage the child to get an education.

Most parents see secondary education as a form of social security.

Married children may have spouses who refuse to support their in-laws. Educated children, sons or daughters, are likely to make enough money to support their aging parents. Education, however, is a gamble. A child may "forget her studies" and a parent's investment is lost.

Several villagers have attended college, either at the University of Belize (UCB) or the Teachers College. Entrance into college is competitive. Occasionally, government scholarships allow students from the village to travel to the United States for education.

Economic Development

The history of development projects in Toledo is sporadic (Wilk 1991: xvi). Development seems haphazard and somewhat dependent on national and foreign theories of what will work rather than on locally defined needs. Therefore, walking though the village you will see street lights and thatch houses, fax machines and kerosene lanterns.

The village seems to be on the wane. People nostalgically tell stories of what the village was like "when we sold pigs," or "when it looked like the village was going big." Unfortunately, the history of development projects in the village is a history of failed cooperatives.

Tales and accusations of embezzlement, told in surroundings dotted with evidence of better days, temper the "growing atmosphere of change," James Gregory (1972, 1984, 1987) felt in the 1960s. Electric wiring rots in the rafters of thatch houses. The buildings that once housed the beekeepers' cooperative and the Social Office, where the government taught new farming techniques and home economics classes, are abandoned and collapsing. People often sigh and exclaim, "We Indians can't work together."

When I left the village in 1995, the government was surveying the land in order to collect property tax and installing a "pay-for-use" water system. At the same time new forest use plans restrict farming, hunting, and collecting forest products. The government is moving toward collecting taxes and restricting the use of things that were once free and plentiful. While the hardship isn't severe yet, some people see bad times coming.

Most people in the village want to improve their lot. Most of the time, this means that they are interested in making money: another legacy of earlier days of development projects. For women, making money is important for buying household items that they can't easily make: soap, salt, sugar, cooking pots, kerosene, and cloth. It is also important for buying school supplies.

Women have few ways to make money, and they can't always rely on their husbands to buy what they need or to save for a child's educational needs. For this reason, many are involved in women's craft groups, co-operatives which help the women market crafts. In their spare time, they embroider wall hangings for tourists and cross-stitched strips of cloth for the neckline and armbands of traditional blouses. Some make pottery; most make baskets.

There were four such women's groups in the village in 1994–1995. All had fissioned off a government development project administered by a pair of Catholic nuns living in the village at the time, and a Peace Corps worker, also stationed in the village. The original craft project grew out of several efforts by the government to help women create and market goods for tourists (see Gregory 1984:74–75 for a brief history of Peace Corps women's projects).

Factions developed around accusations of embezzlement. As factions broke off, some women encouraged others to act as chairladies for new groups. The new chairlady may not have been enthusiastic about her new position, but she decided to "try her best." This fissioning still occurs among the women's groups, since more and more women are gaining the skills needed to be a chairlady: basic bookkeeping and simple literacy.

A corn-milling cooperative also splintered off the original craft group. Unlike the craft cooperatives, the corn mill requires greater bookkeeping skills, as well as maintenance, housing, and operation of the diesel-powered corn grinder. It is expensive to run. Members of the co-op work long hours for little pay, but they do it because the little money they make is helpful. Also, since the mill house is rarely too busy, the long hours give members time to work on their crafts.

During my stay, membership in the grinding co-op declined, making the work of those remaining even harder and their hours longer. Recruiting new members is hard, since only women who can find the time (usually those with no small children, or with older unmarried girls at home) and those with willing partners (or without a partner) can stay away from home for such a long time (see Chapter 4: Daughters).

When I returned to the United States I received a letter from the woman who diligently served as chairlady for the grinding cooperative while I was in the village. She had resigned, she wrote, and was now living with her daughter in the Cayo District. She expressed concern about the cooperative because she had heard that the machine was broken and repairs expensive. The cooperative's failure seems inevitable.

During my stay in the village, the government began a sixth women's group, a sewing project for young women. It is a continuing-certification program which teaches sewing skills to a new group of young women each year. Women can use these sewing skills to make clothing for their families or products for the tourist trade. Certification can also help to secure a job in Belize's growing textile industry. Most see the program as an exceptional opportunity. Few are aware of or interested in the problems workers face in the textile factories in Ladyville and Belize City.

2: Marriage

Each section of Part 2 describes a different aspect of Mayan marriage and gender relations, from a simple description of Mopan marriages to an examination of the Mayan gender hierarchy. Subsequent chapters illustrate and embody the information presented here.

Mopan Marriages

This "ideal-type" description of Mopan marriages rests on my observations and discussions with women about marriage in the village. Despite variations, marriage for most older women in the village, as well as for many younger ones, follows the pattern I sketch here. Many Mopan women criticize these "traditional" ways, and marriages are changing. I will discuss these criticisms and changes later in the chapter, under the heading "The Young Women's Revolt."

Young women are marriageable at fourteen. Parents encourage their sons to think of marriage by sixteen. When the boy agrees that it is time for him to marry, he approaches his father with the name of a young woman he is interested in. Sometimes his parents choose a bride for him. In either case, it is best if the young people have never spoken to one another. Maya interpret a lack of verbal communication between the two as an indication that the girl is virtuous and will not seek extramarital lovers. It is probable, however, that the two have communicated nonverbally. For example, most teenagers interested in each other smile at one another. Such nonverbal communication encourages the young man and shows him that the young woman is interested in him. On rare occasions, for example when the boy's parents pursue a daughter-in-law from outside their own village, the couple may not ever have seen each other until the marriage negotiations.

The boy's parents, and possibly a couple bound to them through *compadrazgo,* visit the girl's family four times. Each time they ask for the girl, promise to treat her well, offer respect to the girl's family, and arrange the logistics of the marriage. If each meeting is successful, the fourth meeting is an engagement party or *hobol u k'aat,* literally "the end of the asking" (Danziger 1991).

During the negotiation period, the young woman may ask her parents to refuse the marriage offer. Some parents honor their daughter's request and tell the young man's family that she is too young or otherwise not ready for marriage. Other parents ignore their daughter's requests and continue to negotiate. Parents teach their children, especially daughters, to listen to and respect their elders. This makes it difficult for daughters to express displeasure even though they may be unhappy about their parents' marriage choice.

Hobol u k'aat, the engagement party, brings the two families together, usually in the bride's home. Her brothers and father may slaughter and butcher a pig the night before. That night, her family may enjoy a festive meal of liver and tortilla, which the women cook, and *chicarone,* which the men have made by frying the pig's skin.

The next day, members of both families arrive. The bride's sisters, aunts, mother, and brother's wife make pork soup (*caldo*) and tortillas for everyone, while a brother or perhaps the bride's father circulates through the crowd offering guests rum, soda pop, beer, or *chicha,* a homemade fermented corn drink. Men typically sit outside and drink alcohol. Women typically sit inside and sip soda pop.

Eventually, the groom's father introduces the bride to the significant members of his family. This formal introduction involves promises of respect and support from both parties. After this, the groom's family presents the bride with gifts to begin her new life: cloth, soap, cooking pots, and large gold earrings to replace the medium-sized ones she typically has worn since she was much younger. After this, everyone enjoys more food and drink. Some people, sufficiently drunk, may dance to cassettes of traditional marimba music. The party may last until sunset, with some guests, having passed out during the day, staying until late at night.

A few weeks later, the groom's family arranges a church ceremony at the Catholic church. After this Catholic ceremony another ceremony ensues at the groom's parents' house. When all the guests have arrived, the groom's parents welcome the newlyweds, especially the bride, into their home. The newlyweds then kneel just inside the threshold, and both the bride's and groom's parents, and possibly their *compadres* and *comadres,* stand before the two and bless them. Later, they all sit together and give the newlyweds advice on how to have a successful marriage. These long formal speeches emphasize the importance of work and respect for one's spouse and in-laws.

After the welcome and the advice, the groom's female relatives serve food and coffee, while a male relative serves alcohol and soda pop. Both the groom's parents circulate among the guests, encouraging them to eat and drink and thanking them for coming. Later, the groom's mother gives the bride a tour of her house and compound, giving her more gifts, such as hair clips, cloth, and possibly chickens.

Postmarital residence is most often patrilocal, so the tour of the compound is a tour of the bride's new home. Sometimes, the newlyweds live their first year in the same house as the groom's parents. Often, however, just before the wedding, the groom constructs a new house a few feet away from his parents' house.

Although the bride and groom are married, no one considers them fully adult. Instead, the first year or so of marriage is a training period during which the bride learns how to be a wife, or "how to do her work," from her mother-in-law. Likewise, the groom's parents tell him how to be a husband.

A woman becomes adult with the birth of her first child. At this time, the couple moves out of the groom's parents' house, if that is where they were living, and into a separate house within the compound. If they have been living in a separate house since marriage, the groom's parents simply cut back on unsolicited advice.

The first year of marriage can be hard for the bride. She may never have left her family's compound for an overnight visit before. Now, strangers surround her. She is under the authority and tutelage of her mother-in-law, a woman she may have only recently met. Marital success depends not only on the wife "getting used to" her husband, but also on "getting used to" his mother's authority. Discussing their marriages, older women often talk about the cruelty they suffered or the kindness they enjoyed under their mothers-in-law.

Sometimes marriage negotiations require bride service. During the first year of marriage, the bride's father expects his new son-in-law to provide labor, such as clearing fields and helping to plant and to harvest. Although this obligation lasts only a year, a son-in-law usually continues to help his father-in-law until the old man relinquishes his share of the communal lands and begins to rely on his sons to provide his food.

During bride service, the bride usually visits her father's house to help her mother and sisters prepare food for those working in the fields. In this way, a bride is able to visit her natal family frequently. Sometimes a mother-in-law worries that the new daughter-in-law might gossip about her when she visits her mother and sisters. Discreet young women avoid discussing their mother-in-law's household.

Marriage as a Complementary Union

Mopan men and women live in separate spheres, women *ix nah,* "inside the house," men *yok'ol kab,* "out in the world" (Danziger 1991:35). Women's primary responsibilities and authority rest within the household. Women do household chores, especially cooking and washing laundry, and raise children. Men's primary responsibilities and prestige lie outside the home. Of primary importance is food production: farming and hunting. Men also hold community-wide positions of authority such as *alcalde* and member of the village council. Furthermore, they are more likely than women to hold professional positions such as police constable, construction worker, or soldier.

Marriage forms an economic dyad, linking *ix nah* with *yok'ol kab.* By performing the duties of a husband or a wife, spouses help their partners to survive, gaining a sense of being a "complete" or "true" man and woman (Eber 1995:67, Arias 1973 as cited in Eber 1995, Rosenbaum 1993:50, Maynard 1963:87, Redfield and Villa Rojas 1934:70, 97, Bunzel 1967:122). The Maya sense of being focuses on service; marriage is service to one's spouse.

By working hard for each other, couples say they "get used to each other." While in the United States this phrase may indicate a rather lukewarm relationship, in the village it indicates a close connection marked by mutual love and respect. When one partner dies, the other may discuss this love and respect in economic terms. However, "Who will make my tortilla?" or "Who will bring me corn?" does not simply reflect the loss of a servant. It reflects the loss of a life partner, someone who cre-

A newly married Mopan couple. This arranged marriage will develop into a strong and intimate partnership in the years to come.

ates and shares joys and provides support in difficult times and makes you complete.

To some extent, Mayan emphasis on a couple's responsibility to each other makes Mayan marriages equal partnerships. Perhaps the best example of how Mayan couples take on life's projects with equal responsibilities and respect is childbirth. A Mayan husband assists in childbirth by supporting his wife by the waist as she kneels, hands clasped behind his neck, laboring until the child emerges (Eber 1995:108–109).

Among Quiche' in Momostenago, Guatemala, diviners or *chuchkajawib* (literally mother-fathers) are ideally husband-wife teams (B. Tedlock 1992:85), like Xmucane and Xpiyacoc, the matchmaker and midwife in Quiche' mythology. According to the *Popul Voh,* the sixteenth-century Quiche' Mayan text, the gods consulted the team before beginning their third and final attempt to create humanity (D. Tedlock 1985:34, 71–86, 163–167).

Even more earthly projects, some of which anthropologists once thought solely in men's domain, are mutual. For example, the civic-religious cargo system, where men gain prestige through serving the community by sponsoring festivals in honor of the saints, continues in many Mayan villages. Anthropologists now recognize that both men and women share this honor and the commitment of sponsoring saints' festivals (Eber 1995, Mathews 1985, Rosenbaum 1993:152–153, Maynard 1963:94, Bunzel 1967:123). No husband can sponsor a festival without his wife's help, and no husband would commit to such an event without first consulting his wife. Furthermore, they both gain prestige for such service.

Although the villagers have almost fully abandoned their cargo system (Gregory 1984), couples sponsor novenas in their homes at Christmas time. No one, man or woman, would consider sponsoring a novena without the support of his or her spouse. Similarly, men consult their wives if they feel that someone might nominate them as *alcalde* or they might gain a position within the village council. Shopkeepers also consult their wives before making major business transactions or investments. Therefore, in the absence of a formal system of prestige, men still consult their wives when faced with important decisions, and women still share their husband's status when providing community service (Gregory 1984).

This equality is especially obvious in *compadrazgo,* the most important community service in the village (Danziger 1991). This system of fictive kinship ties husbands and wives to other couples throughout the village. As *comadres* and *compadres,* they build honor and respect throughout the village. *Compadrazgo* is a manifestation of and a means to perpetuate embeddedness within the community. Maya strongly emphasize the interdependence that human beings have with each other, not just as couples, but also as members of the same community. No one can survive by themselves; everyone survives because they have a place within their family and within their community. *Compadrazgo* helps to emphasize and create people's relationships with one another as relationships of respect and service.

Some Mayanists have suggested that Mayan marriages are more than economic partnerships; they are also a merging of two souls (Bunzel 1967:122, Vogt 1976:22). While, to my knowledge, no Mayanist has elaborated as to what that might mean, some have presented gender complementarity in other areas of Mayan spirituality. Chorti consider the spirits of beans and corn, the two major foodstuffs, as female and male lovers (Wisdom 1940:402–403). They also consider the god of earth to be both male and female, whose offspring are cultivated crops (Wisdom 1940:402). Tzotzil associate the numbers three and four with women and men, respectively, and consider both numbers equally important symbols (Eber 1995:66–67). Chamula, like ancient Maya, recognize both Our Father the Sun/Christ and Our Mother the Moon/the Virgin as important deities (Rosenbaum 1993:67).

Marriage and the Mayan Gender Hierarchy

Despite the complementarity of Mayan marriage roles and Mayan emphasis on the interdependence between husbands and wives, Mayan gender relations are nevertheless hierarchical. Men dominate women.

In the village, people justify the gender hierarchy with the argument that men's work is harder than women's. Women say that men spend long, arduous hours in the hot sun working in the fields. Women, however, enjoy their cool dark homes, laughing and gossiping with friends while shelling and grinding corn, making baskets and sewing embroidery, or caring for their children. A woman can easily dispel the heat from cooking by stepping out of the kitchen into the living room for a moment. A man's work does not allow him easy relief from the hot, humid climate.

Men's domination over women is evident in a sexual double standard. While Maya do not condone premarital and extramarital sexual intercourse for either sex, most consider them lesser offenses for men. A man's lack of virginity rarely affects his ability to marry a "good woman." For men, extramarital affairs are common, and as long as men support both families, few consider it a serious offense. Most men try hard to support both families. Many, however, eventually abandon their first wives and the children from their marriage. It is this abandonment that people consider objectionable.

Women who are not virgins find it difficult to marry. People feel that women who have sex before marriage cannot control sexual urges and may seek lovers. Most husbands are jealous, and many act violently upon suspicions of their wives' extramarital affairs. Few forgive actual occurrences. Men's jealousies restrict women's mobility. Women who walk or travel alone, whether to do their work, to attend a political meeting, or to attend a literacy program, are in danger of igniting husbands' suspicions.

Women, however, often joke about the idea of having "two husbands." The amount of work it would take to support them, they say, would leave little energy to enjoy the benefits. Women often complain about their husband's "outside" families. Such complaints often focus on the resources that their husbands are providing to the other family, instead of those to whom he is legitimately responsible. A wife may sometimes act on suspicions of a husband's infidelity, but rarely through violence. Instead, she may return to her parents' home until her husband retrieves her and reaffirms his devotion to her. If unable to leave, an angry wife may just refuse to work for her husband.

The Mayan gender hierarchy takes other forms as well. Since the male sphere of influence has traditionally been outside the home, men can control more financial resources than women. They control all money they make selling produce or hogs, either on the national market or at the district market in Punta Gorda.

Women complain, however, that their husbands spend their money on alcohol, leaving little to run the household. Therefore, some women sell tamales, sweet tortillas, roasted hot pepper powder, and other small food items at the market or among their friends. Others sell crafts. While women control the money they make, it is rarely enough to support a family.

Likewise, women without men have little access to the means to produce food. Divorced, deserted, or widowed women must "do the work of a man" as well as "the work of a woman" to survive. It is easier if a woman has a son, who can work in the fields when he gets old enough. A son, however, doesn't have the kinship and *compadrazgo* ties an adult man would have, and therefore has few men obligated to help him clear fields, plant, or harvest. The poorest people in the village are the elderly and women without husbands (Mohrmann and Nelson 1993:16).

Mayan Domestic Violence

Although few Maya would say that a man has the right to beat his wife, as an *alcalde* in the village once ruled, many men beat their wives and few suffer any punishment. Anthropologists working in the village have noted that domestic violence is common (Thompson 1930:81), "somewhat of a norm" (Danziger 1991:90), and culturally sanctioned (Gregory 1984:38, 1987:18).

Mayanists, for the most part, have discussed domestic violence only briefly. Wagley (1949) tells of Mam men beating their wives in order to initiate divorce. Wisdom (1940:302) mentions that Chorti husbands lash adulterous wives with leather horse whips, and feel justified in killing those who repeat the offense. Bunzel (1967:128) suggests that all the men in Chichicastenango beat their wives "compulsively."

Mayan women can sometimes escape abusive relationships by returning to their parents. Newlywed women have the best chance at this option (Danziger 1991:92–93). Sometimes, after a wife returns, her father and brothers find the husband and beat him (Wagley 1949, Rosenbaum 1993:109).

Returning to their parents' home permanently, however, is not an option for many women, especially if they are in an arranged marriage that provides their father with powerful political allies or strong economic connections. Similarly, women who have refused arranged marriages and have sought husbands independently of their parents have trouble convincing their parents to help them (Rosenbaum 1993:98). Women with young children also have difficulty returning home since they bring the burden of extra mouths to feed. Because Maya tend to be patrilineal, children are their father's responsibility. The mother's parents may feel little obligation to care for them.

Even if parents accept their daughters back into their home, solace is most often temporary. Fathers usually negotiate with abusive husbands and their parents to return daughters to their husbands. Women return to their husbands if they promise to curb their violence (Danziger 1991:91, Bunzel 1967:128, 131, Rosenbaum 1993:108–110).

Older women with money and good status within the community sometimes leave their husbands and set up a new household or join the household of one of their married adult children. Some even return the beatings (Danziger 1991:92–93).

Women can appeal to legal authorities for help. In 1993, Belize adopted a Domestic Violence Act making domestic violence punishable by law (Johnson and Moreno 1994:37). Police constables are required to take such cases seriously. In the village, women can report abuses either to the police constable or to the *alcalde,* or both. The officials then usually speak to the violent husband, appeal to his Mayan sense of complementarity in marriage relationships, and tell him he should respect his wife. Sometimes, especially if the man is drunk, the constable will lock up him up for the evening. If the beating is severe enough, either the police constable or the *alcalde* may set a fine (Gregory 1984:38, Danziger 1991:92).

Few women approach the constable, since he drinks rum and beer with men. They feel his friendships may taint his sense of justice. Generally, the constable's attitude is that couples will "sweet up" again no matter what he does. Most cases of domestic abuse I became aware of went unreported to either the constable or the *alcalde* (Chapter 3: Another Legitimate Beating provides one exception).

A Responsible Patriarchy

Despite the existence of a gender hierarchy, some anthropologists have maintained that Maya gender complementarity and emphasis on the partnership of marriage provide women with respect and economic support that other gender systems deny them (Eber 1995:239–242; Rosenbaum 1993:136–142; Maynard 1963). Indeed, Maynard (1963) describes Mayan gender relations as a "responsible patriarchy."

Gender complementarity and the emphasis on marriage as a partnership imply that a husband is responsible for certain duties, has certain economic responsibilities, and is expected to respect his wife. This provides her with psychological security and justifies her garnering support from others if he fails to meet these requirements (Maynard 1963).

To some extent, Mayan "responsible patriarchy" allows Mayan women to understand that they do not cause their husbands to be violent.

It may also help abused women gain support from others. Responsible patriarchy may account for the lack of self-blame and the maintenance of high self-esteem among abused Mayan women. Self-blame and lack of self-esteem are both characteristic of "battered-wife syndrome," a common syndrome in the United States (Dobash and Dobash 1979, Mills 1984, Hoff 1990:38–53).

"Responsible patriarchy" also complicates domestic violence. A widely held, sexually rigid division of labor reinforced by a strong sense of duty and responsibility helps to legitimize some cases of domestic violence. A woman seeking support to leave her husband and trying to maintain a good reputation can be undermined because the definitions of "laziness" or "adultery," the two most common reasons men beat women in the village, are open to interpretation. Chapters 2 and 3 both elaborate on this point.

The Young Women's Revolt

In one village in southern Belize, prior to 1960, *pasados,* men who had previously served as *alcalde,* would, as a group, choose their successors. In 1960, a group of young men, recently gaining economic strength, challenged this traditional political system by rejecting the man the *pasados* had chosen (Gregory 1984, 1987). They argued that their newly acquired wealth showed that they understood the economic changes facing the village better and therefore knew whom to choose for *alcalde.*

This challenge to the elders' authority led to the eventual decline of the civic-religious system in the village. Men no longer gained authority solely through serving the community. Now, they gain authority through economic success (Gregory 1984, 1987). Many men in the village today are in conflict, both with others and within themselves, about the balance between community service and economic success.

What Gregory (1984, 1987) calls "the young men's revolt" has, to some extent, led to a growing disrespect of the elders and of traditional ways. Within this new criticism of "old heads," women, especially those under sixty or so, have started speaking out against traditional marriages. Most feel women should not marry as young as age fourteen, and many reject the idea of arranged marriages. Popular culture and Creole and Garifuna government workers, who consider Mayan women the most oppressed in the nation, reinforce such criticisms, encouraging women to "rise themself up."

Some parents, especially abandoned, widowed, and never-married single mothers, now encourage their daughters to continue education beyond primary school and to take part in development projects in order to gain skills that will make them economically independent from men. Likewise, many young women now reject arranged marriages. Some try to avoid marriage altogether, a trend also among young Mayan women artisans in Chiapas (Nash 1993:7, Eber 1995:241). The most common reason women give for these changes is to avoid marrying and becoming dependent on a "jealous man," someone who will beat them.

Gregory (1984, 1987) predicted that a "young women's revolt" would topple the gender hierarchy, as the "young men's revolt" toppled the age hierarchy in southern Belize. He cited several examples of young women's refusal of arranged marriages and several other examples of women professionals, such as seamstresses and shopkeepers, gaining prestige and economic success within the village. His prediction rested on the belief that, as villages became more a part of the national economy, economic opportunities would allow women the same kind of advantages young men had over their elders in 1960.

The "young women's revolt" is not without problems. Economic opportunities for young Mayan women in Belize are meager. Some make women vulnerable to sexual abuse, and to negative gossip that damages their reputations and chances for gaining respect within the community. Furthermore, continuing education requires young women to rethink or transform their identities. Some forge new identities by blending what they feel is "traditional" with what they feel is "modern." Others create new identities in ways they feel oppose tradition.

These problems are discussed and illustrated throughout the narrative chapters. I have devoted so much space to "the young women's revolt" because many women see the new opportunities it presents as a way to avoid domestic violence.

3: Fieldwork

I mention some events from my first stay in the village in the introduction and later in Chapter 3: Another Legitimate Beating. This stay lasted just under two weeks. During this time, I arranged with the family of a local shopkeeper to return one day and stay "a long while." This "long while" began nearly four years later.

During those four years I tried to secure funding from granting agencies, without success. Therefore, I worked several odd jobs to fund my research. Most notably I worked as a housing activist and community organizer in Buffalo's inner city, where I lived. I led neighborhood activists onto the lawns of some of the most notorious slumlords in Buffalo, to call attention to the urban decay which underwrote suburban credit lines.

I nearly changed my research topic when a fellow "slumbuster" faced the death of her teenage son. He was shot in the face execution-style over drugs. Shortly after that, another "slumbuster" faced the possibility of losing her 16-year-old son to prison for attempted murder. I wanted to tell their stories, the stories of African American mothers trying to save their neighborhoods even while facing the violent loss of their children. For many reasons, some good, some bad, I chose instead to temporarily leave the neighborhood, believing that foreign fieldwork would expand my perspective and help me understand what was happening in my own backyard. Perhaps, one day, I will return to that other project.

When my bank account reached four thousand dollars, my in-laws bought me a laptop computer and I bought an open-ended, round-trip ticket to Belize. I packed my bags and left, alone, leaving Michael, my partner, behind. I missed him greatly almost every minute I was gone.

I stayed in the village from April 1994 to February 1995. At first I rented a cement house from the shopkeeper with whom I had previously made arrangements. As I watched my money dwindle, I decided I needed cheaper accommodations and moved into a thatch house that the merchant also owned. While the thatch house took more maintenance, living there made rapport with everyone easier. The idea of a gringa living in a thatch house drew several visitors who otherwise might have stayed away.

Not having much money made my ethnographic relationship with the villagers different from what they were used to. I couldn't afford a language tutor since the rates established by previous anthropologists were beyond my means. I also had little money to pay informants. I could, however, buy occasional small gifts for people and a few crafts from the members of women's groups. I also had enough to "lend" a few dollars to young people trying to attend high school and mothers needing bus fare to take sick babies to the hospital.

I wish I had had more to give. In many ways, I poorly compensated those who tried to teach me language and those who taught me Mayan ways. I am more indebted to people's kindness than I am comfortable with. However, I did help a lot of women with their work, shelling and grinding corn, making tortillas and hauling water. I also listened to them, and developed some good friendships. I think my lack of money helped some people to accept me as a person, rather than as a source of money.

At least one anthropologist warned me to make sure that people knew why I was there, and that the things they told me might appear in writing. Honesty is part of ethnographic ethics. I presented my project to the village council and to the *alcalde* as a desire to learn about women's lives and the changes that were taking place. My presence, I explained, was an effort to conduct research for my doctorate in anthropology. I chose not to tell the village council or the *alcalde* that I was specifically interested in domestic violence. I was afraid that I might make my informants targets for harassment or violent retaliation by their husbands for speaking against them.

I told the women who befriended me that I was in the village to learn about women's lives and that I might publish the things they told me in my research findings. This alone elicited a great many stories of violence. Mopan women see domestic violence as a distinctive part of their life, something that distinguishes them from white women from the United States, like myself. I was surprised women spoke so openly about their experiences with violence. The topic always caused me discomfort, as it did that day when Antonia approached me on the veranda. For months, both in the field and when I returned to the United States, I tried to think of another topic I could write about. I couldn't stop thinking of the stories that women told me. Nor could I escape from those that unfolded before me, even though at times I did my best to avoid hearing about them.

For the most part, I tried to make the interviews and focus groups as informal as possible. Most took place while we shelled corn in women's homes or washed clothes together at the river. I taped only a few interviews. Instead, after each day, sometimes several times a day, I would return to my home and write out, verbatim, as much as I could remember about my conversations and the day's events. Only during bouts of depression did I fail to make extensive field notes.

The line between friend and informant was as hard for me to understand as it was for them. How could I tell when I was a friend discussing the day's events and when I was a researcher asking questions? I found it impossible, and as a result I may have included things in these stories that were told to a friend, not a researcher. Using pseudonyms and conflating certain people helps to retain the information people gave me without betraying friendships.

I have no statistics concerning domestic violence in the village; no numbers to express how many women are beaten or how badly. I relied on women's voluntary reports to me and felt uncomfortable formalizing my curiosity. I could not conduct a household survey on the topic. Since few women report abuse to the *alcalde* or to the police constable, formal records are of little help. Most women I talked with, however, told me about abuse they had suffered. The problem is substantial. I cannot tell, however, if it is as bad as it is in the United States.

I enjoyed my stay in the village and look forward to future visits. My field stay was not without difficulties, however. I found Mopan a difficult language, partly due to my inability to afford a language tutor. I could converse in Mopan somewhat, but usually reverted to English, which most of my informants spoke fluently. I was, however, able to understand much of the Mopan spoken around me, sometimes to the surprise of those trying to make jokes or lewd comments about me in my presence.

Another anthropologist arrived in the village about six months into my field stay. Although friendly to each other, we never formed the kind of cooperative relationship that would have benefitted us both. Instead, we tried to stay out of each other's way as much as possible. Mutual friends would often play us off against each other, fostering a subtle competition between us and adding to the manic-depressive emotional surges that characterized my field stay.

I suffered a lot of unwanted sexual attention during my stay. My landlord offered lower rent in exchange for sexual favors. Others suggested I could learn the language quicker if I "sucked on a man's tongue." One man, a friend, tried to climb in my window one night. He became verbally abusive when I refused to let him in and even worse when his wife showed up to retrieve him. Drunk older men would almost always make passes at me when I entered a shop where they were drinking. I learned to hide myself and peek into a shop before entering. While the harassment decreased when Michael, my partner/husband visited, it increased significantly after he left. Men assumed that I "missed my husband too much" and needed sex. Although the constant need to reject sexual overtures was annoying, I never really felt threatened.

Certainly not all men in the village harassed me. I befriended a few men who helped me to understand important issues in national politics and the fight for land rights. As my friendships with men grew, I sometimes had to face the fact that they abused their wives, who were also my friends. It made for complex relationships. I hope that the intricacies of my relationships to both men and women in the village are evident in the narratives.

CHAPTER TWO

Laziness and Work

The Good Life

"Francesca, you know, I'd like it, if one day you could tell me the story about your life." I pluck an orange from one of the lower branches and toss it on the pile on the ground. We'll gather the oranges just before we move to the next tree. We are alone on "the plantation," her husband's farm. She asked me to help her "pull some oranges" to sell in the shop.

Francesca stands up straight, laughing. "Jesus Christo, my life." She is still chuckling as she reaches up high for another orange.

As she chuckles, I continue to circle the tree and stretch for one last orange high on a thick branch. Francesca would need to use the giant stick to knock this one down. I stand about a foot taller than her.

"My life." She's still laughing. We gather the oranges we just tossed on the ground, stuff them into our net bags, and move on to the next tree. "Yes, I can tell you about my life." She stands and swings her machete in the air. "If you want to hear it."

I smile to encourage her. She thinks my request is absurd. "Please, I'd like to hear it." I look at her eyes as I pull the first orange from this big tree and toss it on the ground. I reward her with my work and my attention.

"Well, *ix* Laura, my life has not been so good as you see it now." She picks a few easy-to-reach oranges. "Now, with Mr. Coc, I have my little shop, my little house, my little plantation. I have my oranges, my *ku'la*, my ginger." She lists the things we have been harvesting today. "I can buy things for Angela. But when I was small, huh, I had nothing."

"Nothing?" I try for an orange that's just too far away and nearly lose my balance.

"Mind you fall, gal." She giggles and then continues, "We had nothing. My mother made dresses for us from sacks. But not like the sacks we have now. No, these were made from cloth, not plastic. But the cloth was rough, gal. It made our skin itch." She laughs, her plumpness jiggling slightly. "All the time I was scratching, the sacks were so itchy.

"And my mother was poor. She had nothing. My father, he died when I was small small. I never saw him, gal. Never." She pauses. "But my mother, she sells *chicha,* to make her little money. Aiy, so much *chicha.* I don't know why the people have to drink like so. I don't like it." She lifts her net bag to her back and maneuvers the strap onto her forehead. Francesca's fifty years have made her strong and agile.

I do the same, but with less grace. Together, we head back down the hill to the path leading back to the plantation house. When we get to the bottom, we meet the path to the house. She walks in front of me. Our conversation is on hold.

When we reach the plantation house, we both slip our *tumplines* off and sit on the bench in front of the house next to each other, close as sisters. I rub my neck to relieve a cramped muscle.

"When I was young, my mother promises one man that he can marry me. My mother told him he can marry me, but not until I am old enough."

"How old were you when he asked to marry you?"

"Maybe twelve, gal."

"Twelve, that's young."

"Yes, gal." She chooses an orange from her net bag and I hand her my Swiss Army knife. She takes the knife to the orange and begins to peel it. "My mother tell him to come back when I'm older. And yes, it's true, he left me alone for a while. But he comes back again and asks my mother again. This time I'm only thirteen, gal." Handing me half of the orange, she nods her head to show me I should take it.

I bite into it and suck the juice. "Thirteen," I manage between slurps. The juice is sweet, tangy; the orange is perfect.

"This time he tell my mother, 'Why should I wait, the girl is old enough, it is only a few months before she is fourteen.' And my mother, she says, 'Yes, it is true, she will be fourteen in a few months. But she is only thirteen now and she is too young to be married.' "

"So she wouldn't let you go?"

A cloud of tangy citrus aroma surrounds us, penetrating the hot, humid air. "No, but the man, he starts to convince my mother, he says, 'Look, you have nothing. How can you care for this child? Let me take her and she will at least have her tortilla. It's better that she have something to eat. You have nothing.' That is what he tell my mother."

"So, what happened?"

"My mother say, 'Yes, okay. Better this child stay with you. You can marry my child. It is only a few months before she will be fourteen. Better she have something to eat. Better she have her tortilla, her little beans, her *caldo*.' " Francesca nods. "So that's when I get to be married." Holding the remains of her orange in her hand, she turns her head to me and says, "But it's not long before the man likes to lash me too much.[1] Maybe he start to lash me after two months.[2] Then, all the time he lash me."

"But why?"

"I don't know, gal. Maybe he likes to drink too much." Francesca stands and tosses the orange into the bush. It lands far away, next to a cacao tree. Then she sits on the bench again and stretches out her legs. "When he drinks he gets jealous. But I don't go anywhere, I stay at home, I wash the clothes, I cook the corn, I sweep my house. Only sometimes, I like to go visit my mother. But he thinks I go all kinds of places."

"So he lash you."

"Yes, he lash me. Every day, he like to lash me. I say to myself, why do I have to live like this? I have done nothing wrong. I only do my work. I don't go all kinds of places. I grind corn, I make tortilla, I sweep, I do my work good." She walks over to the rainwater vat, turns on the spigot, and rinses her hands.

I do the same.

"So, I decide to lef him." She stands waving the excess water off her hands.

"You left your husband?"

"Yes, I tell him I will not stay with him because he likes to lash me too much." She nods with finality. "When I tell him I'm going to lef him he gets vexed, gal." She laughs, "Aiy, he grabs my hair."

I suck air through my teeth. "Aiy!"

"Yes, gal." She mimes his actions while narrating the story. "He pulls

my clip from my hair and he say, 'If you leave I will take everything I
have given you.' But what has he given me?" She shrugs. "Only one small
hair clip and my earrings, that's all. So I take my earrings and I throw
them. Make him find them in the dirt. Then I lef him." The finality in
her voice and a long pause make it seem that leaving him was easy. "I
go back to my mother." Shaking her head and frowning, "I go back to
my poor mother."

"How old were you then?"

"I don't know, gal. Maybe sixteen, that's all." She repeats it, perhaps
to make it more certain. "Maybe, I was sixteen when I went back to my
poor mother."

We are silent for a few moments. I can't think of anything to ask her.
Maybe she can't think of what to say next.

"He find a next wife and leave this place to work picking oranges in
Pomona."[3] She laughs. "That man picks oranges, just like we!"

I laugh too.

When our laughter subsides, she leans close to me and whispers, "But
someone tell me, gal, that man has no hand now."

"No hand?"

She pouts and nods. "That's what they say, gal. He gets into a fight
and someone chopped him good with a machete. They say he has no
hand now." She shivers. "He likes to fight too much, it's true."

Disembodied hands give me the creeps, and the incentive to ask another question. "So what happened after you left him?"

"Nothing. He just goes to Pomona and I go with Mr. Coc." She stands,
wipes off the skirt of her dress, and picks up her net bag. She gathers her
little bundles of ginger and *ku'la* that we left on the other bench earlier
this morning and puts them in the bag.

I follow, gathering my little bundles and packing them so the oranges
won't smash the *ku'la,* a treat I have come to savor.

"Mr. Coc, he left his wife because she was bad, too." She puts her bag
on the bench where she was sitting and begins to close up the house.

I follow her, closing the kitchen window and then the side door,
throwing the bolt to the lock, making sure it is deep enough into the
small hole drilled into the smooth round log that makes the door frame.
We meet outside again, where she takes a Master Lock and slips it
through the heavy wire latch that closes the front door. We then balance
our net bags on our backs and place their straps onto our foreheads,
immobilizing our heads.

"Come, gal. *Watac a haa.*" Here comes the rain.

"Rain?" I lift my head as far as I can under the tump, but all I see is bright blue sky.

"Yes, gal. You can't see the clouds?" She points off into the distant east. I look but still don't see anything. Francesca quickens her pace and leads the way down the path, down the hillside. We step on the stepping stones which help us secure our footing as we cross over the fence. The wire fence itself has been bent down at this spot to make it easier to get over. "Mind your step, gal," Francesca says as I carefully keep my load balanced on my back.

Crossing over this fence, we leave Mr. Coc's property. Property he leased for five years and now owns. Property Francesca has helped him develop, planting cacao trees, bananas, oranges, ginger, peppers, and of course corn. We begin the walk back home. The way seems longer because of the weight of the oranges. When we reach the main road, we are able to walk next to each other and continue our conversation, the story of her life.

"Mr. Coc's wife was bad?"

"Yes, lazy, gal." Her words are breathy at first, but take more form as she continues. "But me, I do my work." She smiles and laughs.

"You've made a good life with Mr. Coc."

"Yes, gal. When you work for your husband and he is a good man, you can have a good life. It's not hard, you just have to make up your mind and do it. That's all, gal."

A few minutes later it is sprinkling. The bright blue sky is menaced by a heavy gray cloud. I feel foolish now for doubting Francesca's ability as a meteorologist.

The soil at the steepest part of the trail has worn away, leaving a slick rock surface. The few drops of moisture falling from the sky lubricate its slickness. I watch Francesca move ahead of me, my eyes focusing on her clear plastic sandals. I remember my mother, just a bit younger than Francesca is now, slipping down the bank of Shedd Brook on one of our trips to "The Farm," the place where my mother grew up. Her family lost the small dairy farm to bankruptcy in the 1950s. Her knee was never the same after that fall. I fear Francesca will fall, and wonder how that might affect her ability to "work for her husband."

She slows her pace and takes careful, graceful steps. I slip off my flip-flops, knowing I am sure to lose my footing with them on, and I follow her. I put my feet in the same places she has stepped, twisting my ankles so my feet will land at the same angles that Francesca's feet fall. I watch each step I take and trust my feet to let me know if they can't maintain a grip. When I look up, I see Francesca halfway down the hill, waiting for me.

When I catch up, she whispers, "I hear that gal in hospital."

"What girl?" We continue to walk.

"You don't see that house?" Her whisper is louder. Exasperated, she adds, "Where it's slippy, gal!"

I sense the look of confusion on my face. I just don't understand.

"Aiy! Where the children are crying!"

Maybe I did hear sobbing. I was so focused on my feet, I don't really know. "There's a house over there?" I turn around to look. We are far away from that area now. I am not surprised I don't see it.

"Yes, gal. You can't see it?"

"No, maybe there's too much bush."

"Too much bush, yes, you see. That man don't like work."

I am confused. I trust her that there is a house with crying children by the slippery part of the road. "She's in the hospital?"

"Yes, gal. I get to hear that her husband kicks her, right here." She places her hand over her kidney. "And now she's sick sick."

"Her father just went to get what *fu she*. Everything he takes; her dress, her cook pots, her chickens, everything *fu she*. Only the babies he leaves." She frowns. "And now they cry for their poor mama." She speaks with pity. "Maybe she'll die, gal."

"But why does he leave the children?"

"I don't know, gal. Maybe he wants to make that man know what he did. If he kills her, who will care for his children? Who? Who will marry him again if he kills his wife?"

The sprinkles are getting heavier. We speed up. "Why did he kick her?"

"I don't know, gal. But they are both bad. She is lazy, all the time she just stay in her hammock. She don't want to do work. And that man, huh, all he wants to do is drink." She pauses. "You don't see him at Prim's shop? Every day he drinks."

My imagination conjures up all the men I have seen drinking at Prim's. "I'm not sure which one he is." I am not sure she hears me, we are walking very fast now.

"They're both bad, gal. Neither one wants work! Can't you see? They don't chop the bush by their house! They are too lazy, gal. All the time drink; all the time sleep." I hear her as the rain finally lets us know it isn't toying with us. She jumps over a stream that now flows across the road at the bottom of the hill. It is an instant flood.

I jump, too, holding my tumpline so it won't fall off my forehead. We quickly and silently walk past the football field, up the small hill, and back to Francesca's house, out of the rain.

Risa

"So." I sit next to Risa on the car seat, the most comfortable seat on Coc's veranda. I look her in the eye. "When are you going to have a baby?" She blushes and giggles, then turns her head. She covers her face to cover her laugh. Modesto, her husband, is standing in the doorway, not three feet from us. He looks away.

"I don't know." She looks back at me after taking her hand away from her mouth and gripping the car seat. She extends her arms fully, pressing lightly against the car seat, swinging her legs. "And how about you?" Another giggle and a smile.

"Oh, me? Never." We laugh together. This time she covers her entire face with her hand, fingers spread so we can still look at each other. I smile and sit for a few more moments before I get up and go home. Francesca and I have just returned from church, and I am anxious to type up my notes about the sermon.

"I'll come see you," she says as I get up.

"Okay, good." I tell everyone I am leaving. Modesto waves a tiny good-bye.

At home, in my thatch house, I turn on my computer and start writing. After a few minutes, a quiet, invisible *"deyoos,"* a hello sounds at my door. Sounds like Risa. I didn't think she would get away so soon.

"Yeah, come on in, I'm in the kitchen." This is the greeting I give her, just like an American. I am at the other end of the house, not twenty feet from her. I know it is Risa, but I don't take the three steps it would take to go to the door and welcome her in. I don't want the formality, I want a friend. I want to ignore "respect" for awhile. I want the informality of an American friendship.

She doesn't respond. She forces me to do the right thing. I stand and take those three steps of formality, those three steps of respect. I welcome her into my house. *"O ken, tel a banco."* Come in, there is a seat.

Then she enters. She comes right through into the kitchen area, where I am working on my computer. She stands next to the table, so I take my seat again. She is quiet.

I try to make conversation. "So you are visiting the Cocs. This is the first time you visit since your wedding."

"Yes, this is the first time. My husband thinks it's good to visit my family." She bites her lip and picks up a pencil from the table. She looks closely at the point, and picks at the wood. "What is that?" She points to the computer with her lips.

"It's a computer. I use it to write." I type a few words so she can see how it works.

"Then you don't use this?" She holds up the pencil.

"Well, I use that to draw." I pick up the computer and move it over a few inches. Under it is a calendar I bought in the States. Each month shows a different Mayan artifact or site in Mexico. It also keeps the Mayan days. Under that are the enlargements I made of the glyphs for Mayan day names.

"So, you like draw." Risa's eyes twinkle and she smiles.

"Yes, I like it." I hand them to her; she flips through them. "I made these glyphs big. Maybe I can use them as patterns to sew. Everybody makes the small calendars, but maybe some people can make just one glyph."[4]

She nods her head as she slowly looks at each one. "Maybe I can sew them."

I am happy she likes them. "Do you want? I can make patterns for you, if you want."

She bites her lip again, nods her head, and speaks slowly. "Maybe that's good."

"Yeah, I can make them, no problem." I pull out a few sheets of typing paper. "Which ones do you like?"

"Maybe all of them." She smiles.

I am flattered. I wasn't so sure people would like the idea. I trace the first one, *Zotz*. It is probably a tapir, but I always think of an elephant.

She quietly watches as I begin to trace the next one, *Kayab*. She breaks our silence. "Why don't you have a baby?"

I look up at her, she looks down at the drawing. Her fingers play with one of my piles of papers. I answer, "Because my husband don't want."

"Your husband don't want?" She shakes her head, her eyes squinting with puzzlement. "Maybe you drink medicine."

"Yes," I look up at her, "I do."

She knows a little bit about birth control. Different members of her family have asked me about birth control before. They, unlike other families, seem obsessed with it.[5]

I continue, "But I don't take it now, because my husband is not here. When he comes to Belize, I will take it again." No man; no babies. It's easy.

"Oh." She bites her lip again. "But you take it every day?"

"Yes. When I stay with my husband."

She nods slowly.

"I'll show you, if you want." Without waiting for a response, I lean over to my food preparation table. Under this table I keep medicines, insect repellent, bleach, and bungee cords. I grab the plastic case for my birth control pills, open it, and hand it to her. Her eyes are wide.

"This is what you drink." Not a question, a statement.

"Yep." I watch her eyes.

She holds the packet in her hands and turns it over. "And you don't get babies."

"That's right." I smile.

She turns it in her hands again and looks at me. "But how?"

Hormones. How can I explain hormones? But Modesto steps into my house, without "deyoosing." Somewhat startled, I turn toward him. Risa hides the pills under a stack of papers on my desk. She looks at me. I nod, trying to make the nod look like a greeting for Modesto.

"Modesto, welcome to my little house. I was showing Risa"—her eyes nearly pop out—"my computer and some drawings I made." I can feel her relief; I am covering for her.

"Yes, you have a small house." He cranes his neck looking around, standing next to Risa. "But you have so many things."

"Not so many, really." I continue to trace the next drawing.

Modesto turns to Risa and speaks in a whisper.

Risa nods and looks down. "My husband says we should go."

"Oh, here, you can take this drawing." I turn to Modesto, "Risa says she wants to sew. I'm giving her some patterns."

"Yes?" Smiling, he looks at the one I am tracing. "That's good. Maybe she can sew." He smiles a broad, handsome smile.

I smile at Risa. "I can bring the others to you another day." She smiles back.

Modesto leads us outside to the veranda, where we stand for a moment. "Maybe you will come to my little house again, Risa."

"Yes, maybe." Modesto smiles cheerfully as he looks back at me. A statement from her husband. He might let her come to my house again sometime. It is approved. Maybe then I can tell her about birth control.

"Bye, *ix* Laura." She smiles at me again, and they are gone.

Remalda, Risa's mother, is sitting on my *banco,* the piece of carved tree trunk I sit on when I am cooking. She is trying to get my fire to burn more steadily. Prudencia, Risa's younger sister, is sitting on my tall stool, the one I sit on when I am writing. She is sitting with her arms in her lap watching her mother. I am watching her, too, from the doorway of my kitchen. The three of us fill the house, it is so tiny.

"So how is Risa? Have you seen her lately?" A conversation starter. I am uncomfortable without conversation. I am also a little annoyed that Remalda has taken over my kitchen. I didn't ask for help. I know how to cook.

"Yes, she come two days ago." Remalda leans down closer to the flame and blows. I don't have much firewood left. Her need for bigger flames is going to waste my wood. It is burning fine. I don't say anything. She blows again, until big flames tickle the sides of my rice pot. "Sometimes she's a little bit sick."

"Sick? I never knew." I like Risa, even though we don't really communicate well. Her English is rough and my Mopan is bad. But she giggles a lot, and that makes all the difference in the world. She seems even more private than most Mayan girls her age. I like to tease her about getting pregnant, now that she is married. She seems to enjoy the joke.

"She's not sick all the time." Remalda sits back from the fire. "She just gets sick in the mornings."

"Maybe she's pregnant." I say it without thinking. It is what I always say. It's my joke.

Prudencia giggles on cue.

"Maybe." A quiet fills the air as Remalda looks at the fire. I still don't get it. I don't get it until later, much later, when it is obvious to everyone.

Evangelista, Risa's mother-in-law, is spreading rice on a blue tarp in front of her wooden house. She looks up as I approach. "So you come." She stands, straightens her hair, and smiles.

"Yes, I just come to see Risa." I stand on the tarp next to her and help spread rice. She smiles broadly as she bends down at the waist, to continue her work.

"She's home." Still bending, Evangelista stretches her arm out far, pointing to Risa's house. When I turn my head to look, her arm gracefully returns to spreading the rice. "It mus dry inna dey sun." [6] She stands again, arms at her sides, and looks at the sky. "I jus spread it now," she laughs, "cause inna dey morning it look like de rain dey come."

"Yes, but it don look like dey rain will come again." I use the "again" like the Creoles use "again." It doesn't indicate repetition as much as it is a statement about the outcome. It means "after all." It hasn't rained in days.

Just as we finish spreading the rice evenly across the tarps, Evangelista instructs me, "Mind the holes." She doesn't want to lose even a grain. We stand for a second looking up at the sky. My hands are on my hips, hers at her sides. She breaks the stance first and sits on a stool in the doorway of the wooden building. "No, it can't rain again."

"I come because I want to give Risa these patterns." I sit on the rotting porch steps of the wooden house and pull some drawings of Mayan glyphs from my backpack. Each boldly drawn glyph fills an $8\frac{1}{2} \times 11$ piece of typing paper. "I made them for sewing. Risa said she wanted some, so I made some for her."

Evangelista laughs a big "can you believe that" laugh. "So she say she wants to sew." I am silent. Evangelista holds the patterns at arm's length and looks at them, turning them around, trying to find which way is up. "Maybe she will sew all day." Her laugh turns to chuckles as she hands them back to me.

"I hear she's sick." I slowly turn my gaze from the glyphs to Evangelista's face.

She looks straight ahead, into nothingness, tilting her head high. "Maybe she eat too much." She motions an upward swirl in front of her chest. Nausea. She turns her head in my direction, but doesn't look at me.

I giggle to indicate that I am about to tell a joke. I am going to tell the joke I always tell. Everyone else enjoys the joke, why shouldn't she? "Maybe she's pregnant."

Evangelista doesn't find it funny. She shrugs her shoulders and turns her head to look into the house. Smacking her lips, she says, "Nobody tell me." Then a cold silence.

Quick rapid speech, "I don't know. I'm just saying that. Maybe she's just sick." I'm sorry, it was just a joke. Am I making it worse? I stand to make my getaway. "I'm going to see her now."

Evangelista looks up at me, nods, and smiles at me. It is okay. "When you finish, I will give you some rice." She stands up energetically and goes inside. There is more work to be done.

As I near Risa's house, I remember the last time I was here. It was shortly after their wedding. I was bringing her and Modesto their wedding present. I approached the door and saw Modesto lying in the hammock in the living room, his back to me. Risa was standing next to him, smiling, her hand on his shoulder. Like a snapshot, the image frozen in my head. I saw his hand under her dress, high up on her thigh. Risa broke the snapshot when she looked up at me. Her deep nasal laugh spilled out as she put her hand to her face and yanked at the hem of her dress. She turned, almost a full spin, which way do I go? A smile behind her hand as she darted into the bedroom. I was embarrassed, too.

Modesto put his hand on his belly, as if it were never on her thigh. But the way he turned his head to the wall, I knew it had been. It wasn't just a trick of the eye.

I turned and began to walk back the way I came. Modesto stood up, came to the door, and called me back. I came back giggling and blushing. Risa stayed in the bedroom for a few more seconds.

Now, I am passing the point I reached when he called me back that day. I smile at the memory and approach the door. This time I stand beside the doorway, so I can't see in. I don't want to invade their privacy. "*Deyoos.*" I wait, no answer. I peek into the house. Risa is lying in the hammock. She sees me peering at her.

"*O ken, tel a banco.*" She sits up, smiles when I enter.

I sit on the bench by the bedroom, quiet for a moment. "I came to bring you these patterns." I take them out of my backpack again.

She flips through the pile. "Did you sew these?" she asks, looking up at me.

"No, I don't have that much time to sew. I just do that same one I started a long time ago." I look at the ground. I feel guilty whenever I have to admit I haven't finished it yet.

"Make I see." Her eyes are bright, she reaches her hand out to me.

"I don't bring it." I never bring what I should, it seems.

"But why?" She leans back down into the hammock and swings.

"I don't know." I shrug and smile. "I'm tired of it already."

"Because you're laaazzzy." She laughs. Then she stands and goes into the kitchen.

I protest, under my breath. "I'm not lazy. I do lots of work."

A minute later, she returns and hands me a bowl of warm tea.

"*Boticex.*" I grumble thanks and sip the sweet tan liquid.

"But if you are not lazy, why don't you finish? You are lazy, *ix* Laura." She giggles.

If I wanted revenge I could tell her what Evangelista tells me. I could tell her that she is the laziest woman around; unfit to be a wife. But I don't say a thing. I take the abuse, I pretend nothing is wrong. She is just teasing. Everyone teases the gringa. All gringas are lazy.

"Maybe I do other kinds of work." I grumble louder, sipping my tea.

"But you don't know Maya yet."

Yes, my Maya is poor, but it will get better. Risa senses it is a sensitive topic, but does nothing to make me feel better. I am angry. I look out the door sternly. I see a rooster jumping to reach berries on a tree branch. He jumps, pulls at the branch and falls. Again, stretching his neck, he jumps and falls. I can't help but laugh. Risa sees him and laughs, too; we are friends again.

Resistance

In the road, in front of the footpath that leads to the Sho compound, is a mountain of dirt and sand. It doesn't matter that the pile blocks the road. Few vehicles come this way anyway.

When closer, I see Modesto's thirteen-year-old brother, Alejandro, come down the path with a shovel and a bucket. He smiles and nods, and gets right to work shoveling dirt into his bucket. I smile at him. "You've got plenty work."

"For true." He throws another shovelful of dirt into the bucket. He doesn't have time to chat, so I walk past him, up the footpath, to see his mother, Evangelista, and his sister-in-law, Risa.

I pass the empty two-story wooden house. It has been empty for a long time, long before I came to the village. Its blue paint is worn away in spots, chipping in others. The porch floor is rotten, but the steps are still there. The house still stands. The Shos use the cement foundation and first floor for storage. They live in a thatch house next to it. I think of the wooden house as a monument to better times. Not too long ago people with a little extra cash built wooden houses in this style. Maybe that was in the 1960s, when James Gregory, another anthropologist, was in southern Belize. Maybe it was a little more recently.

Now, I am standing where the Shos' thatch house should be, but it's not here. The frame and the roof are still standing, but the walls are gone. I am confused. Modesto and Risa's new-style wooden house is still over there to my far right. Modesto's older brother's thatch house is still to my left. What's going on? Are they moving? I spy a pile of cement blocks and remember them covered in vines during Risa's wedding celebration. Alejandro, I finally realize, is starting the work of building a cement house for his father. Cement is the newest material for those with a little extra cash.

Hesitantly, as if the thatch house were still there, I stand by the front door frame and say, "*Deyoos*." I'm not sure how to visit someone whose house is missing.

"I am here." I hear Evangelista's voice to my left. It is coming from the chicken coop. I turn to see her standing in the coop with a large butcher knife. Her hair is a mess.

"So, now you live with the chickens. Many things happen when I don't visit for a long time." I laugh, counting on her sense of humor to understand I am joking.

"Yes, my children tell me it is good to live wid a de chickens." She is stooped over to fit in the coop, but she turns toward me to finish. "It is good for their mother, dey say, because den she can watch her chickens good." She sighs and then laughs as she grabs a fuzzy chick.

I come closer and lean on the coop as I peer inside. "I never knew."

We laugh together. She has a chick in one hand and the butcher knife in the other. She bends down even further and stretches the chick's toe out on a piece of carpentered wood. She raises her knife and chops about a quarter inch off the toe, leaving a tiny stump after the first knuckle. The chick blinks, opens its beak wide, swallows, and wiggles. She holds tight and singles out another toe until all of its toes, on both feet, are mutilated. "Yes, now I live wid a dey chickens." She lets it go.

I am still leaning and watching. "It's nice, but maybe you want to put a hammock in there."

She grabs another chick and repeats the mutilation. "Yes. It is like dat mon." I have gotten used to Mayan indirect references. I will know who she means if I keep listening. If I am especially dim, she might say his name. "He has no place to live. You see his house? It's de one by the church." A clue, but I can't picture the house. I ponder for a second how a man can have a house, but no place to live. I wait for the next clue. "His dautta don't want him to live wid she no more. So she make him live inna dat small small house, wid no roof." Evangelista has finished trimming the feet of her five chicks. She opens the coop door and lets them run. "Dat is what happens to de poor man. His dautta don't want him no more." She steps out of the coop, and stretches.

"Which house is that? Maybe I don't see it." I am not surprised I haven't noticed a house next to the church, even though the church is the most visible structure in the village. Every day the village seems completely different to me, but exactly the same to everyone else.

"It is by de church." I guess there is no other way to describe it. "He live there for many years, until he die. He die with nothing, wid no one. He only have his little chickens." She closes the coop behind her and straightens out her graying hair. She brushes off her dark blue *p'ik* [7] and *pach caan camesa* [8]. She looks especially beautiful in these clothes. "A storm come one day and tek his roof, he neva fix it. He too old, too poor. He got no one. No one to work fu he." She straightens up and laughs. "Just like me."

I ignore her complaints; they are too uncomfortable to listen to, even if she does laugh about them. After a little thought I think I know the man she is talking about. If I am right, he would be her husband's fraternal uncle. "Why do you cut your chicks?"

"I cut them so I know dey fu me. When dey get older, dey will walk far. Sometimes dey walk inna da utter pipple's coops." She nods her head as she waves her hand to indicate the compound across the road. "Sometimes you can't tell if dey fu you or no." She looks at me and nods again. "Yes, it's happened already."

My eyes follow her hand, and continue to look in the direction of the next compound. "So you're marking them, to know they are yours." I look at her.

"Yes, because, sometimes you have to say dey fu you. It happen already. Some of my chickens walk that side. But de pipple say de chick fu dey. Dey look jus like the chick dat fu dey. How can I say it not for true?"

I look at the butcher knife in her hand. I have tied blue cloth, scraps from the *p'ik* Rosa made for me, around my chickens' feet to indicate they are mine. I have had to replace the cloth a few times as the chicks grew or pulled the cloth off. "Yes, I see."

"But come, come res yourself." She walks toward the wooden house and enters a room on the first-floor foundation. "Dis is my kitchen now, just like before." She chuckles.

I step in behind her. It is a small dark room with two windows. The room is dark because the walls are covered with soot. She has done a lot of cooking here. The room smells of roasting peccary. I can see a cut of meat lying on the grill over the fire, sizzling. Peccary has a foul, nephridial smell, like skunk, but it also smells appetizing.

Evangelista places a tall stool by the door, motioning me to sit. She sits on another tall stool near the table, not far from me, to my left, and picks up a large flat metal tin. Inside, the bottom of the tin is covered with dried beans. She begins picking through them, throwing tiny shriveled ones and small stones onto the cement floor. She will cook the beans with lard for her husband Estevan and her youngest son, Alejandro. "Yes, this is where I cook now." She doesn't look up at me, but continues her work.

"I miss your old hearth." I look over to where it used to be.

She smiles. "Yes. A thatch house is good, the smoke don stay." She reaches over to the new hearth and turns the peccary meat. "And thatch is cooler denna de cement." Then she looks back down at her beans and continues to sort them out.

I am silent for a few seconds. "I come to tell you that I will leave the village soon. I will go back to the States." I look at her but she doesn't look up.

I wait for her response.

"So, now it is time for you to leave us. I tink you stay til April." I look out the door, she still doesn't look up.

"Yes, at first I was to leave in April, but now, I miss my husband too much." He left the village about a month ago, after a two-month visit. Having him in the village made my homesickness worse. "I will go back to him, in the States." I am glad a tear didn't form in my eye. I miss him so.

Finally, she looks up at me. "That is good, you miss your husband. It's because you love him. You like to tek care of he, cook fu he, work fu he. That is good." Then she looks back down at her beans. "But maybe you will neva come back to us in the village."

This thought saddens me. I watch a chick come through the doorway. It is examining the beans and pebbles Evangelista has tossed on the floor. She looks up and shoos it away. The quarter-inch missing from each toe doesn't seem to impede it.

"I would like to come back. Maybe after I get my job in the States, then I can save money and come again. Only God knows." I feel self-conscious saying "only God knows." It's the one phrase people say here that makes me uncomfortable. I am not sure I believe in God. I have been hearing it a lot these last few weeks, especially when I tell people I am leaving. "Only God knows when we will see *ix* Laura again." Only God knows.

She says it too. "Yes, only God knows." She says it while tossing another pebble on the floor.

I see Risa come out of the back door of her house, maybe a hundred feet away. She picks up a large flat tin like the one Evangelista is holding. It is the one I gave her as a wedding present. She walks over to the rice mortar that stands in the house without walls, near where the hearth used to be. She puts the tin down and scoops out some rice with a calabash. I watch as she pours it into the mortar, holding the calabash high to winnow the grain. Then she reaches down and picks up the large heavy wooden pestle, raises it over her head and begins to beat the rice. One, two, THREE, pause, one, two, THREE, pause, one, two, THREE, pause. She turns and looks at me, smiles, and begins again. One, two, THREE, pause, one, two, THREE, pause, one, two, THREE, pause, one, two, THREE.

I am watching Risa, and I say, "So Risa works now."

Evangelista doesn't respond but continues to sort her beans.

I met Risa when I first came to the village. Three weeks into my field-work, her parents invited me to her engagement party at their house "in the bush." It was *hobol u k'aat,* "the end of the asking," the time when wedding negotiations are completed. Risa, at the end of this engagement party, was obliged to marry Modesto.

Modesto and Risa were a good match. Modesto's father, Estevan Sho, is the "second *alcalde,*" an assistant to the *alcalde.* It is a prestigious position. It signals that the men of the village trust him and feel he is good. He and his son are hard-working men. They raise beans, they hunt. The groom's family was willing to have a traditional wedding.

Risa came from a family of twelve. As the second oldest daughter, Modesto's family knew she would know how to cook, how to wash, how to care for children. They knew she could work hard for her husband, as hard as he would work for her. Besides, Risa's grandfather is one of the richest men in the village. That connection could help them if they ever needed to borrow money.

The arrangement was good. The bride and groom were from the same village; she could visit her mother if she wanted, it was not too far. Throughout the negotiations, Risa's soon-to-be mother-in-law, Evange-lista, promised to help her learn her work, promised to teach her how to take care of her son, Modesto.

Modesto, at the request of Risa's grandmother, promised not to get vexed at Risa if she did not quickly learn how to cook, how to wash his clothes, how to live away from her family. He said he understood that it takes time to get used to a new place away from your mother, away from your sisters, away from your father.

It takes time to learn how to be a wife. It takes time to get used to being alone, in a new house, with only your husband's family to talk with. It takes time.

Modesto also promised to respect his new family, Risa's family. He promised to respect her father, her mother. He promised to respect her grandfather, her grandmother. He would help them when they asked for help, he would not laugh at their mistakes. He would never laugh at Risa's family. He promised respect. He would always address them with a title of respect, signifying and reinforcing their obligation to each other as family.

He had proven himself a hard-working man. He had gone to Belize City and worked hard in a restaurant as a busboy cleaning the dishes left by tourists and the Belizean elite. He worked hard and didn't drink his money. He didn't spend it on "all kinds of foolishness." He saved it. Modesto came back to the village and listened to his father. His father told him to build a house with his money and to find a wife. He could have stayed in Belize City to find a wife, but he came home to find a Mayan girl. Maya work hard for their family. He listened to his father when he told him to find someone who will work hard for him and his children.

Soon after he returned to the village, Modesto built a wooden house with a zinc roof. It wasn't an elaborate house like his father's wooden house, but it was stylish. He was inspired by the hotels and restaurants built for tourists.

He built it near his father's house and his brother's house. Family is nearby. His father's compound is near a new USAID water pump. There is also a stream nearby that has water even in the dry season. Water is not too far. Hauling water would not be a difficult chore for his wife.

I vividly remember Risa's father and grandmother trying to convince her that it was good. I remember Risa lying in her hammock covering her face, hiding the tears. She cried throughout the meeting before the engagement was official. She cried for four hours. She cried while her sisters prepared tortilla and chicken *caldo*. She cried while her brother talked to the newly arrived gringa. She cried while her younger sisters and brothers played. She cried while her mother, father, and grandmother and grandfather sat in the front room with Modesto's parents and godparents making sure she would be treated well and that they would be respected. She lay still in her hammock, almost invisible while her life was mutating into something unknown. For four hours she expressed her fear, her unhappiness, her refusal. It would take time to learn to be away from her sisters, her mother. It would take time.

One, two, THREE, pause, one, two, THREE, pause, one, two, THREE, pause. Risa raises the giant pestle over her head. She looks over at me again, but this time her eyes are squinting, her mouth slightly pursed.

"It seem she work good," I offer, hoping a second mention of Risa's work would make Evangelista respond. I want her to admit that Risa is working; I want to hear her say how well Risa is caring for her husband.

"Yes, she work." She said it. I feel joy hearing her admit Risa is working. Then I realize she plans to continue, she is only pausing. She has more to say. "Maybe she listen to her father and grandmother."⁹ Evangelista tosses another pebble to the ground.

"Her grandmother come?" I am surprised. I had asked her grandmother, Francesca, many times if she would come with me on my trips to visit Risa and Evangelista. She always laughed and told me she had no reason to go. Then she would say I knew more places in the village than she.

"You don know?" Evangelista looks at me.

"No, no one tell me." I speak slowly, trying to remember if I could have missed the point of a recent interchange with Francesca. Maybe she did tell me, indirectly.

"Yes, her grandmother and her father come two days ago now." Evangelista's eyes squint with seriousness. "I send for dem to talk to her." She pauses and puts her tin of beans on the table. "Dey tell she, she mus work. I neva see a gal like this. She don want work." Evangelista stands and puts the beans into an orange plastic bowl.

Since I have known Evangelista, she has complained to me about Risa. Risa, she says, refuses to care for her son the way she cared for him. Once, I told Risa what her mother-in-law said about her. I said it as a warning, so she would know she should try harder. I believed Evangelista's complaints about Risa because I had seen her ignore Modesto. Modesto even mentioned it to me once. I thought maybe, if I told her that her mother-in-law complained to me, then she would change her ways and be more accommodating. Maybe she would be more like a wife instead of a captured prisoner with exceptional privileges.

Now, I remember my missed opportunity to come with Francesca and Juan, Risa's father, to talk to Risa. I was heading to the corn grinder. Francesca was hanging her wash. Juan was standing next to her talking in a whisper. She called me over and hinted that I should go with her. I just didn't feel like it.

"So that is why Francesca ask me to come to visit Risa. She ask me to come with her, but I never knew. I think maybe she don't know the place. She was talking with Risa's father, Juan. He was upset, but I never knew." I am upset. I am caught between thinking Evangelista is taking drastic measures against Risa and being angry at Risa for letting it go so far as to have Evangelista summon her father.

In a quicker, higher-pitched voice, Evangelista sums up their visit. "Yes, dey come. Dey tell she my son is good. Dey say 'why you no work.' Dey tell her so."

"Yes, I know, it's true. He don't drink. He like to hunt. I see him work all the time with Juan, with Andres, with Emilio. He just help them plant corn not too long ago." I stand for a second to reach a stick Evangelista keeps near the hearth. I use it to shoo a bald fledgling chick from the house.

Evangelista slows her speech. Her voice is lower, calm, disgusted. "Yes. I neva see a gal like this. She tek de comb we give she and she tek it like dis," Evangelista puts her two fists side by side and mimes breaking something in two. "And den de pieces," she mimes more breakage. "Why would a gal do dat?"

I shake my head. "I don't know." But I do know. Risa doesn't want to be married to Modesto. She did her best to refuse the marriage, everything except voice her refusal.

"My son, he spend plenty onna dey wedding, if she don want, why she don say? We buy her cloth, we buy her new gold earrings, soap. We buy her plenty, but she throw it or break it. She don want anything. She don even cook for my son. He come yestaday from hunting. He shoot dis peccary." She motions with her lips to the roasting meat on her hearth. "Good meat. But she don want cook. He come onto me for food. When

I tek care of my son he neva go hungry, but wid she, he get hungry."
Her voice is high again and rapid. She seems angry, perplexed, and frustrated.

"It has been a long time since the wedding." I had thought, in time,
Risa would get used to being married. I thought, maybe, she was acting a role to let everyone know she had never talked to this boy before;
to show she was a virtuous girl. I had heard a lot of gossip about girls
who talked to boys. Women always talked about them with intonations
expressing disgrace. Maybe, I had thought, it is important to express
resistance in order to maintain innocence.

"Yes! Long time!" She holds out her hand in frustration. "Look, you
are leaving now, she married when a you first come." She slaps her thigh,
stands, and turns the peccary meat again.

"Well, she engage when I first come. The wedding was after that. But
maybe eight months she's married." It is important to figure out how
long it has been in order to figure out if she has had time to "learn her
work." I am hesitant to admit it has been quite a long time. Even I have
learned my work.

"Yes! And she see her mother everytime." She sits on the tall stool
again; her legs are spread. She has one hand braced on each knee. In
another hand movement of exasperation, she says, "I don know maybe
she don work for she Ma." She shakes her head. "But how is that, she
Ma got plenty *pickney* (children). Maybe she Ma de only one wants
work."

One, two, THREE, pause, one, two, THREE, pause. One, two,
THREE, pause. She doesn't look my way at all this time.

Evangelista and I are silent for a moment. I remember the time I helped
Risa and her sisters, Prudencia and Anna, carry cooked corn to the
grinder. We were making tortillas and *caldo* for the men their father,
Juan, had asked to help him plant his new corn. We carried thirty-one
pounds of corn in small plastic buckets down the steep hill, along the
river, and down the road past the football field, past the church, past
Prim's shop down another steep, slippery hill to the grinder. After chatting with Pia and paying $2.48 BZ for her services, we hauled it back.
The work was tiring. The roads and footpaths were muddy. I spent a lot
of energy just trying to stay upright. Their mother is not the only one
who works for her family.

One, two, THREE, pause, one, two, THREE, pause, one, two,
THREE. I remember the time Felicia taught me to "bust rice." She did

Busting rice.

it so effortlessly. As usual, I watched her for a few moments and then asked her to teach me. I remember the weight of the giant pestle. I remember the smooth finish it had where you hold it. It was shiny smooth, the kind of smooth wood gets when it has been handled a lot. I remember the blisters that formed almost immediately, and the back pain that came the next day. Busting rice is not easy. I never knew rice was so much work.

One, two, THREE, pause, one, two, THREE, pause, one, two, THREE. I remember I bought rice this morning at Coc's shop. It was forty-five Belizean a pound. That is twenty-two U.S. cents.

I break the silence and look at Evangelista. "What did they say?"

She looks back at me, "When dey come?"

"Yes. When they come." I shoo a chicken out the door with the stick again.

Evangelista prepares for the telling. It is a subtle preparation. She doesn't look at me directly, but turns her head away, keeping her eyes low. The telling voice is slow, methodical, quiet. These are not her words but someone else's. Maya rituals of telling help the listener to understand that the speaker is not speaking for someone else, just repeating their words.[10]

"Dey say, 'Modesto is good. He works for you, but you don work for he.' Den her father tell she, 'You are married now, you can't come home. You mus work for your husband.' Dat is what he say. 'If you don want Modesto maybe you want to leave.[11] If you leave, who will have you again?' Dat is what dey say. 'If you leave he, maybe you can't find the next husband.'[12] Dat is what dey come and tell she."

Evangelista pauses, but keeps her eyes low. "She grandmutta know. She tell her to think. She tell her she husband is good. 'He don't lash you; he works hard.' She tell she, 'If you don want your husband, you should leave, but if you leave you mus neva think about him again. You must neva think about the way you once lived.' Dat is what she say. She grandmutta know."

I am quiet.

"She grandmutta know, because it's de same wid Mr. Coc. Dat is what she say. She say, 'Mr. Coc have a wife who was no good. She don like work. Dat woman is the mother of your mother. Dat woman don want Mr. Coc, so she lef him. And Mr. Coc work hard den, he was a young man.' Dat is what she say. 'So he find himself a new wife. Now you can see dat if you work hard for your husband you can have a good life. If you both work for each other, like Mr. Coc and me' she said, 'you can have your nice house, you can have your little shop, you can raise your little pigs.' She tell she, 'You both have to work for each other. That is life, that is the way you live.' She says she knows, because now Mr. Coc's wife she is a poor lady, but she and Mr. Coc, they have a shop. 'It is not just for your husband dat you work.' That is how she tell dis gal."

Evangelista looks up at me to indicate her telling is over.

I complete the telling by reaffirming her words. "So that is how it is with Mr. Coc's wife." I nod my head, I understand.

"Yes, and maybe dat is why Risa don want work." She shrugs her shoulders. "Maybe it is like her mother's mother. Maybe my son will find the next lady." Evangelista stands and moves behind the hearth. She takes a stick and stokes the fire. "But if she don want my son she should say so. How can he spend money for a wedding again? He spend so much fu she."

"I don't know." I barely get my words out before she starts again.

"And he build dat pig house." She points with her lips at an empty pigpen next to Risa's house. "He thinks maybe dey can make dey money and raise a few pigs. But look, it sits, she says not to finish, cause she don want to raise de pigs. She say dey stink too much. She won't care for pigs." Evangelista pauses, takes a breath and looks me in the eye. "How can she live if she don want to work? Wid no work you have no food, you have no clothes, you can't buy your sugar, your soap." She counts these necessities of life on her fingers, finishing with her hands in the air. "How can you live?"

I picture the pigpens at Risa's father's house. "Raising pigs is good. Her father raise pigs. She can get them from him."

"Yes, but she no want. I don know why de gal go so." She stokes her fire again and turns the peccary meat.

I repeat some of the words I had heard her grandmother say about Risa's situation. "And her husband is good. I know he doesn't drink."

"No, he don't drink. He keep his money good." She puts her stick back and returns to the tall stool.

Risa puts the giant pestle down by her feet and gently leans over the mortar. She scoops up a few grains of rice and examines them. They must still have their hulls, because she tosses them back into the mortar and raises the pestle again. One, two, THREE, pause, one, two, THREE, pause, one, two, THREE. She wipes sweat from her brow and lifts it again. One, two, THREE, pause, one, two, THREE, pause, one, two, THREE.

"And he don't lash her." I say as I keep my eye on Risa. My ears, however, are tuned to Evangelista.

"If a man lash his wife when he drunk, that's one thing. But if he does it when she no work, that's something else."

We are both silent for a long time. Risa wipes the sweat from her brow again, then, again, lifts the giant pestle.

A few minutes later, Risa's sister-in-law, Juanna, comes out of her thatch house and walks over to her. She has a big bucket of laundry. She stops, puts the bucket down, and talks with Risa. I can't hear what they are saying. Risa nods her head, and Juanna takes the bucket up again and heads toward the stream.

"She go wash at de riva now." Evangelista points at Risa with her lips. "Maybe you bring your clothes to wash wid she."

"No, I didn't bring them this time." The idea of carrying a bucket of laundry through the village never appealed to me. "But I think I will go see her." I stand and look out the door. I watch Risa leave the giant mortar and pestle after scooping her rice back into her tin.

"Yes, you go ta she." She is quiet for a moment, maybe remembering that I am leaving the village. "When you go to States, maybe you'll write to me."

"It's hard when you get back to the States sometimes. Especially when you get your job. But I will try." I turn to her and smile. "But I will think of you. And I will visit you when I come back. I don't know when, but I will be back."

She smiles, and nods. "Go talk wid dat gal. You don't know when you will see her again."

"Only God knows."

As I approach, Risa winnows the rice she has just pounded. She is on her back veranda, where her husband and his friends made *chicarone*, fried pig skin, the night before they were married. I quietly cross the Sho compound's common space and stand on the ridge above her veranda. "*Deyoos*," I say. Her back is to me, so she looks over her shoulder and forces a smile.

I come onto the veranda, and she winnows the rice again. Chickens gather around her feet to catch the hulls and stray grains of rice. I notice some of them have red cloth tied around their feet, others have toes missing.

"I come for a visit." I can tell that she thinks I am here to talk to her, the way her father and grandmother talked to her. Maybe she thinks her mother-in-law sent for me, too. I want to warn her, Risa, it is true, you are going to get a beating unless you act differently. Please give in, he's not so bad. He is a good husband. Please. But how do I say this?

She is curt. "I have to go to the river. I have work." I am standing next to her now, towering a foot above her. I'm uncomfortable, she's uncomfortable. She picks up her rice and goes inside. Should I follow?

She reemerges, but into her open-air kitchen. She puts rice in a pot with some water and balances it on top of two twelve-inch lengths of rebar over the fire. Her back is still toward me. I think I should leave.

She disappears again into the house. Bravely and perhaps rudely, I enter the house too. She gathers up what she will need to wash, filling her bucket with clothes: two men's white shirts, her fluorescent green dress, a pair of muddy work pants, a man's white T-shirt, a red half-slip, white panties, her bridal veil.

"I know you have work." I look down. I am standing by the door. "Maybe I can come to the river with you?"

She smiles and continues to assemble what she needs. In the kitchen she adds a large plastic margarine tub, a small plastic tub with ball soap in it, a five-pound bag of FOCA-brand powder soap, biodegradable, and a bar of pink "sweet soap" for bathing. Then, from the bedroom, a dark blue dress with yellow zigzag trim, a bright yellow half-slip, and pink panties. These she puts in a plastic bag. This is what she will wear after bathing.

"Yes," she giggles, "you can come." I smile, taking her permission as a sign of forgiveness. Though I have been in the village a long time, I still have trouble remembering that everybody is responsible for her own actions. It is up to me if I want to follow her around all day. That is what she is giggling about. She won't tell me what I can or cannot do. She won't even tell me what I should or shouldn't do. That is up to me to decide. We are not tied into a relationship of kinship, a relationship of respect.

I follow her as she walks past the half-built pigpen, then down the path to the river. I slip in the mud going down the hill, but regain my balance without falling. She laughs and keeps walking. I laugh, too, trying to deflect the fact that I am the butt of the joke. Scarlet haliconias line the path. We walk single file, in silence; I am behind her.

When we reach the river, Juanna is still washing laundry. A stack of clean clothes sits nearby on a rock. More clothes soak in her bucket. She is washing a child's flowered dress; one braced foot supports her movements. The stream area is low, the shore steep. The river is just a trickle here, with a few pools made by the careful placement of a few rocks. The trees around here are beautiful. The stream bed is lined with mossy rocks. I find a big, clean one to sit on.

Risa takes her place in the stream. After saying hello to Juanna, I am quiet. I tell myself I am doing the observing part of participant-observation. It eases the feeling of being unwelcome. It eases the need to talk to Risa seriously.

Risa is close to her sister-in-law. She whispers something, but I can't hear. Both giggle. Juanna looks up at me. "So you come to wash?" Risa giggles loudly. She is enjoying making me feel uncomfortable.

"No, I just come for a visit. I'm leaving soon. Going back to the States. I just wanted to see Risa again. Before I go." They both look at me. Risa agitates the clothes in her bucket, now filled with water and a little soap.

Juanna folds the child's dress. "You never come to visit me." She tosses the dress on top of the folded clean pile.

"I'm visiting you now." Silence.

"Why you go so soon?" Risa's nasal voice.

"I miss my husband too much." I look away from the stream. I can see some men walking on a path a few hundred yards away. They have guns. Risa laughs.

"You have a husband?" Juanna looks up at me again, starting on another piece of clothing.

"Yes." I am frustrated. I have had this same introductory conversation a million times since I came to the village. Now, I have to tell it again on the day I come to say goodbye. We follow the usual script. Yes, I have no children. No, my husband don't want. Yes, we have been together many years now, and so on, until we hear a baby cry. I look around, but don't see it. Juanna climbs up the stream bed and crosses the path. There is a white sling hanging from a tree; her baby has awakened from its nap and is crying. She rocks it in the sling until it quiets again.

Risa is scrubbing her wedding veil with a scrub brush.

"Til now you wash your veil." I smile.

She looks up at me and smiles, sincerely this time. "Yes, 'til now." She rinses it and folds it, then tosses it on top of her clean-clothes pile.

When she finishes the laundry in her bucket, she hides herself from me and takes off her clothes and washes them. There is a bend in the stream; she is hidden by the bank. We have bathed together before, but she was never so shy. Her modesty now entices me to catch a peek. I look for bruises. No, I don't see any bruises. She reaches over to get her "sweet soap" when I notice what she is keeping from me. Her belly is big. She is pregnant. I had almost forgotten about the rumor I unknowingly helped to spread.

Juanna returns with her baby, a two-year-old boy with big rosy cheeks. She sits him down on the bank, across from me, near where she is finishing up her laundry. The script continues. Do you have a big house? Do you still have your parents? It is hard when you have only one. Why did you come here? Where do you stay?

Risa is dressed now and is putting her clean clothes and washing supplies back into her bucket. Juanna will stay longer, she has more to do. She has three children. Risa climbs out of the stream bed. We begin the walk to her house, side by side.

She stops and turns to me. "My hands got pain from the rice." She shows me her blisters.

What can I tell her? She has to work harder, blisters turn to calluses. "Yes, it's hard work to bust rice."

She makes a strained smile and looks at the ground. We continue to walk silently. Climbing back up the hill, her bridal veil falls from her bucket, into the mud. I pick it up and hand it to her on top of the hill.

With a growl of frustration, she mumbles to me, under her breath. "I want to throw it!" She puts it in the house, in the hammock, then returns outside to hang the clothes. I stand on the veranda waiting, debating whether I should help her or not. Normally, I would, but Evangelista is watching from her kitchen doorway. I decide to watch, too.

When she finishes, I follow her into the house. As she passes the hammock, she puts the veil in the bucket. In the kitchen, she adds some water and a little soap. I follow. She kneels next to the bucket and swishes the veil around in the water. "It's only a little dirty," she mutters.

I nod my head in agreement.

She shakes the veil out, checking to see if it is clean. It is, so she dumps the soapy water out her kitchen window, adds fresh water to the bucket, and rinses the veil. Then she hangs it on the line outside, next to her fluorescent green dress.

I wait inside, sitting on a bench along the bedroom wall. I can feel Evangelista still watching. Her eyes are burning through the wooden walls. It is beginning to get unnerving. Risa returns and sits across from me, sighs, and smiles. "So you are going."

"Yes, I'm going." I want to talk to her about her situation, but I still can't seem to find the words. She is smiling at me. I start, she looks away. I am unable to say anything to her; my mind is clouded. I am trying to understand why Evangelista thinks Risa doesn't work, and why Risa continues to reject Modesto. I can't even think to tell her "Thank you, it was a pleasure knowing you."

She stands up and goes into the kitchen. I hear the clanking of pots and pans. She returns with a small covered plastic tub. "It's peccary." She hands it to me. "My husband shoot it. You can take it to your house."

"Oh, thank you." I accept the food and place it on the bench next to me.

Just then, Modesto enters the back door.

"Hi, Modesto." I am nervous. I fidget with my plastic peccary bucket. "Risa just give me some peccary." I hold it up.

"Yes, she cooks it good." He smiles at her. She turns away from him.

"I just come to say I'm leaving." He looks puzzled. "Back to the States, I mean. In a few weeks."

"Oh, so you will go back to Michael." He sits in the hammock, smiling. Risa stands, goes into the kitchen, and sits down again.

I feel awkward. I look down. "I wanted to thank you, and Risa, and your family, for being so nice to me." I can see Risa in the kitchen. She smiles.

He smiles, too. "Yes." He begins to rock.

"I will remember you when I'm in the States." I look at Risa when I say this. I am quiet for a second, then I stand. "I have to go back home now, I have to do my wash."

Risa comes out of the kitchen. Modesto still swings in his hammock. I walk out the door. Risa stands in the doorway and calls me back. She points to the take-out peccary. "How can I get my plastic?"

I smile. "I can leave it with your mother, I will see her tomorrow."

"Yes, that's good." She watches me find my way to the road. Alejandro is still filling buckets with dirt and carrying them up to his father's compound. He is building another house.

ANALYSIS: REBELLION AND THE NEGOTIATION OF VIOLENCE

Introduction

I had no idea Francesca would respond to my request for her life history with a tale of battery and abuse. Yet hers was not an atypical response. Women in the village often incorporated accounts of abuse into their life stories.

It is difficult to assess how much or how many women suffer domestic violence in the village. Few people report such abuse to the police constable. A household census on the topic would be unreliable, since husbands often take control over such formal interactions and may not choose to discuss the topic. My knowledge about domestic violence comes from women who came to know me; women who felt comfortable telling me about their lives. Not all of the women I came to know told me tales of domestic violence, but many did. It is impossible for me to know how many may have had such experiences but chose not to talk about it.

What interests me here, therefore, is people's reactions to domestic violence, the situations that gave rise to it, and the ways women talk about it. Francesca's story begins the narratives in this chapter because her tale is one about husbands and wives working together to create economic success. Men and women have a social contract in Mayan marriages. That contract dictates that they work for each other. As a unit, as a team, they can find happiness. Without this teamwork, without hard work in general, couples cannot find happiness or success. Violence is often a part of these unhappy unions.

Besides her own story of spousal abuse, Francesca relates another story about a couple who are both bad. They are both lazy. She tells this story with pity for the children of that union. It is clear to Francesca that children are victims of domestic abuse, whether or not they witness it, whether or not they are physically bruised.

Francesca's story, therefore, sets the common theme of this chapter. It is Risa's story, however, that takes center stage in the analysis.

Risa's Resistance

Risa is taking part in a rebellion in the village. It is not the kind of rebellion Mayan women in Chiapas are fighting, where organized groups make plans in an air of revolution much like women did during Nicaragua's Sandinista revolution (Hernández Castillo 1997, Randall 1981). Instead, it is a rebellion individuals negotiate within their own specific social settings. Women are in a rebellion against the "old heads," those who think in the old ways, those who preserve the old traditions. James Gregory (1987) predicted this rebellion, and saw evidence of its beginnings in 1977.

Risa's part in the rebellion is courageous. For her, it is a rebellion against a long tradition of arranged marriages. In such arrangements, parents evaluate the likelihood that a young woman's suitor will provide their daughter with economic stability, and that he and his family will develop and honor a relationship of respect with them and their family members (Danziger 1991). Mayan parents try hard to choose a man who will treat their daughter and her family well.

Risa's wedding and engagement were special to many people. At the *hobol u k'aat,* the last of four meetings between her family and his before the wedding, nearly every man present approached me to say, "This is the way it is supposed to be done. This is a traditional marriage. It's good you came here today, so that you can see the way we Indians live; the way that is changing." No woman told me that, they did not seem to feel the same sense of loss that the men were feeling.

Risa is not the first to rebel against arranged marriages. Many women her age and older have done the same (Gregory 1987:17). Other women have run away or convinced their parents that they never want to marry. I will tell some of their stories later. Risa's form of rebellion, "not working for her husband," is idiosyncratic and perhaps dangerous. Her actions, however, can help us understand the negotiations involved in some acts of spousal abuse among Maya.

Marriage as a Perfect Union and the Importance of Family

> *Pedranos say that men and women are indispensable to one*
> *another.*   (Eber 1995:67)

> *[T]he husband/wife dyad functions as a true economic and status*
> *partnership. The contributions of both are indispensable to the*
> *family's precarious economic life as well as to accrue prestige in*
> *the community.*   (Rosenbaum 1993:50)

Central to Mayan thoughts on womanhood and manhood is the idea that marriage forms a man and a woman into an economic team (Eber 1995:67, Rosenbaum 1993:50). Without a man, a woman suffers. She must do "a man's work," clearing fields, planting, and harvesting corn. Likewise, a man without a woman also suffers. He cannot make his tortilla, his food. He cannot have clean clothes. Many widows and widowers and divorced people in the Maya world will tell you of these gender-based hardships. Others might point out a passerby and tell you the pitiful tale about how she must "do a man's work," or how he must "make his own tortilla."

Economic hardships are not limited to the presence or absence of a spouse. Other missing family members, like fathers, sons, and daughters frame Mayan discussions of hardships. Women shook their heads with sympathy when I told them about my family in the States. The loss of my father and two sisters, the lack of brothers in my family meant much more in terms of hardship and social status than did my long explanations about working-class roots and class consciousness. Without family you have no labor. You must work alone. Sometimes, when an old man or woman walked by on a path noticeable from any number of the houses I visited, my hostess would begin a long tale about how difficult it is to live "when your children have forgotten you." Occasionally, she would dot her story with comments about how important it is to treat your family well, or they might desert you.

Working fulfills the contractual agreement of Mayan marriages. Significant persons in a husband or wife's life (like fathers, mothers, and godparents) continually remind them of their responsibilities to respect each other and work for each other (Eber 1995:67–68). During the wedding ceremony, they give this advice using special ritual "beautiful speech" or *kichpan t'an* (Danziger 1991). For the young bride, advice-givers emphasize the fact that the young woman's work is no longer with her mother, or for her father; it is for her husband. Some may mention that the young woman must now listen to and respect her mother-in-law.

Until her marriage, a young woman learns from and works for her mother. After her wedding day, her mother-in-law teaches her the specifics of working for her husband's family (Rosenbaum 1993:50).

Mayan postmarital residence is usually patrilocal, allowing a bride's mother-in-law to cast a watchful eye on the newlyweds, making sure the new bride "learns her work" quickly and completely and that her son acts as a "good husband." This arrangement often causes friction (Rosenbaum 1993:50). It has caused enough friction for Risa that Evangelista asked her father and godmother to talk to her. But even after their counsel, Risa still rebels, she is still "lazy."

Laziness

Maya women worry that others might think them lazy. Therefore they never stop their work when visitors come (Eber 1995:68–69, Siverts 1993:232). To be considered lazy is perhaps the second-worst slander that could spread about a woman in the village. The worst is that a woman is promiscuous. People often link the two, so that lazy women are said to be promiscuous as well. For a young girl, a reputation for laziness can prevent marriage; for married women, it can destroy respect.

A good Mayan woman works constantly, cooking dishes her mother or mother-in-law taught her to make. She quickly responds to her children's needs, sweeps her house daily, and keeps her appearance tidy, with her hair tightly wrapped in a ponytail twisted into a bun and secured behind her head. Although she cooks over a wood fire, her pots sparkle clean with no dull soot covering the bottom. She grinds corn for tortillas at least once a day, and occasionally goes into "the bush" with a female companion to collect wild foods and sometimes medicines. A good woman might also be active in women's groups, making baskets and embroidery to sell for tourists, foreign and domestic alike, or raising chickens for making tamales. If so, she spends spare moments making crafts. If not, she will find something else to occupy her time, perhaps tending livestock or growing flowers. Good women wouldn't think of relaxing.

A bad woman is lazy. She spends her day in her hammock, finding her daily chores too taxing. Her laziness makes her family suffer.

Risa's lack of enthusiasm for her work, her rebellion, her resistance to an arranged marriage, translates as laziness. Onlookers like Evangelista, Francesca, and Juan see her as lazy no matter how much she works because she works without enthusiasm. She also shows disrespect and rejects symbols of her marriage. She breaks wedding gifts. Evangelista, however, focuses on Risa's "laziness" when she complains about her daughter-in-law. It is laziness that puts Risa in danger of a beating.

Negotiating Laziness

Risa's mother-in-law worries about her son. She is also worried about herself. Without economically successful children, children who have married hard-working people, she and her family will suffer. It is with worry that she labels her daughter-in-law lazy, and works hard to have others agree with her.

Evangelista negotiates Risa's laziness with her family, with Risa's family, and even with me. Our recognition of Risa's laziness lets Evangelista prepare more drastic means by which to relieve her worry, and to protect herself and her family from hard times. Evangelista is preparing to ask her son to beat his wife to make her more willing to work.

Other anthropologists have reported that men beat their wives for being lazy (Danziger 1991, Wagley 1949:16). The example of Evangelista and Risa suggests, however, that laziness can legitimize Mayan wife-beating even though no one, not even Evangelista, is comfortable with it.

Getting Out of Abusive Marriages

Important to Evangelista's negotiation of Risa's laziness is the fact that her son is a good man, a desirable mate. Engaging Francesca in the negotiation is significant, not just because she is Risa's godmother, but because she herself has suffered at the hands of an abusive husband. She has experience with illegitimate violence, violence that justified her divorce.

Among Mopan, as among Chamula, families usually support their daughter's decisions to leave abusive partners (Rosenbaum 1993:53). Francesca is one of several women I met who had escaped from abusive husbands. Francesca's story, a narration of an event that happened nearly twenty years ago, clearly depicts her husband as abusive. He had a drinking problem. He continued his violence even after Francesca left him. Later, many years after Francesca leaves him, his violence costs him his hand in a machete fight. Francesca's story clearly identifies her husband as the problem.

Although Francesca grew up in a family with much hardship due to the loss of her father, her mother was willing to take her back. She was clearly the victim of domestic violence, and there was no doubt that her husband was not a good man.

Risa's situation is different. She has no legitimate complaints. Everyone agrees that her husband Modesto works hard for her and respects her. He doesn't drink; he doesn't hit her. Therefore, Risa's resistance bothers Francesca, her godmother. Juan, her father, responds by telling her that she cannot return to his home. However, Risa continues to resist and isolates herself from the social network designed to protect her from an abusive husband, the network that would allow her to return home.

The Baby

Risa's pregnancy also makes her situation different from Francesca's. Childbirth marks the end or at least a lessening of the watchful relationship between mother-in-law and newlywed bride in Mayan society. Sometimes, if the bride and groom have been living in the same house as the groom's parents, it is at this time they will build their own new house nearby (Wagley 1949:15).

Children, however, also mean an increase in the amount of work a woman must take on, as well as a decrease in household resources. Indeed, Risa's pregnancy may have contributed to her father's insistence that she cannot come back to live in his household. While children are a delight to Mayan families, they are also the responsibility of their father. This is evident when Francesca tells us of the lazy couple whose children cry for their mother in hospital. When her father came to collect what was hers, he left her children with their father. When a woman retains custody of her children and faces the possibility of remarriage or returning to her father's household, she fears for her children's welfare. This fear lies in the fact that her actions sever the children's relationship with their biological father, the one person who is clearly responsible for their welfare. Furthermore, the children would put a strain on the finances of any man she might reside with who is not their father, whether he is her father, brother, or a new husband. Having fatherless children, therefore, limits the possibility that a woman can find another man to live with.

Risa's pregnancy could work as a buffer, limiting Evangelista's authority in requesting sanctions against Risa. The chances, however, are slim. Risa has disrespected her mother-in-law by not telling her about the pregnancy. Furthermore, she already lives outside of her mother-in-law's house. A separate residence for her would not mark her independence from her mother-in-law.

The child, however, could allow Risa another chance to show her willingness to work. Mothers delight in their children, as companions within a lonely environment. As Risa's brother wrote to me, "Now my sister has someone to play with, just like a brother or a sister." Taking care of a baby is taking care of someone who is both part of you and part of your husband's family. By caring for her child, Risa may be able to show enthusiasm for her work, yet simultaneously refuse to work for her husband. The child might even make her forget her rebellion altogether.

This is only a possibility, however; she might just dread the work her child presents to her. This would increase the likelihood that she will suffer sanctioned abuse.

Is It Really Resistance to Tradition?

I choose to frame Risa's actions (or inactions) as a rebellion against a tradition of arranged marriages. Another interpretation is possible. Risa's rebellion could be a sham. Her resistance to marriage might be an attempt to protect her position in the village as a virgin. In fact, this is the interpretation I originally held while attending her wedding and for several months after that.

Virginity is important to young Mopan women. Women, both young and old, spread gossip and rumors at an amazing rate when they see a young girl talking to a young man along the road, in the school yard, or especially at the river. Such rumors always suggest that the young girl is planning a sexual rendezvous with the young man. Unlike the Mayan women Redfield and Villa Rojas (1934) and Elmendorf (1972) write about from Chan Kom, Mexico, here, loss of virginity stigmatizes a young woman. It reduces her chances of marriage and destroys her respectable position. Young women, therefore, try to avoid young men in order to avoid the rumors that can make life difficult. I reevaluated my original interpretation of Risa's actions because she persisted even after her pregnancy was obvious.

Another interpretation, that she is resisting marriage because she doesn't want to leave her family, is, I think, a more plausible alternative. Risa's family is close. At her wedding, her father cried at the thought of losing his daughter. Mary Elmendorf (1972:3–10) tells of a woman who cried for three months after marriage because she missed her family. Anthropologists have also documented cases in which young women violently attack suitors and their family members when they come to petition for them, because they know marriage means leaving everyone close to them (Rosenbaum 1993:94). This alternative interpretation does not negate the interpretation I offer here. Indeed, the rebellion against marriage in the village in many cases may stem from a fear of leaving home. Young women who remain single stay with their mothers. Perhaps their resistance to arranged marriages is partially a rebellion against the lack of power to decide when they are ready to leave home. I see Risa's resistance as partially based on this fear.

In this way Risa's rebellion is part of the ways women have rebelled against Mayan patriarchy, perhaps for centuries. It seems now, however, that other forms of rebellion are developing, as education and development projects affect women's lives. I will discuss the relevance of these types of rebellions to domestic violence later.

CHAPTER THREE

Another Legitimate Beating

Ix Mooch: *The Frog*

I met Justina the first time I was in the village. She was about thirteen or fourteen then. I occasionally thought of her when I returned to the States. I knew she would be married when I went back to Belize four years later.

She was a lot of fun when I first met her. She giggled and teased me a lot. We walked together on the dirt road. We passed the soccer field, then the cemetery. We turned right at the bridge and walked along the river past the Mennonite house. This was the place where her family washed clothes. We carried plastic buckets filled with dirty laundry. I had my own. She had hers, her little sister's, her mother's, her grandmother's, and her father's clothes. She asked me if I was married yet. At the time I had just broken up with Michael, the man I now call "husband."[1] She giggled as I explained to her I was not married and had never really been married, even though I was twenty-six. "You're an old hen, then," she said plainly. She looked at me and laughed. This laugh, like many of her laughs, was not inclusive. I was the joke.

I slowly mimicked her actions, fearful that my ignorance would bring on another bout of excluding laughter. We removed our rubber-bottomed flip-flops and chose a place to wash our laundry. We took washing stations next to each other.

A washing station, as I call it here, is several flat rocks stacked one on top of the next. The one on top tilts back, away from you, slightly, so soapy water can flow down behind it as you pound and rub your clothing on it. She told me to fill my bucket with water and put my clothes in it while I washed each piece individually. This way they could soak and "get clean soon."

She taught me to hold my garments with one hand close to the front of the rock. Take your other hand and sprinkle the cloth with powdered soap. While still holding the cloth near the front of the rock, take the part near the back of the rock and rub it against the front part. Rub hard. She rubbed her clothes with skill and with a rhythm that I was later to encounter almost everywhere. One, two, THREE, pause, one, two, THREE, pause, one, two, THREE. Flip the cloth. One, two, THREE, pause, one, two, THREE, pause, one, two, THREE, flip.

We were silent while washing. One, two, THREE, pause, one, two, THREE, pause, one, two, THREE. She looked up to be sure I got it right. Pause. One, two, THREE, pause, one, two, THREE. Giggles. One, two, THREE, pause, one, two, THREE. Then you rinse it in the river. Turn it inside out, let the water flow through it. If it's a T-shirt, open the collar and let the water run through where your body would be. Then fold it neatly and set it on a clean rock.

When you finish all the clothes in your bucket, you take off your dress and wash that. One, two, THREE, pause, one, two, THREE, leaving your half-slip on. One, two, THREE, pause, one, two, THREE, then you wash your panties. One, two, THREE, pause, one, two, THREE.

Now, you can wash yourself, but be careful never to reveal the area between your knees and your waist. Keep your half-slip on. Wash your hair. Your back. Your legs. Your buttocks, but don't let them be seen. Cover them always.

Because we are young women, we can swim. She doesn't tell me, but I can see that no older women rinse this way. They would rather take a calabash, fill it with water, and pour it on themselves. If you are really old you can carefully take all of your clothing off and sit on a submerged rock. You must keep your legs closed tight and your arms low, in order to hide your lower body.

We splash in the water. She pushes her arms together just at the surface of the water making a thunderous clap. Giggles, smiles, we play tag. The water is warm because it is dry season, but high because it rained the night before. It has been a wet dry season. The trees around us feel pro-

tective. They are so tall, covered in vines and bromeliads. As we splash and giggle, she makes up a story. She says when a boy wants to marry a girl, he brings her a frog, *ix mooch*. It's this frog, she says, that brings the two, the boy and the girl, together. Another bubble of giggles erupts when she can no longer keep a straight face. She dives into the water. Later, I found out that *ix mooch* is slang for "vagina."

Justina

As our bus pulls into Orange Walk,[2] Francesca looks out the window. Angela, seven years old, stands on the seat and looks out, too. I try to look, but Angela blocks my view. I don't think I would recognize Cil anyway. The last time I saw him was four years ago, on my first visit to Belize. All I can remember is a conversation we had sitting on Coc's veranda. It was about bathing in the river. "It's better than a bathtub," he said, "because you get fresh new clean water passing by you every second. Sitting in a tub is like sitting in filth." I think it was Cil I was talking with, it might have been someone else.

I look across the aisle of the bus, craning my neck, trying to get a view out the opposite window. I can't see much, just shops lining the streets, painted bright white; jewelry, yard goods, shoes. The bus makes its first stop, along the main road into town. Across the street is a Shell gas station. A few people gather their belongings and file out. The confusion makes it harder to see out the window.

"I don't see him, gal." Francesca's voice is a loud whisper.

"Maybe he'll meet us at the next stop," I offer.

"But he said he lives over here, near the big Shell, just as you come into town." Francesca turns to examine my face for a moment.

I shrug my shoulders. "Maybe he's late. Do you think we should get off here?" An ounce of worry slips off of Francesca and lands in the pit of my stomach. What will we do if we can't find him?

She stands to get a better view from the front windshield. "I don't know, gal." Chaos has left the bus. The driver closes the door and shifts gears. We're rolling again.

"We can get off at the next stop," I declare.

Francesca sits. Angela begins to point out the window and nod her head. She whispers to Francesca.

Francesca squints her eyes and smiles. "There's Cil. There, on that bike. See, Justina and Martino are with him. See, gal." She points her lips out the window. "Angela found him! See, gal, that's them."

"I'm not sure." The only one I truly remember is Justina, but she was thirteen when I last saw her. I don't remember anyone named Martino. But, I do see a group of three with a bike. "Is that them walking toward the park?"

"Yes, gal. We'll get off at the park." Francesca leans back. Angela continues to stand and look out the window, smiling, jerking her legs with tiny jumps.

When the bus reaches the park, Francesca and Angela push through everyone to get off. I hold back, because Francesca has left me in charge of a box, a midsized but bulky cardboard box. I don't know what is in it. I just know it will be easier to maneuver down off the baggage rack and out the door if there are fewer people in the way.

Standing at the top of the bus stairs, I see Cil, a handsome, mustached man with a beaky nose, talking with Francesca. He looks somewhat familiar. Next to him is a larger, muscular man wearing a wide-brimmed camouflage safari hat. He's smiling. I am sure I have never seen him before. Behind them, a few feet away, is Justina. She is looking at the ground, silent. Her bowed head and slightly hunched back can't hide her beauty. She's a woman now. On her hip is a small child, less than a year old, with huge bright eyes and a delicate tiny mouth. The child wears a diaper and a dirty, striped, multicolored T-shirt. When I get off the bus, I stand next to her. Cil smiles at me and takes the box. He balances it on the bike and our entourage heads back toward the Shell station.

I walk next to Justina. Quiet. "I don't know if you remember me," I say. "Probably not."

She looks up at me, still no smile.

"I met you at the village, about four years ago. We washed in the river." I smile. "I gave you a small ring. Silver."

"Yes, I remember you, *ix* Laura." She looks back down. I am disappointed that she doesn't smile. We cross the street at the Shell station and head down a small side street in silence.

Cil's house is a 20′ × 20′ wooden box on stilts. A bedroom is walled off in the corner. A double bed nearly fills this room. Cardboard boxes and wires strung across the corners of the room hold clothing, including a rifle, a police uniform, and a fishing spear. The two interior walls of the bedroom create two additional spaces in the box, a living space and a kitchen space. The living room contains another bed, a hammock, and an entertainment center. The wooden entertainment center holds a TV, a boom box radio, a box of cassette tapes, and assorted odds and ends: lipstick, photo albums, hair clips, an empty Caribbean-brand rum bottle. The kitchen contains a small refrigerator, a stove top connected to a giant propane tank (both balanced on a small table), a kitchen table, and three wooden chairs painted orange. Toys litter the floor: a pink horse on wheels, a dump truck, a light-skinned baby doll with ragged blond hair, missing its left eye. There seems to be more stuff in this house than in any in the village.

When we enter, Sylvia, Cil's four-year-old and youngest child, is sitting on the floor playing with a dump truck. Michaela, Cil's wife, is scrubbing clothes in a basin, with a washboard. A garden hose snakes up the back steps to Michaela's basin. Angela immediately joins Sylvia in play, while the adults shuffle around searching for a comfortable place to land. Almost all at once, like musical chairs, we sit. Martino and Cil end up on the living room bed, facing the kitchen area. Francesca, in a kitchen chair. Justina, in another kitchen chair leaning against the bedroom wall in the living space. I sit in the most out-of-the-way seat, the hammock.

As soon as Justina puts her baby down, it crawls over to Sylvia and Angela. In a matter of seconds, the baby has grabbed control of the dump truck and Sylvia is crying.

With quick jerky movements, Justina pulls the truck from the baby's hands, throws it towards Sylvia. Then she slaps the baby on the back of the head. Two of the three children are crying now. The baby, eyes watery slits, rubs its head. With a square mouth the baby looks at her father, Martino. Sylvia, sobbing, takes the truck and walks over to Michaela.

Michaela doesn't miss a stroke of scrubbing, but speaks in fast, harsh tones. "*Chicha pul! Tan in mehya!*" I'm working! Stupid! She shakes her head, looks up at me. Chuckling, she says, "Aiy, this baby cry too much." Her gaze shifts to Francesca, who laughs. Sylvia still cries unattended.

Francesca's laughter distracts me from the tension cramped into this tiny box on stilts. "Yes, it looks that way," I mumble. Martino reaches over and picks up Justina's baby. He wipes her tears and announces, "This baby is wet."

Justina stands and quickly rummages through a small plastic woven bag near the door. She returns with a cloth and a tiny dress which she throws on her seat. She grabs the child away from Martino, rekindling its tears. She wrestles with it on her lap, replacing its wet diaper and T-shirt, handling it like a heavy sack of potatoes. "THIS baby," she snaps, "likes to pee-pee too much!" Finished, she puts the child on the floor and tosses the wet diaper and T-shirt onto a pile of dirty children's clothes near the front door. She returns to her seat, this time facing the front door, away from the circle of adults.

We are all silent, except the baby, who gurgles and plays with the pink plastic horse Martino has just handed her. Her tears are gone almost as soon as they began. Sylvia, wiping her eyes, sits back down on the floor and continues playing with Angela.

"Cil, do you mind if I borrow your bike?" I manage to meekly push through the tension filling the air. "I just want to check out Orange Walk."

"Sure," he smiles with enthusiasm. "You know where it is, under the house."

I stand, anticipating the relief the outside will bring, even though I know it will only be temporary. My whole body is still like jelly from the twelve-hour bus trip.

Sylvia and Angela are playing in the shade under the house. Francesca and Michaela sit on the small porch at the top of the front steps, talking. I hop off the bike and walk it under the house where I found it. As I walk up the steps, I comment, "Orange Walk is bigger than I remembered it," and sit on one of the upper steps, just below Michaela. "I was here very briefly four years ago."

"Yes, it grows." Michaela's light, freckled skin accents her sparkling dark eyes and beautiful black hair. Her gentle smile and graceful movements make her especially attractive.

"Do you remember *ix* Laura?" Francesca asks Michaela.

"I stayed in the village for a short time. We went to the river together once. I remember you lived near the hotel." I give as many clues as I can.

She shakes her head gently.

"That's okay. It was a long time ago, and so many people come and go." I watch Angela run up the steps. "This one was just small."

"MAN-GO!" Angela's whiny demand ruins her otherwise delightful demeanor. A gappy smile sprawls across her face. She's losing her baby teeth.

"Aiy, mangos! I nearly forgot." Francesca goes into the house and returns with those we bought during our short rest stop in Belmopan, Belize's capital city. She hands one to each of us, including Sylvia, who has just caught up to Angela. With a kitchen knife, Francesca begins to peel Angela's mango, letting the skins fall off the porch onto the ground below.

Sylvia can't wait. She takes a huge bite of her mango almost immediately.

"Aiy, *chicha pul*, Sylvia." Michaela knocks Sylvia in the head, gently, laughing.

Sylvia smiles and spits the skin out over the stair railing. She constantly wiggles.

"Here, baby. Give me your mango." I take my Swiss Army knife from my pocket, take her mango, and begin to peel it. It is slippery and nearly falls from my hands a few times before I am done. Sylvia looks on, smiling the same gentle smile as Michaela. When I finish I pass my knife to Michaela and wait until she is finished before I peel my own.

The kids sit on the step below me. We are all slurping and chewing; mango juice drips everywhere. These are especially ripe and sweet.

"Where's Justina?" I wipe my sloppy, juiced mouth on my sleeve.

"Martino took her to the doctor, gal. She's sick."

"Sick?"

"Yes, gal. She has fever for four days now, and she can't eat."

"Four days, that's long. How about the baby?"

"The baby sleeps. No fever, only her mother."

Just then Justina's baby crawls to the doorway, sits down, and picks up a rattle that was lying on the floor.

"Jesus Christo," Michaela puts her hand to her mouth. "How did that baby get down from the bed?"

The child looks up at Francesca, whines, and grasps for a piece of mango. Francesca laughs, "Aiy, what if that baby crawled the other way, to the back stairs." She hands it a piece of mango and lifts it onto her lap. "Maybe she'd fall, gal."

I raise my eyebrows, "You mean this baby was just sleeping in the bed?"

"Yes, gal," Francesca whispers with exaggerated pity.

"Aiy," I hold the child's foot. She giggles and kicks it. I continue my hold, pulling on it slightly. She is such a happy baby.

"Jesus Christo!" Francesca laughs, holding the baby away from her with outstretched arms. A stream of urine flows as the child kicks her feet in midair, giggling. I stand just in time to avoid getting wet.

"*Watac a wix.*" I giggle. Here comes the piss.

Michaela, surprised by my Maya, giggles too. Still laughing, she pulls a fresh cloth from Justina's plastic handbag, as Francesca removes the baby's wet diaper and dress. Before reclothing her, Francesca examines a few black-and-blue marks on her buttocks and back.

I squint my eyes and ask softly, "Are those bruises?"

"Yes," Michaela nods her head, "they're from Justina. She likes to be rough with this baby too much."[3]

"Aiy, poor Ronny." Francesca moans as she diapers the baby. "Who knows what will happen to her? This little Veronica, this little Ronny."

The child squeals excitedly and then babbles, holding her toy high in one hand. Francesca puts her back on the floor after Michaela sweeps the urine away with a worn corn broom.

"There's her mommie." Francesca points her lips toward the street. Justina and Martino walk side by side, a few feet between them. Justina has several pamphlets in her hand.

Both climb the steps. At the top, Martino leans on the porch railing next to Francesca. Justina silently passes us and enters the house.

We have stopped talking now. We just continue to eat our mangos, silent except for a few slurps. Francesca finishes hers and tosses the pit over the railing. A rooster runs to examine the discarded treasure.

I go inside and look for Justina. She's sitting on the bed, holding one of the pamphlets in her hand, staring at it.

"Francesca says you're sick." I sit in a kitchen chair next to the bed. "What did the doctor say?"

She responds, in a flat voice, almost a monotone. "He gave me some medicine, but it's too expensive." She continues to stare blankly at the pamphlet.

"Medicine is expensive," I mumble.

"I just wish I was dead." She stands, tosses the pamphlets on the bed, and walks down the back steps. I stand and watch her begin to fill Michaela's washbasin with water. She's going to wash Ronny's dirty diapers. The title of the top pamphlet is "Symptoms of Syphilis."

The doors and windows of the little box on stilts are closed up now. Insecticide still lingers in the stale, hot humid air. Cil sprayed Baygon about an hour ago, to kill the mosquitos, so we can all get a good night's rest. Sylvia and Ronny are sleeping on the living room bed, little rumps raised in the air. Angela lies on the bed, too, but she's still wiggly. Perhaps the adults are keeping her up.

Martino is on the edge of the bed, with Cil. Justina, keeping her head low and her face blank, sits slouched on a chair in the kitchen. Michaela quiet, observing, sits next to her. I am outside of the circle, lying in the hammock, swinging slightly. Cil's bike, leaning against the living room wall, makes it difficult to swing any harder. Like Michaela, I am quiet, observing, listening. Unlike Michaela, I can't understand much. I have only been in Belize for a month, so my Mopan is limited.

Francesca has been speaking nonstop for about forty minutes now. Her head is tilted down, her eyes averted. Occasionally Cil or Martino speaks, but only briefly. Justina says nothing. It is Francesca's monologue. Several times she has moved her hand in Ronny's direction, as she is doing now. She also sweeps her hand across the stale poisoned air toward Martino. A few times, she has paused, shifted her weight, taken a breath and continued.

She's lecturing Justina. I know this because it is Justina's gaze that she avoids the most, even though Justina makes no attempt to look at anyone. Justina just sits, slouched in her chair, looking down. Martino and Cil have also directed their words to Justina, but they are less humble. They sometimes lift their eyes, especially Martino. I don't know what they are saying.

About twenty minutes later, it is over. Cil stands and enters his bedroom. Francesca has stopped talking. Martino stands, too, and takes

Justina's hand; he guides her to the edge of the bed in the living room where Sylvia and Angela are sleeping. She swings her legs over and lies down. Francesca and Michaela stand and begin to put the leftover food into the refrigerator. Cil returns from the bedroom in his police uniform.

"Tonight, I have to guard the MIN-is-ter." He smiles at me. His speech has a curious rhythm, like poetry. "SOME pipple say, de MIN-is-ter needs guards because dey HATE him, too much. If he HELped de pipple, instead of HIMSELF, he wouldN'T NEED a guard." He laughs.

"The minister's no good?" I'm thankful for Cil's conversation.

"No, it's BEcause of him, we have an IN-crease in crime you know. He has made certain DEALS wid de GANGS, de DRUG dealers. We can't ar-REST any of DEM. If we do, they JUST go free." He sits on the chair Francesca was in, takes one of his shoes, and examines its shine. "I HATE these shoes." He spits on it and rubs it into the shine with a cloth. Then he examines the other.

"Which minister is this?" I stop swinging, afraid I'll crash into him.

"De one who LIVES in OR-ange WALK. I'll show de house tomor-row. It's a BIG house because he's COR-rupt." Cil slips his feet into his polished shoes and stands. He opens the front door and guides his bike onto the porch. "I'll be back tomorrow. Sweet dreams." He tilts his head, laughs, and salutes as he closes the door behind him.

Michaela giggles, "Aiy, Cil. 'Sweet dreams.'" Both she and Francesca laugh as they make their way into the bedroom. Martino turns off the light and takes his place next to Justina. I do my best to sleep in the hammock.

In the morning Justina takes Michaela's washbasin under the house and washes clothes. Martino goes out, and Cil sleeps in the bedroom. Angela and Sylvia play outside on the front steps. Francesca and Michaela cook.

"Where's Martino going?" I sit on the floor with Ronny. She babbles, blowing bubbles with her spit, and holds up a plastic army soldier for me to see. Curiously he has a pinwheel coming out of his head. I take him in my hand and examine him. He has *Hecho in Guatemala* embossed on his buttocks. He's an attempt to lessen people's fear of their army, I suppose. I give him back to Ronny before she cries.

"He looks for work, gal." Francesca draws water from the garden hose. "He lef his job in Pomona because of Justina." Pomona is a plan-tation town in the Stann Creek District of Belize. It consists of citrus orchards, a schoolhouse, a small shop, and a bar.[4]

"Why? What happened?" I roll a pink plastic horse around on the floor on its back wheels. The front wheels are missing.

"Because Justina was talking with a boy.[5] He's only seventeen. Why does his mother let him do such things?" Francesca shakes her head and lights the stove top.

"That's how they go in Pomona." Michaela peels an onion.

"Martino feels shame, so he lef Pomona. He can't work there again." Francesca puts a few cups of flour in a big white bowl.

"Is that what you talked about last night?" I stop my play and look at Francesca.

"Last night I told Justina that she has to make up her mind. She has to decide if she wants to go back to that boy, or to stay with her husband and her baby." Francesca adds a cup of lard to the flour. "The girl likes to treat Ronny bad, because in her mind she is still with that boy. She don't want her baby, she don't want her husband. She wants that boy."

Francesca begins to knead the flour and lard mixture. With each phrase, she turns the dough again. "I told that girl that if she makes up her mind, I can accept it; Martino can accept it; Ronny can accept it. But now, because she doesn't know what she wants, it's not good. No one can help her, because she has to make up her mind. Let Martino find the next lady; let Ronny have a new mother." Francesca motions with a dough-covered hand to Ronny. "She don't love her baby, but no one gave her that baby."[6] She rubs her hands together rolling the excess dough off them, and adds more flour to her mixture. "That baby is fu she." She kneads again. "If she don't want it, better she give it away. It's not right for that baby to suffer. It's wet, dirty, nobody cares for the poor child."

Ronny shrieks with laughter as I roll the horse down her arm onto her leg and then onto the floor. I tweak her nose, ruffle her hair, and echo Francesca's words, "The poor child."

"You can see where the baby gets bruise," Michaela nods with raised eyebrows. "She push that baby, she knock that baby. She can't treat the baby like so. The baby will get sick!"

Francesca looks up from her work and sadly adds, "Yes, maybe one day she kill that baby."

I let the silence linger before I ask, "Where did she meet this boy?"

"In Pomona, gal. He picks oranges." Francesca begins to tear pieces of dough off the larger clump and roll them into balls.

"Did Martino pick oranges, too?"

"No, gal. Martino was a security." She places the smaller balls onto a plate. Michaela moves in to help roll dough. "But now he looks for the next job. Poor Martino. That baby favors Martino, not true?"

"For true. She looks like him." I wave a red plastic block in front of Ronny's face. She grabs at it and laughs when she grasps it.

Just then Martino appears in the doorway, cooling himself by waving his hand in front of his face, making a slight breeze. He comes in and sits in the hammock.

"I was just saying how this baby looks like you." I smile at him.

"Yes," he speaks slowly from a charming smile. "The poor baby favors her dad." Ronny crawls to him excitedly. He reaches down, picks her up, and sits her on his belly. "But maybe she has no ma."

Francesca holds Ronny as she and Michaela sit in the shade of a big mango tree, on a park bench. I am playing with Sylvia and Angela on the slide. It is a huge concrete monster of a slide, with one set of stairs and three slides. It's not very fast. Two other kids, both mestizo, are also playing; a boy of four or so and a girl, maybe eight, in a frilly dress. They stay to themselves. Neither said anything when I greeted them. They just stood and stared.

From the top of the slide, I can see Cil, Martino, and Justina through the branches of the mango tree. They are waiting for a sugarcane truck to pass so they can cross the street and meet us at the park. Cil is smiling and laughing; he is talking with Martino. Martino has his arm around Justina, resting it on her shoulder. She doesn't seem resistant, but she doesn't look happy, either.

I point to them, "See Cil. See your father." I exaggerate my enthusiasm, hoping Angela and Sylvia will want to leave the slide to see their father. Cil, Martino, and Justina left us earlier this morning and headed out toward the clinic. I want to find out what's up.

"Let's goooo!" Angela yells as she slides down.

I smile and follow with Sylvia.

"Angela!" Francesca's familiar call doesn't stop Angela from taking one last slide. I grab Sylvia and tickle her belly as I carry her over to the bench.

Everyone is quiet as Cil and I gather up Francesca's packages of plastic cups, cans of sardines, and hair clips, stock for Coc's shop back in the village. Everyone is quiet on the way back to Cil's house.

It isn't until we are all in the house again that Cil announces, "The tests are NEG-a-TIVE; lucky! You can catch all kinds of DISeases: AIDS, herpes." He didn't seem to be talking to anyone in particular. "The boys in PoMONA, they go ALL night with PROS-ti-TUTES. Maybe that's what you want."

Justina just stares at the floor. Ronny, wet again, begins to cry.

"She's coming, gal." Francesca is standing in my doorway, in the village. We've been back for a few days now.

Angela stands next to Francesca, bouncing a young white and tan cat. Its belly is sticking out from under her grip; its back legs are dangling down and its front paws jut out just over Angela's arm hold. Its tail is twitching. It is a patient cat.

"Who?" I stand up from my hammock and meet her at the door. "Who's coming?"

"Justina, gal." She frowns, "She just called. I got a message from Chen that they were going to call. They just called, gal. Justina says she's coming." There is one phone in the village, not far from my house. Chen operates it. The usual practice is for the caller to arrange a time when Chen can try to get the caller's party to be at the telephone office. Chen then takes responsibility to summon the party at the right time. Sometimes his kids speed through the village on bikes telling people that they are about to get a phone call.

"They're coming here to the village?"

Her response is a loud whisper. Her eyes are wide. "Yes, gal. Martino get drunk and lash her."

I breathe deeply and shake my head in pity. "No. When will she reach?"

"I don't know, gal. Maybe tomorrow, on Chun's bus." Francesca enhances her already sorrowful face with a frown. "Michaela, too, gal."

"Michaela? Why is Michaela coming?"

"Cil just lash her, gal." She shakes her head, "Chen say he called, too. I have to go to the phone at four, gal. Cil will call then." Francesca pulls her long ponytail and squeezes the water from it. She must have gone to the river before she got the phone call. "Chen say Cil is drunk, gal." A small, longish puddle forms on the ground where Francesca has squeezed out her ponytail.

"But why? Why would Cil lash Mik?"

"I don't know, gal. She doesn't do anything." She frowns again. "The poor gal."

"Yes," I whisper, "the poor gal." I shake my head. What else can we do?

The next day, Francesca and I sit quietly on her veranda. She is in the canvas chair and I am on the car seat. When I hear Chun's bus roar up the hill, I turn my head to see the cloud of dust and trail of diesel smoke it leaves behind. Francesca watches intently, squinting her eyes so she can see.

"Justina and Mik are coming," Francesca announces.

The cloud of dust settles as Chun's bus rounds the corner and stops. Several passengers unload. Two young girls, sisters, get off the bus and stand a few yards away, whispering to each other.

A few seconds later, Justina, holding Ronny, and Michaela, guiding Sylvia, make their way off the bus. Pablo, the bus driver, opens the back of the bus and hands each of them her small cardboard box, tied with jute. These are their belongings.

Justina opens the gate, and they approach the veranda. We continue to watch them. Michaela keeps her head down, Sylvia walks slowly and must be prodded into continuing. She's tired. Justina walks tall, Ronny wiggling on her hip. Ronny's eyes are bright; she's smiling. They stop at the veranda and greet us. Francesca frowns and tells them to go up the stairs to the other house. The place where they will sleep.

I carry their boxes up the stairs, then leave. If they want to tell me about what happened, about Michaela's black eye and the ring of bruises around Justina's neck, they will, in their own time. Right now, they will tell Francesca.

"Are you married?" Michaela asks as we walk down to the river, buckets of dirty clothes in our hands.

"Well, I have a man, but we're not married. We just live together. Kinda like a common-law marriage. We're domestic partners." I swing my bucket as I walk; it is light compared to Mik's. "Sometimes I call him my husband."

"Oh," and we are quiet again.

When we reach the river we take our places at two washing stations next to each other. "So you like the river?" Michaela smiles. Her black eye is less noticeable now. It is healing quickly.

"Yeah, I like to wash with people; to talk." I slap a wet skirt on a washing stone. "It's nice. Which do you like better, the river or your washbasin in Orange Walk?"

"The river." She doesn't hesitate. "But maybe, I'd like a machine. They have them in Orange Walk, a machine to wash clothes. Maybe it's easy that way." She slaps one of Sylvia's little dresses on a rock, sprinkles some soap on it and begins to scrub. "How about in the States?"

"In the States," I flip my skirt and scrub the other side, "in the States, I have a machine."

"Is it easy?" She rinses Sylvia's dress, holding it into the river flow.

"Yes. But, in the States I have to work a job, too." I rinse my skirt in the same way. "So I don't have time, sometimes, even to use the machine. So sometimes it's hard, because you don't have time."

"Oh," Michaela makes a crooked smile and slaps another one of Sylvia's dresses on the rocks.

We're silent for a long time, until Michaela, continuing her work, looks up at me and says, "This is not the first time I lef Cil."

"No?" I stop my work for a second and look at her.

"I lef him three times now." She rinses Sylvia's dress.

"Three times," I repeat her words. "Is it for the same reason, because he hit you?"

"No." She doesn't miss a beat in the rhythm of washing, starting on one of her blouses. "It's because of the next lady."

"Cil's got another woman?"

"Not now. Before, yes. I lef him then, but he comes and finds me. So," she shrugs, and continues to scrub the blouse, "I go back."

After hanging my clothes on the line, I sit down and begin typing some notes. Justina stands at the door of my cement house.[7] "*Deyoos.*"

"*Deyoos*, Tina. Come on in." I darken my computer screen, embarrassed that I was writing about her and Michaela. "What's up?"

"Mik's going back to Orange Walk." She leans against the wall of my bedroom.

I nod. I figured she'd be going back soon. "Yeah?"

Justina nods with a determined face. She's cool. "Cil called. He wants Miss Coc to send her back."

I stretch my lips across my face. "How about you? Are you going, too?"

She shakes her head. "No. Cil says Martino is on the bus now, he's coming here to find me." Her eyes are bright with panic, but her movements are still calm, collected. "I won't go with him again. I'm going to lef him one time. Miss Coc say I can leave my baby with her. I can find my job in Belize City. I'm better alone, without Martino. He lash me, that's why these bruises." She holds her neck. "My mouth, too. He did that, he beat me."

"No, you don't deserve it. Maybe you can make a new life." I attempt a small smile, feeling sympathy. She is so young to experience all this. I miss the happy girl I knew four years ago. I never knew she would grow into such an unhappy woman.

"It's better for my baby. Make she stay with Miss Coc. She christened it, she cares for it. She likes children because she has none of her own." Justina sways, putting her weight into her back, leaning against the wall. "She was there for the birth. She wants it."

I nod, and without commitment say, "Maybe that's better."

"He will come tomorrow." She sways again. "Maybe he will lash me, I don't care. Me no afraid. Let him come. In Orange Walk, he say he gonna stab me, but I'm not afraid for my life. I don't care if I live."

"He was going to stab you?"

"Yes, my godfather was going to take a machete to me. He says he has the authority to do it, but he never do. He never touch me. He only encouraged Martino, that's all. They drink a bottle of Caribbean and my godfather encourages Martino to hit me." She sways, "He only lash Michaela."

"Why did Cil hit Michaela?"

"I don't know." She shrugs. "Maybe he thinks she is like me." She looks up at me. "Now he is sober and he calls for her."

"Justina, if there is anything I can do to help you, you let me know, okay." I feel relief in offering, but am clueless as to what I can do.

She nods. "Me no afraid. There is nothing you can do. I will leave Martino and find my job. I'm better alone. I will feel sad to lef my baby, that's all. But maybe it's better. I can find my job."

"Maybe you can get help from Social.[8] Make him pay child support. Maybe you can get some money from him," I nod, "for Ronny."

"Yes, they will make him pay." She shakes her head. "But I don't want it. If he pays then one day he will come for my baby. He'll take Ronny to the next lady." She pauses, "I don't want it. Maybe she will punish my baby; she won't care for my baby." Nodding yes, she continues. "Better he not pay, then if he wants she, he has to pay back all the expenses. Better Miss Coc take the baby, she cares for it. She can raise it."

"Then you can come and see her again." I smile. "She can stay with Miss Coc, just like her mother did, not true?"

Softly, Justina says, "Yes, just like me." She looks down, and sucks in her lips into her mouth. "It's better for she."

Martino and Justina stand together by the chicken coop. She holds her arms crossed over her chest. Occasionally, she turns away from him. But he talks, quietly, persistently, humbly; he frequently looks down. Once, I thought I saw him wipe a tear from his eye.

"When did he get here?" I try to avoid watching the two by the coop. I am sitting on the veranda, maybe two hundred feet away from them.

Francesca, holding Ronny in her lap, ignores them. Her focus is on Ronny. "Just now, gal. He hitchhiked from P.G."

"Do you think she'll really leave him?" I hand Ronny the pink plastic horse, a toy from Orange Walk. Justina must have brought it with her. It must have been in that cardboard box.

Francesca chuckles. "I don't know, gal." She stands Ronny on the floor, making sure she holds onto the car seat for support.

Ronny makes a high-pitched squeal of laughter and excitedly runs the length of the car seat, then stops, looking up at me with a giant smile.

Francesca laughs with the child. "Only God knows what will happen to this baby."

"Do you think it's good if she leaves him?"

"Yes, gal! You don't see how he lash her! Like an animal. Maybe one day he'll kill her." Francesca goes into her kitchen and begins patting out tortillas.

I stand, take Ronny in the house, and sit her on the floor, placing the pink horse in front of her. I make sure she will be satisfied with it for awhile before I go and wash my hands.

Standing by the outdoor sink, I peek around the water vat to see Martino put his arm around Justina. She smiles with a happiness in her eyes I have not seen since four years ago. He guides her toward the house.

I wash my hands, and enter the rhythm of household production, patting out tortillas and turning them to keep them round. One, two, THREE, turn, one, two, THREE, turn, one, two, THREE, turn. By the time I have made my first tortilla, Martino stands in the doorway, while Justina gathers Ronny's belongings.

"We'll come tomorrow for the rest." She smiles at Francesca. "We're going that side," she points with her lips down the road, "to stay with he pa."

"You don't want tortilla?" Francesca asks matter-of-factly.

"No. I'll cook for he pa. He wants to see he pa."

Francesca says nothing but continues her work. One, two, THREE, turn, one, two, THREE, turn, one, two, THREE, turn. Justina sets Ronny on her hip and walks side by side with Martino down the road and over the hill.

Tzimin: *Horse*

Justina sits with me in my house. A few days ago, I moved from a big cement house into a small thatch-roofed house. The rent is much less and it is much cooler. It is like other small thatch houses that often stand a few yards away from larger, roomier ones. The smaller houses usually house a tiny *na'chiin,* a grandmother. She is the mother of either the man or the woman living in the larger, roomier house. The one I live in was built for Francesca's mother, Evarista. It sits just outside the Coc compound. Evarista helped Justina give birth to Ronny in this house. I like the idea of living where Ronny was born. It gives the house a history.

Francesca had told me how she, Evarista, Justina, and Martino were the only people present when Ronny came into the world. Justina gave birth to Ronny while sitting in a hammock, "just like we Indians do." She pushed and strained. She pushed her legs hard on the floor, sometimes standing upright with pain, and sometimes, perhaps, with resistance.

"Ronny was ugly when she was born. She looked just like a rat to me. But now I'm used to my baby,"[9] Justina once told me.

Now that Justina lives in the village with Martino, she visits often. This visit is different, however. This time we are quiet. The door and windows are closed. We are pretending no one is home. It isn't easy because Ronny is with us. She is just over a year old now and is enjoying exploring the various jars, bottles, plastic containers, books, papers, notebooks, etc. that are crammed into my tiny living space. Her eyes are wide as she picks up whatever she can, holds it high, and drops it. An occasional burst of glee followed by a rhythmic stamping of her tiny feet lets us know she is enjoying her visit.

I am roasting coffee on my hearth. The fire stubbornly keeps trying to go out. Billows of smoke rise between the cracks where the metal grill doesn't quite match the curve of the ash-constructed hearth. Trying to keep the fire going, while simultaneously limiting the damage the child might do to my stuff and to herself, is getting too much for me. So far, Justina has ignored the nearly silent cues Americans give each other when someone's baby is a bother. The "tsk"s and moans I occasionally emit as I jump up to pull something out of Ronny's hands haven't suggested to Justina that she should watch her daughter more closely.

"Tina, can you help me roast this coffee? I'll watch Ronny to be sure she doesn't hurt herself." Or my stuff.

"Okay." She takes the spatula from my hand and stirs the coffee beans. She leans over, her face near the fire, and blows. The smoke immediately subsides and the flame strengthens. She repositions some of the wood in the fire and stirs the coffee beans again. The smoke is gone.

"I don't know, *ix* Laura." Justina's eyes are focused past me, over my head. "His sister told me that he would beat me like a horse, like an animal, and that is what he does." She should be stirring the coffee beans again, but she's just staring over my head. Just before they start to burn, she looks down and stirs them. "I'm not a horse."

Fragrant oil begins to burst from the beans. The house fills with the smell of strong bitter coffee oil and wood smoke. We sit quietly.

Justina doesn't seem melancholy or angry to me. She seems frightened. But I don't think she would admit that fear. She has a thick streak of defiant coolness about her, machismo in a sense. I don't get this cool feel from any other women her age in the village. Most are meek and shy. She is forceful. I do get the same feel from kids back home in my neighborhood. Buffalo's inner city forces kids to cultivate an air of aloofness. They try not to show emotion, especially fear. Coolness is a sign of inner strength. In Buffalo's young people, as in Justina, this aloofness is sometimes thin and transparent, like Saran wrap stretching tight to keep everything in.

This morning I saw her coolness falter for just a second. Justina came into Coc's shop, where I was keeping Francesca company while she stocked shelves. The gouges on Justina's face were bright red and swollen, then. She didn't hide them from us, but sat Ronny on the counter and stood tall, ready to begin her story.

Francesca also played cool. She looked at Justina for a moment, then continued to unpack a carton of canned sardines, stacking them on the counter. She never asked what happened. If Justina wanted to tell it, she would.

In a small but clear voice, Justina began. "Martino lash me again."

Silence. Francesca moved three cans of sardines from the counter to the shelf, next to the Vienna sausages. I didn't say anything either, but watched Justina as she continued.

"He grabbed my face like so," she held her hands inches from her face, fingers spread wide. "Then, he trew me and say he goan kill me."

Francesca stacked three more cans on the shelf.

Justina was silent for a moment, then a tiny quiver of stress broke through. With a crack in her voice, she said, "He push Ronny."

Francesca lowered her chin and opened her eyes wide. She slowly shook her head. Martino had never touched Ronny in a harmful way before.

Justina stretched the Saran wrap tighter. "I just come now. When I wake up, I wash my clothes, like nothing ever happened. When he wakes, he goes to find more rum. That's when I take Ronny and come here."

Francesca stood Ronny on the counter. "Why does he push Ronny?" She knows why he hit Justina. She held Ronny's arm, carefully inspecting it for bruises, then she inspected her other arm, then her legs. Finally she lifted Ronny's dress over her head and began to examine her torso.

Justina explained. "He knock her because she cries. She fall onna dey ground. De baby cry cause she pa lash she ma. When he took my face I cry and Ronny gets to hear me cry. Ronny jumped, and she cry too. When he trows me, I fall onna me shoulder and dis finger gives me pain." She held up her left hand and touched her ring finger. It was swollen and dark around the first joint. "Then he kick me, here." She tenderly touched her right side. "He kick me and say, 'I can never forgive you for what you did. Maybe, I can't forgive you until you die.' That is what he said, then he say, 'Maybe I have to kill you to relieve my mind.' I just stay on the ground and my baby is crying, but I'm afraid to go to her. I'm afraid he'll get vexed again. Let him kill me if he wants." [10]

"He pushed her after she jump?" Francesca looked up from Ronny's torso.

"Yes," Justina nodded slowly to indicate the seriousness of the offense, "and Ronny cry again. Then he lef. I don't see him til nighttime. That's when he comes and sleeps because of too much rum."

Francesca looked Justina in the eye for the first time this morning. It was then that I saw Justina's strength break. She held her right hand over her brow and wept.

Justina's last beating was worse. She cried then, too. Francesca and I had just returned from a trip to Orange Walk when Amelia, her grand-daughter, who was taking care of Evarista while we were gone, told us that Justina was hiding at her godmother's house. We went immediately to find Justina in a blood-soaked dress, sitting in a hammock. The blood was from a cut just above her ear. It had stopped bleeding a while ago and the blood on her dress was drying. Francesca pulled a chair up close to the hammock and gave Justina one of the dresses she keeps for her. Justina tried not to look at Francesca, but when she caught her eye, Justina's tears began to flow and her shoulders heaved and dropped in sorrow.

I went to get the nurse that night, to examine Justina. She shined her flashlight in Justina's eyes, looked at the black-and-blue marks on her back and felt her leg, where she was suffering the most pain. The nurse's six-year-old son had his own flashlight and liked shining it on Justina's ear, to see the gash just above it. The nurse eventually stopped him by threatening him with a belt. He sat quiet for a few seconds but, still curi-ous, tried it again. His mother grabbed him by the arm, lifting his whole left side off the ground, and spanked him hard. She made him sit out-side, in the dark. When she returned, she suggested Justina get X rays. We spent the next hour trying to figure out how to get her there. "It's unfair to make Pablo go again," Nurse said. "He just come back with the bus today."

Cho, the replacement police constable filling in for Vernon Cayetano, tried to get a police vehicle to come out to the village. None were avail-able, however, because they had all been transported to Belize City for a parade the next day.

Francesca let Justina stay at her house that night, despite Mr. Coc's objections. "He feels sorry for the boy," Francesca told me. He was re-luctant to help Justina. Two years ago, Mr. Coc discovered that Justina and Martino were "talking." It was this discovery that led to their mar-riage.

The next day, Justina convinced Martino to take her to the hospital to get X rays. He found someone with a truck willing to take a large sum of money to make the trip. Hiring a truck is expensive. Vehicles use a lot of gas and the roads cause a lot of damage. She took this as a sign of good faith and went back with him, keeping their little family intact. The doctor's prescription of aspirin helped ease the pain, until Martino got drunk again.

This time, the sympathy in Francesca's voice was for the child. This was a much more serious situation. This time, Francesca didn't examine Justina for bruises; she didn't ask any questions about Justina. She only asked about Ronny.

Then she looked away as she spoke. "I tell you that you and Martino live like animals. Now look, Ronny might get sick. I tell you maybe you don't need that husband. But every time you go back. What can I tell you? Maybe you should think about Ronny."

Justina stood, picked Ronny up, and put her onto her hip. She went to Francesca's house, giving me a strained smile as she passed.

"The poor baby, gal." Francesca's voice was just above a whisper. "Martino frighten her. Maybe now she'll get sick, gal."

"Sick?"

"Yes, gal. Maybe Martino scare her . . ." Francesca waves her hand in frustration, "spirit, gal. Maybe she gets loose stool. Justina takes her to my mother now. Maybe she can save that baby."

"How?"

"I don't know, gal. She'll try to get Ronny's spirit back, or build up what she has left." Francesca's brow wrinkles, "I don't know, gal. That baby might die." [11]

I left the shop about an hour ago. Now, Justina is roasting my coffee, hiding. The smoke is starting to clear because she knows how to attend the fire.

"My mother says I should lef that man. She say we live like animals, it's true." She begins to scoop the beans with a metal spatula from the grill into a bowl. When she is finished she puts more beans onto the grill. "He beat me five times now, three times I was naked. The first time he made me kneel down, and he told me it was my punishment. He doesn't drink that time, he beat me sober." She stirs the beans. "Another time he starts when I'm sleeping. I don't even know what is happening, I just feel him hit me." A pause. "And you know the time in Orange Walk."

I have Ronny on my lap now. Her hair smells of copal incense. "Yes, that's the time you come back to the village." Ronny squirms, so I put her down. "You told me then you were going to leave him." I try not to make it sound like she had made me a promise. I am just telling her what happened.

She looks at me. "But yes, I left him to come here. I never knew he would come find me again. It was then that he told me he would stop drinking, and would never lash me again. Because mostly he lash me when he drinks." She looks down at the coffee beans and stirs them again.

"It seems he's drinking again," I offer.

We are quiet for a long time. I show Ronny how to put shells I gathered during visits with an anthropologist friend in Dangriga into a basket I bought from Ma.[12] After I put three or four small shells in the basket, I tip it over, spilling them out. Ronny squeals with glee and does it herself.

"I want to go to my house and take my things." She is going to leave him. "Maybe you can help me."

"Yes, anytime. We can let the fire go out. I can finish the coffee another time." I right the basket Ronny is playing with. She fills it, again.

"But what if Martino comes? He went to get more rum. I don't know when he will come home again." Leaving won't be easy.

"Where do you think he's drinking?"

"I don't know, maybe Prim's." She is silent for a second. "I think I should leave him one time! It's not right that he hit me. I'm not an animal. I can leave him and find my job somewhere, maybe in Belize City. I can go to my mother, she lives there. I can leave my baby with Miss Coc. She was there when I give birth. She was there when I baptize my baby. She already cares for her."

"Yes, I know she will take Ronny." I try to emphasize her available resources. Justina looks off into the distance again. We sit in silence.

"If we go, we should go soon. We don't know when he will go back home."

Justina has terror in her eyes, but the rest of her face hides it. "He is drinking." She speaks in a soft whisper.

"But he will go home after he drinks, not true? We should go before he goes home. I don't want to see him drunk." I really don't want to deal with a drunken, angry Martino. He stands at least 5′10″ and weighs about 200 lbs. He is the Maya version of a defensive end.

She remains silent. All the coffee is nearly finished.

"SHHH. I think that's him." She stops, puts the spatula down, and silently moves closer to the door, where she stands completely still and listens. A voice calls *"Deyoos."*

It's a woman's voice, Antonia, the same woman I met four years ago on the veranda, the first to tell me that she was beaten by her husband. I say nothing. Justina relaxes a bit, but still remains silent.

Antonia is a good friend, but the worst gossip I know. I don't want

Justina to have to tell her story to Antonia. If she wants to hide, telling Antonia is not the smartest thing to do.

Again *"Deyoos, ko manech wa?"* Hello, are you home?

I stay quiet. So does Tina. But Ronny squeals with excitement. Tina and I giggle silently, holding our mouths. Justina looks at me with twinkling eyes; she loves to be devious. "Is she home?" Antonia's voice.

"Mine weile." I don't know. "I jus hear one baby," Leita, Antonia's eldest daughter, responds.

"Aj nene?" A baby. Antonia giggles. In my mind, I can see Antonia's face crinkle up and her hand raise up to hide it, as she always does when she giggles.

"Deyoos." Leita tries again. Silence. "She must be gone."

We can hear their footsteps moving away from my house. I know we didn't fool them, but they knew we were not going to let them in. After we know they are far enough away, Justina and I laugh long and hard until tears stream from our eyes.

Justina catches her breath, "They think you've changed into a baby." We laugh again.

After awhile, we settle into our routine, attending the coffee. Justina's eyes change from twinkling joy back to seriousness. The heat of fire under the grill makes this batch of coffee beans release their oil; a few pop. Most are dark, or mostly dark, and the smell is invigorating. I take the spatula and scoop roasted coffee into a yellow plastic bowl I bought from the *Cobaneros,* traveling salesmen, in Punta Gorda. The colors go well together.

As I put the next batch of beans on, Ronny twists from her mother's arms and runs for the door. Justina stands and follows, leading her back to the kitchen area by the hand. Ronny takes her mother's lead, but stops halfway, looks up at me with worried eyes. With a smile she widens her stance and urinates. Justina giggles, "She knows to go outside now." Ronny's urine soaks into the hard dirt floor, leaving a large, dark, wet spot.

I smile.

"Ix Laura." It's a man's voice at the door.

I can see Justina's arm muscles tense as she twists her head toward the sound. She pulls Ronny up from the ground onto her lap and quietly says my name. "Laura."

I stand, and slowly move closer. I listen for a moment.

"Ix Laura."

Roasting coffee.

I recognize Andres' voice and quickly shoo him inside, closing the door behind him. I return to Justina, in the cooking area. Andres follows and sits on the high stool, the one I use when I write. He sits with his legs spread wide, maintaining his usual handsome smile.

Justina avoids his gaze, gathers up Ronny, and slides into the sleeping area. She sits on the bed with Ronny in her lap, where he can't see her. I continue roasting coffee.

"Justina is here with me. Don't tell anyone. It is a secret." I speak in a low whisper.

Andres doesn't seem to care. He makes no attempt to be quiet. "I want to borrow a tape. Something good this time." Then, he smiles. "Maybe you got some country."

"I don't HAVE any country, Andres." It is a loud whisper.

Again, at normal volume, "What's good?"

"Shhh, we're trying to be quiet. Justina doesn't want to see Martino. He hit her again, and now she wants to hide."

Confusion masks his face, his head cocks to the left. Without blinking, he says, "Do you know why he hit?" He never thinks I know the whole story.

I reply sternly, "Yes, and that doesn't mean she deserves to be hit." To protect him from Justina's laughter, I don't say what I want to say. I don't mention that Andres has come to my house twice, late at night, drunk, asking me to let him in. Justina's "talking" in Pomona was somewhat unclear to me, but Andres' attempts at infidelity to his wife were not. The only difference between his actions and hers was that she was more successful. If I wanted to hurt him, I would say that. I think Justina would find it funny. There seems to be a tension between them.[13]

I stand abruptly and reach over Andres' head, where I store my cassette tapes. He jerks back, startled, eyes wide. I put a *Clash* tape in his hand and sit as quickly as I have stood. "This is my favorite. Maybe you will like it." I stir the coffee beans.

Andres muffles a laugh as he turns the tape over a few times in his hand and smiles. "So you roast coffee."

"Yes," I snap.

Then he makes the smile that tickles my stomach. "Who show you?"

I stay firm. "I hear how to do it from Francesca, then Justina show me. Now I roast coffee."

Nodding arrogantly: "That's good."

I don't respond with the smile I might have otherwise made. Instead, we all sit a few inches apart, in silence. Justina averts her eyes. Andres looks at me; I look at the coffee, wanting to look at Andres. Ronny breaks the spell by overturning a few books that were balancing on a bench near my bed. Andres leaves and Justina and I continue roasting coffee, quietly.

"Maybe we can go now to get my things." Justina plays nervously with her skirt. We finished the coffee a long time ago.

"Yes, maybe now would be good." I nod slowly and look at her.

"It's like his sister said. He beats me like a horse." She straightens the bow in Ronny's hair.

"Yes. He does." Pause. If we're going to do this we had better do it soon. "He's probably drunk at Prim's shop. Now's a good time, he won't go home for awhile." I have already pulled the larger pieces of wood out of the fire, covered the coffee, and changed my shoes.

"Yes, now is best because we don't want him to find us."

But she sits immobile. I sense her fear and imagine it is a mixture of fear that he will hit her again and fear that he will convince her to stay. I can feel my own fear, too, the fear that he will come home just as we gather up her belongings. I am afraid of being trapped in their house, holding Justina's stuff. I fear his wrath.

We sit together wrapped in our fear for nearly an hour. By then, my fear has dissipated, replaced with calm. I am calm because I know she won't leave him. I won't have to face his rage. She will sit here until he comes for her. Then she'll follow him home. If I had let Antonia in, he would have come sooner. Now I must wait until he discovers her hiding place.

For over an hour we have quietly talked about how we need to act soon and how waiting would increase the chance that Martino would catch us. I am humoring her. I know she won't do it. She's not ready. If she wanted to do it, we would be back with her stuff by now.

I am lounging in my hammock. Justina is sitting on my bed, her legs dangling over the edge, swinging. Ronny, having ransacked my house, now naps.

Justina leans over her baby and picks up the white cloth she uses to carry her on her back. "He's at Prim's drinking."

"Yes," I mutter.

She adeptly slips Ronny into the cloth without waking her. Justina's eyes are bright. "Better we go now, when he's away from the house. We can run along the river, maybe he won't see us."

"Yeah. We could do that." I nod and swing gently. She has said this already, a dozen times.

"Come, *ix* Laura, before he gets back!" Ronny's tumpline is on her back with one quick movement.

I race to catch up with her. She is headed to Francesca's. Here, Justina hangs Ronny's instant hammock from Francesca's rafters. Francesca hands us each a plastic-coated burlap sack, and we rush down the hill to the river.

Quickly, she leads me down a path along the river that I have never taken before. It is slippery, but I don't fall. I follow her lead, even though she is moving at a pace too fast for me. My heart clamors to stop, but we don't. Two of Martino's nieces, Theofila and Zoila, are on the path ahead. They are on their way home from school for lunch.

I can't understand her Maya, but Justina harshly whispers something to them, and they rush ahead, excited. Justina hides behind a tree. I do the same. My heart is pounding. I am out of breath.

Before my body rests, Theofila and Zoila are back. "Martino's not home."

Justina bolts up the hill to her house, Theofila, Zoila, and I trailing behind. Martino's sister Reina meets us there. I stuff the things Justina indicates into my sack, including Ronny's toys. Almost as soon as I put things into my sack, Reina pulls them out to admire. "Justina has many nice pots. This fry pan is nice."

Justina agrees. Surrealistically, her movements slow down. She admires her pots as well, pulling others out. "This is my favorite. I got it in Orange Walk. They have so many nice pots there."

I take it from her and put it back into my sack. She glides outside and begins to take her laundry off the line. "It's still wet." She stands holding a dark blue dress, looking at me.

"We'll hang it later," I snap, taking it from her and wrapping her favorite pot in it so it won't clank against the others.

"That's good." Justina compliments my idea. "We might have to hide in the bush. I don't know how to get back to my mother's. I don't know where he is. Which way will he come?" She looks at me.

My heart sinks. What am I doing? Why am I here? How do I stop this? Why did I interfere? How do I get out of here?

Reina takes Justina's arm and begins to lead her down the path to her house, but Justina gently pulls away. She lifts a rock that sits next to the door frame outside. Under it is a set of keys. She pulls the door shut and closes the Master Lock. Pausing for a moment, she stares at the closed door and finally hangs the key on a nub protruding from the doorframe. Turning to me: "If I put it under the rock, he might not find it. He's drunk."

Reina leads Justina down the path to her house. I follow, pots clanking softly in the sack on my back. The girls trail. Reina hides Justina in her kitchen, under a counter. The girls stuff me in a tiny bedroom, and cover me with clothing. The sacks disappear with the girls. I can hear them clanking off into the distance.

After a few seconds, I emerge from the bedroom, a shambling mound of clothing. "This won't do. I can't hide like this." Standing in the kitchen, I can see Justina hiding under the counter. "No. Something else, not this."

Reina rounds us up again and shoos us across the compound to a small house next door. A tiny wrinkled woman dressed in a torn dark green *p'ik* and a greying *camesa* trimmed with a floral design hobbles quickly to help us in. Her house is silent. It feels safe. This is Dionesia's house, Reina's mother-in-law. She has agreed to hide us.

With a quiet wavering whisper she brings me a tall stool, the kind gringas like to sit on. Slowly, she drags another one from the kitchen into the living space for Justina. She smiles at me, a big smile, exposing her two teeth, one on the top, the other on the bottom. Slowly she lowers herself to sit on a *banco*. As we settle, the kitchen window opens. Giggling wafts in. The two sacks loom through the window and fall to the ground. The old woman stands and attends to them, replacing what has fallen out, quietly rebuking the girls. She is so quiet, I don't think the girls hear her. She drags the sacks under her food prep table in the kitchen, then returns to the living space and gives us each an orange.

In hushed tones, Justina relates her story to Dionesia, looking over to me occasionally. I am quiet. I nod when appropriate. Eating my orange, I smile at Dionesia.

"I think I might be pregnant. How will I find a job if I'm pregnant?" Justina whispers to me, taking the last bite of her orange. "What can I do?"

"Don't worry. You don't even know yet. Don't worry about what you don't know."

She is quiet. I am quiet. The old lady sits still.

Justina is the first to stir. Seconds later, Theofila is at the old woman's door, whispering between the slats. "He's at the house. He's breaking it up. Can't you hear?"

Dionesia moves to the door and locks it. She whispers harshly. "Be quiet. Go away. He'll come here. Go away." The girl clomps away.

Now, Reina is at the door, whispering. "I'm going to go see. I'll hide in the bush. He's drunk, he won't see me. I'll tell you what he is doing." Then she is gone.

Justina and I try desperately to see through the slats of Dionesia's house. Nothing. I don't hear anything. Nothing.

Reina is back. Justina unlocks the door and lets her in. Both seem calm. "He's not there. I didn't see anything. The door is still locked. He was never at the house. I don't know where he is. Who knows what that sound was, maybe the pigs."

Justina seems neither relieved nor upset. She sits down again and thanks her sister-in-law. Reina leaves, and we continue to wait.

"I don't know how to get back to Miss Coc's house." Justina is quiet, calm. "We can go in the bush, but we still have to go in the road to get there." She looks at me. "We can go the long way, but still, we have to go up the hill on the road."

"Whichever way you want to go, you know best." I have nothing to offer. "I'll follow you."

"I don't know where he is." She looks down.

"He's either at Prim's or Matt's if he's drinking rum."

"Yes. But we have to go soon, before the schoolchildren get out." If we are anywhere when the children are walking home, we are found. They will ask us questions, and if we don't say anything, they'll make up their own answers. The school is in the center of the village. Anything that happens while the kids are on their way home spreads like smallpox. No one is immune.

"Best we go now." Justina gathers up the sacks and brings them to the living space. I thank Dionesia for the orange and promise to visit another time, then I put the heaviest sack on my back. Justina leads the way down to the river, on yet another path I have never taken.

I am quickly out of breath, but Justina, fourteen years younger and used to the humidity, has no problem. I watch her feet as they seem to cling to the slippery rocks along the river. She is barefoot. Her feet are shaped differently from mine, wider. They seem attached to her ankles at a different angle. She doesn't walk with her feet parallel: the ball of each foot points inward, the heel out, just the opposite of mine. Her big toe is far from the others, not close like mine. I watch her feet move quickly over the rocks, over the moss, finding footholds in the roots of trees. I watch her, while I think about what people will think when they see me helping her.

A young woman thigh-deep in the water pauses from washing clothes to watch us pass. Her two children, a boy of four and a girl of eight, splash and play nearby.

"Did you see Martino?" Justina grunts.

"No." She shakes her head, eyebrows raised.

We don't pause, but concentrate on little judgements about which rock to step on, which root will act as the best foothold, and which we should avoid. Finally, we come to the area where she taught me to wash, years ago. Here we begin up the hill, past the Mennonite house to the road, where everyone can see us.

Marta, a fourteen-year-old girl, runs down a path from her house. She stops just before the road and watches us. "What are you doing?" she asks me.

"*Max!*" Nothing! I yell, not losing a step. Marta runs back up the hill to report to her mother, nothing.

We slow down as we near the top of the hill. If Martino is on the other side of the hill, we won't be able to see him until we top the rise. If he is on his way home from Prim's, this is his most likely path. There is no way to avoid danger.

When we reach the top of the hill, we can't see him anywhere, so we slow our pace and finish our journey to Francesca's.

I put my sack down with a thud, and Francesca attends to the contents. She takes the pots she had given to Justina, and stores the rest behind the partition in her kitchen with her store of dried corn. Then she hangs Justina's wet clothes out to dry. Justina and I rest in silence for a while, until I leave. I have clothes to wash. It is already afternoon. If I don't do it now, there won't be enough sun to dry them. I have gotten lazy too many times already on a sunny day, only to have my clothes stink of mildew by morning.

Ronny

I stop by Francesca's on my way to the river, just a few minutes later.

Justina is making tortillas, while Francesca stirs up a pot of pork she cooked yesterday. "I'll go to the police, *ix* Laura. I'm gonna tell him he hit me, so I can go to Social tomorrow and sign the papers for Miss Coc to take Ronny."

"Francesca's taking Ronny?"

"Yes, *ix* Laura." Francesca smiles. "Better I take the child. How can Justina find her job if she has this baby with her?"

"Maybe Justina can take her back someday." I look at Justina, her head bowed over the *comal,* flipping tortillas.

Without emotion, without looking at me, she responds, "How can I get my job if I have Ronny? Miss Coc can take care of her. She wants my baby. Let her take her."

"So you're going to the police." I look outside. "Vernon Cayetano is back."

"Yes, gal. He come back last week." The pork dish is bubbling. "She mus tell the police so she can get the papers from Social." Francesca fumbles through her dishes to find two plastic bowls.

"Adoption papers?" I nod.

"Yes, gal. You don't see how this baby suffers?" Francesca brings her bowls to the hearth, carefully lifts the pot of pork off the flames onto the edge of the hearth. "You want lunch?"

"No. No, thanks. I gotta wash my clothes before there's no sun left to dry."

Francesca laughs, "Yes, mind they don't stink." She is happy she's getting another child to raise, another child to one day help her with her work.

The river is calm today. It is not always so. Sometimes women beckon me to wash with them, torturing me by testing my Mopan, or kids call me to play when I am tired and cranky. Sometimes, fish pick at my feet. It is a sickening irritation to be eaten alive in the jungles of Belize by minnows of some sort. On days like that, the river creates excitement and danger. It threatens to drag your clothes down the river, to knock over your soap, and to soak the clothes you planned to wear after bathing. Sometimes I hate the river.

Today, however, the river is calm. No one is washing, no one is playing. I am thankful for the reprieve. No one is here to ask me what I was doing, running with Justina. No one is here to torture me with language. No one. Not even the fish.

I wash my clothes, and enjoy how the river has gently engulfed my feet, my calves, my knees. I can clearly see my feet below me, somehow attached an inch or two to the right of where they should be. Refraction, illusion. The river gently flows.

Then I bathe. Slowly rubbing a bar of "sweet soap" over my body, I massage my upper body as the river massages my legs and feet. I swim, rinsing the soap from my body, from my hair. This is the first real calm I can remember in a long time. It is a different calm from the resignation I felt in my house when I convinced myself Justina would never leave. This is a true calm. Things settled. Maybe it is best for Ronny to stay with Francesca. She raised Justina this way, and Cil. Now she is raising Cil's daughter, Angela. She is a kind of foster mother, taking care of children who need a home for whatever reason. A good woman unable to have her own. Maybe it is best for Ronny.

Walking back home, the weight of my bucket full of clean wet clothing tugs at my arm. I can feel a smile on my face as the sun begins to dry my hair. I will hang my clothes and sit in my hammock when I get home; a hectic day has come to an end.

When I reach the top of the hill, the same hill on which Justina and I slowed our pace, I see him. Martino is standing by Coc's shop, unsteady, drunk. Holding Ronny. Standing next to him is Lucio in his school uniform, just off the school bus. A huge smelly billow of diesel exhaust hangs heavy in the air as the bus rumbles down the road to its next stop.

I am still with fright. I have to pass Martino in order to get home.

"*Ix* Laura," Martino mumbles.

I try to ignore him.

"Laura." He speaks a little louder. "Excuse me, *ix* Laura." Maya always say "excuse me" before asking a favor. It is a humbling. They also seem to say it just before they express anger.

I brace myself for his words, his condemnation. I brace myself for his violence. Drunks in the States seem to take offense at things much less important than people helping their wives leave them.

"Excuse me, Laura."

"Yes." I clear my throat.

Ronny looks at me when she hears my voice, "LaLA." She yells my name and squeals with excitement, giggling, "hee hee hee."

Martino looks down. "I'm sorry," he says. "I'm unable to buy the radio from you now."

Radio?

"But this boy," Martino motions to Lucio, who steps forward and smiles, "this boy wants it."

I move toward them.

Martino continues, "I don't know if it is possible. I don't know if you can sell it to him. Maybe you can. I can't buy it now. Maybe you want to sell it to someone else. I don't know. It's a good radio, but I can't buy it now."

"I need a radio for my school." Lucio smiles again. "We have an assignment to listen to weather reports, but I don't have a radio. Maybe you have one for me."

I take the tone of Mayan negotiation. "Maybe you want to see it before you buy." Everything must be agreed upon. There can be no ambiguity. I know now that Martino's humbleness was to begin the negotiation. He isn't angry. "Maybe it is not good for you. Maybe you don't like it." Emphasize the negative: The purchase must be his idea.

"It's good." Martino offers his opinion, and stumbles for a moment as he turns to Lucio. Regaining his balance, he whispers, "*Kichpan.*" Beautiful.

"Maybe you should see it," I suggest.

"Okay." Lucio smiles hard, his dimples showing, his teeth straight, clean, like a toothpaste commercial. They both turn toward my house and begin to walk.

"Oh, but not now. I have too much work." I motion my head toward my bucket, smiling. No, not now.

"Okay." Another smile. "Maybe tomorrow, when the bus comes again."

"Yes, good. This time tomorrow." I turn to leave and sense Martino waver a little. I can hear him say good-bye to Lucio. From the corner of my eye, I see him head down the road toward the river, toward his house, taking his baby home.

On the veranda: "Martino has the baby," I announce to everyone at Francesca's—Francesca, Angela, Evarista.

"I know, gal. Justina is with the police." Then, whining, "Angela won't go to get her." Angela is lying on the ground, in her dark blue satin dress, playing with a kitten. She wiggles and moans when Francesca mentions her name.

I am furious. I put my bucket down hard, summoning the image of what happened in my head. Martino, drunk, looking for Justina. Justina gone, already talking to Vernon, trusting Francesca to watch Ronny, trusting her to keep her safe. Francesca's mouth pouting with the realization that Martino wants his daughter, but too cowardly to stop him. Without protest, she lets Ronny go with him, and he is barely able to walk.

"He is drunk!" I say, for the first time letting myself express anger with Francesca. "Why did you let him take her?" I don't wait for an answer but leave my bucket and go to the police station.

At the highest point, the green and yellow police station overlooks the village. It houses both the jail and the constable's family. His family lives upstairs, in the wooden part. His office and two jail cells are on the ground level. They are made of cement blocks. One cell is about 8′ × 12′, "for men," Vernon once told me. The other is about 8′ × 6′, "for women." The 8′ × 6′ cell is full of the constable's empty cases of soda pop and beer bottles. He doesn't jail women very often.

The door to the office is open. Justina is sitting with Police Constable Vernon Cayetano. Vernon is Creole, proud of himself and his position. Cho, the Mayan police constable who lived and grew up in the village, the man who replaced Vernon while he was on vacation for a month, is sitting on the ground near the office door. He is listening to Justina tell

Vernon her story. He is picking up pebbles and tossing them down the hill. He nods to me as I come up the hill.

"Hey, Cho." I nod and smile at him, but walk past him and enter the office. Ignoring Vernon, I tell Justina, "He has Ronny."

"Martino?" Her eyes are big and watery. She has a tissue in her hand. "He's got Ronny?"

I acknowledge Vernon. "He's drunk."

Immediately, Vernon begins to resonate. It is a deep rumbling sound he makes before he speaks, sometimes he makes it instead of speaking. His heavy Creole accent made it difficult for me to understand him when I first met him. Now I understand him all too well. "Where is he?"

"He's headed home, walking down the road toward the river."

"It's not safe for the baby. He's drunk. I tell you, he knock her. What will he do? What if he sleep? I lef Ronny with Miss Coc, why she let him take her?" Justina fires off the questions that have been running through my mind.

"I don't know." I look at Cho.

"She like to make trouble for da police too much." Grumble. "Dat's why." Moan. "Now where my cap. Dees pipple wanna mek trouble too much." Vernon puts on his beret, tilting it with style, examining himself in the mirror. His voice and grumble resonate through his body and his office as he picks up his nightstick. "They can't rest themselves, they wanna mek trouble." Grumble. "Come on, Cho, the pipple done mek trouble again, dey doan wan rest."

Cho jumps to his feet. He isn't in uniform, but he's ready. He is wearing his bright white Nike sneakers, a pair of dark blue work pants, and a black and white vertically striped cotton shirt, neatly tucked into his pants. He looks like a referee. His sparse mustache never seems to get much fuller. He nods and smiles at me, then carefully at Justina, as he and Vernon head down the hill. His white sneakers defy grime.

"I'm going, Tina. I don't want to be here when they come back. I don't want him to know I was the one who told Vernon where to find him."

Justina nods. "But why did she let him take her?" She looks up, her dark watery eyes shining through the gouges on her face. The gouges seemed bigger before, redder. Her body is already healing itself. She stays behind, sitting in Vernon's office, hands in her lap, looking out the door.

I head back to Francesca's to get my laundry.

As soon as she sees me, Francesca asks, "Where's Justina?"

Sharp and direct, with no additional information, I say, "At the police station, waiting for them to come back with Ronny." I pick up my bucket and continue on to my house. I am not going to tell her anything else. If she was so interested, she should have been the one to go to the police. She has relied on me too much.

I see Justina on the path to my house, Ronny on her hip. I welcome her into my house and put Ronny on the bed. Justina sits next to her, with a heavy sigh. Surprisingly, Ronny sits still and quiet.

"So you have Ronny." I smile.

"LaLA," Ronny squeals.

"She says your name now." Justina smiles.

I smile wide. "Yes."

"Martino's in jail." Justina frowns, swinging her feet as they dangle over the edge of the bed. "Tomorrow, I go to Social and give my baby to Miss Coc. Then, I try to find my job." She sighs.

"Where will you go?"

"I don't know. Caye Caulker maybe.[14] I know a woman there, maybe she has work." Her mouth is crooked. "Maybe I'll go back to Stann Creek[15] and find my job." She pauses for a moment. "But Ronny stay here. It's too hard to find work if you have a baby. Miss Coc will take her. Ronny will stay here like her mommy. I was nearly Ronny's age when Miss Coc take me." She plays with Ronny's hair. "She want her."

"Miss Coc made you work hard," I offer.

"Yes. I do every thing for she. I don't want that for my Ronny, but what can I do? I can't take her with me." She sighs and smiles at me. "I think it's best for she. Tomorrow I'll go and get the papers. Miss Coc can take my baby."

"Maybe it's best." I have no other solution. Francesca takes good care of Angela. In fact, she spoils her.

We sit in silence. Then Justina stands and puts Ronny on her hip. "Good-bye, *ix* Laura."

I grab Ronny's leg and shake it. "Good-bye, Tina." When I let go Justina returns to Francesca.

After dinner, I wander down the trail to Francesca's kitchen. I can hear Ronny crying her evening sleepy-time wail. Sometimes she gets too tired and then can't sleep. Francesca and Justina are talking. I stand in the doorway and see Justina has Ronny in her tumpline, gently bouncing up and down to rock her asleep. Francesca is cooking. Mr. Coc sits at the table, a transistor radio in front of him. The back is open, he's trying to fix it. Evarista sits on a *banco,* brushing Angela's hair.

"*Deyoos.*" I smile.

"*Deyoos, ix* Laura." Francesca laughs. "*O ken.*" Come in.

Justina says my name too, playfully.

"Maybe you know how to fix this." Mr. Coc chuckles.

"I don't know. I don't really know anything about radios." I nod to Evarista and sit in the chair across from Mr. Coc.

"Maybe you want to try this." He motions to a piece of roast meat in a bowl in the middle of the table.

"I just ate, but that looks good." In truth it looks too greasy.

"It's *gibnut.*" Paca, a rain forest rodent. He smiles. "The best meat in Belize." He laughs.

"Go ahead, take it." Justina encourages me.

"I like *gibnut.*" I smile.

In a second Francesca takes a flour tortilla and strips some meat off the bone. She places it in the tortilla and hands it to me. "Here, dip it in this." With her lips, she points to a clay bowl of oil on the table.

I dip the tortilla and taste it. The oil is flavored with hot pepper and cilantro. Delicious. *Gibnut* is wonderful meat, especially roasted. Coc laughs as I wiggle my eyebrows and smile between bites to show how much I like it. "Mmmm. Delicious. Why can't we have *gibnut* in the States?" I muse, making Coc chuckle again.

Justina laughs, too, swinging around to take her tumpline off and hang Ronny's instant hammock from the rafters. She's asleep. As I turn to watch her, I see Martino in the doorway. He slowly enters the room, somehow still blocking the doorway. He takes Justina's wrists, tight. He is mumbling something, but I can't hear. Mr. Coc asks him to leave. Martino still holds Justina, he still mumbles. The only way out is through the window, right behind me. I drop my *gibnut* tortilla and jump out the window. I pop my head in the other window by Francesca and tell her I am going to get the constable.

"Yes, go, gal," she breathes.

As I head down the hill, I turn to see Mr. Coc come out the door and grab a shovel leaning against the house. I run. Dogs bark at me fiercely as I pass different houses. I don't stop. Past the shop, past the church, up the hill, across the schoolyard, I am running, out of breath. I slow down but continue until I get to the police station. I walk quickly up the stairs and knock on the door.

Cynthia, Vernon's five-year-old daughter, opens the door. I rush into their living room to find the entire family just finishing dinner. "Sorry. Vernon," I breathe hard for a few seconds, "Martino is at the Cocs', he's got Justina by the wrists, and Mr. Coc just went to get a shovel." I breathe again. "I don't know what's going to happen." I pause. "Can you come?"

The house resonates. "Da pipple can't res themselves. Always trouble."

"I'm sorry, Denise." I turn to his wife.

It seems to take forever for Vernon to get ready. He takes his stick and his beret and kisses his wife. Then he heads off into the dark toward the Cocs' compound. I stay with Denise to catch my breath and repeat the whole story for her in case she didn't know what had happened.

"Why didn't Vernon keep him in jail?" I shake my head, not really expecting an answer.

"Oh, dat man wail all night." She waves her hand in the air, and begins to collect up the dishes from the table. She motions to Cynthia. "My baby can't sleep again. He want his wife, he want his baby; he can't shut up. Cry, cry." She ends it with a nasal hum and dumps the dishes in a plastic basin in the sink.

"So Vernon let him go."

"Yes, gal. But why dat gal go bock home, when she know he gonna come again? Dey all-ways come again an try to sweet it up."

"He didn't look like he was trying to sweet it up." I shake my head. "Where else could she go?"

"Well, you'll see, another day and dey all sweet again. You wan lime juice?" She turns and pours water on the dishes.

"No, thanks. Maybe I'll head back now." I smile at Cynthia.

"Okay. Mind da dogs, gal, dey fierce at night. You know to trow rock at dey." She looks over her shoulder at me.

"Yes. Thanks." As I go down the stairs, I can see the outline of a stumbling figure swaying back and forth as he walks down the road. He pauses for a moment in front of Tzir's house, probably wondering whether Tzir has *chicha*, corn wine, to sell. Tzir's house is dark. The drunk continues on his way. It is Martino, making his way back home. When I get to the road, I see Vernon headed toward Prim's shop. He will have a Belikan stout and fill everyone in on the news before he heads home to Denise.

Cocs' house is dark, so I go home, sit in my hammock, and read.

Martino

One, two, THREE, pause, one, two, THREE. Hammering wakes me the next morning. I can hear Mr. Coc giving orders. I have gotten used to sleeping in my clothing, like a Mayan woman. It makes morning a little easier. I open my door and stand on the veranda. Down the path, I can see Mr. Coc closely supervising Martino's repair of his chicken coop. I watch for a moment and begin my morning chores. I head out to my own coop, open the door, and let the broilers run. I am raising a few "Mennonite chickens," the product of genetic engineering.[16] They are fat already. It will be time to slaughter them soon. I return to the house and sweep.

"*Deyoos.*" The pounding has stopped. Martino stands at my door.

"Martino. Hello." I come out on the veranda and motion for him to sit with me.

"Hello, Miss Laura." He takes off his camouflage hat and frowns as he sits.

"So you work for Mr. Coc today." I smile.

"Yes." He sits with his arms on his thighs, holding his hat between his legs. "By now you should know. Justina is gone." He swings his hat.

"Yes."

"Looks like I'm single again." He looks down, swinging his hat.

I am silent, looking toward Cocs'.

"I tried to get on the bus this morning. I waited by Prim's shop. I wanted to get on as it passed, but," he giggles, "I fell asleep." He stops swinging his hat, looks up at me with a smirk, and nods. "Too much rum."

"Yes, you were drunk last night." I pause. "And the night before."

"Yes. I wanted to stop her, to try again." He looks down, again, hat swinging. "By now you should know why Justina lef me." He looks up at me, eyes glassy. "Looks like I'm single again." His mouth droops into a frown.

"Yes, it looks that way, Martino." I take a breath. "What will you do? Will you stay in the village, with your father?"

"Maybe I'll go back to Pomona and find my job again. My boss say anytime, I can come back." He squints as he looks at me. "But I don't want to go back there. Too much shame."

I nod.

"I can go to Orange Walk, maybe." He smiles and holds his hat still. "I can go anywhere because I'm single again."

"Yep, that's what's nice about being alone." I smile back.

Lowering his head again, he says, "Maybe, I might miss my dautta too much, and my wife."

"Do you want some tea, Martino?"

"No, I'll go back to Coc. He's got work." He puts the hat on his head. "I can use the money." He stands. "Sorry I can't buy your radio. I think Lucio wants it."

"No problem. Good luck, Martino." I stand too, as he heads down the path, back to Coc.

"Justina's gone, gal." Francesca is hanging her laundry in the sun. Angela chases Ronny past us, tickling her belly when she catches her.

"Yes, and I think Martino goes, too."

"LaLA." Ronny runs to me and grabs my leg. "Heeheehee."

"Dat baby gets used to you." Francesca smiles.

"Yes, she's a good baby." I pick her up and put her on my hip. "Ronny," I bounce my head on the last syllable to make her laugh. She giggles with delight.

"But she don't have no mommie now." Francesca turns so I can see her frown. "Who'll take care of the baby?"

"Martino's going to Orange Walk, maybe." I look over my shoulder at Angela. Now she is chasing chickens, laughing.

"Yes, gal. Tomorrow the baby has no father." We are silent for a moment.

"Ron-ny," I say again, to break the silence, to make her laugh. I giggle with her, mimicking her. She is such a wonderful baby.

"Maybe Mike wants to be the father of that baby." She smiles and returns her attention to her laundry. "Maybe you'll take that baby back to the States."

"She's coming, gal." Francesca is standing in my doorway. Ronny is on her hip, nose running in two streams down to her mouth.

"Who? Who's coming?" I come out onto the veranda, holding a cup of hot ginger tea.

"Justina, gal." Her eyes are wide, frightened almost.

"Justina? Coming here?" I sip my tea and cough. I made it strong to help loosen the phlegm. I have had a cold for about a week now.

"Yes, she gets to hear Ronny is sick. So now she comes back to the village."

"When will she reach?" I clear my throat. "Tomorrow maybe, on Chun's bus?"

"Maybe, gal. I don't know." She pouts, rocking Ronny on her hip. "Maybe we have to say good-bye to Ronny."

I take hold of Ronny's foot. "Maybe she needs her mother."

"Yes, gal. She's sick." She rocks Ronny again. "Maybe you want to go to plantation tomorrow, gal."

"Sure, we'll be back by the time the bus comes. Right." I take another sip of my tea.

"Yes, gal."

Francesca and I are resting on her veranda, waiting for the bus to come. I am eating a golden plum, a bittersweet fruit with prickly fibers throughout. Kids like them. I don't, and am beginning to regret starting this one. It is like dental floss and fruit all in one. We harvested two huge bags to sell at the shop. Angela is enjoying hers.

I watch the road for the bus. I haven't seen Justina in months. I will be glad to see her. Ronny sits on my lap. I take her foot in my hand. Francesca's suggestions that I take Ronny back to the States have been more frequent. I am tempted to take the child as my own.

"De bus come, gal." Francesca motions with her lips down the road.

"How can you tell?" I squint, but still can't see anything. Then I can hear it, far in the distance. "Yes, it's coming." I turn to her and smile.

Evarista steps out on the veranda and watches too, coughing the deep phlegmy cough that started a long time before any of us started getting sick.

Slowly the bus follows the road, occasionally stopping and letting people off. Then it stops in front of Cocs'.

"Look, Ronny, look." Francesca points to the bus. Ronny looks.

I can see Justina step off the bus. She moves around to the back and waits for Pablo, the driver, to hand down her box of belongings. But when the back of the bus opens, Martino jumps out and Pablo hands him their boxes. Martino smiles, takes off his hat and nods; they're laughing. I wasn't expecting Martino's return. As the bus leaves, Martino and Justina follow the path to the Cocs' compound. Justina's belly is distended. They have returned to have another child.

ANALYSIS: JEALOUSY, LEGITIMACY, AND THE MAYAN CYCLE OF VIOLENCE

Of all the cases of domestic violence I encountered in the village, Justina's seemed most like those in the United States, perhaps because she and Martino are caught up in a cycle of violence similar to the one many couples in the United States experience (Walker 1979). Mayan domestic violence is often characterized by a husband's bout of drunken violence, a wife's return to her family of origin, and the husband's attempt to convince her to return.[17] The narrative in this chapter provides an example of how the cycle is lived; this analysis section puts Justina's experiences in a wider Mayan perspective to examine the legitimacy of such beatings in the Mayan world. Negotiating legitimacy or illegitimacy is essential to facilitating escape from abusive partners.

The Cycle of Violence

The idea of a three-phase cycle of violence emerged from interviews with women in the United States who had stayed in abusive relationships for a long time (Walker 1979). The cycle encompasses a period of tension that develops between wife and husband, and the release of that tension for both through the husband's violence. After a violent episode, abusive husbands regret their actions and treat their wives with extra kindness in attempts to prevent them from leaving. Walker developed her idea of the cycle of violence in efforts to understand why women don't leave abusive husbands. While economic entrapment or fear of losing a comfortable standard of living are responsible for some women staying in abusive relationships, Walker feels that the problem is more complicated than that. Women stay because abuse is not a constant in their lives. Their husbands express a deep, complex love which has great emotional power (Walker 1979). The cycle of violence Walker describes seems appropriate for Maya.

Watching Justina struggle with her decision to leave Martino, I came to understand that the motive for leaving needs to feel more powerful, more stable, and more secure than any other feelings she might have.

A Mayan Cycle of Violence

When the circumstances are right, abused Mayan women can temporarily return to their family of origin. This is true for Chamula (Rosenbaum 1993:109–111), Zincantecos (Vogt 1969:214), those in Chimaltenango (Wagley 1949:45), and for the Mopan in the village (Justina and
Michaela in this narrative). In fact, beating your wife can be a means for
a man to initiate divorce (Wagley 1949:45, Vogt 1969:214).

Once a woman has returned home, her husband might initiate a "reconciliation." [18] Reconciliation may involve not just the husband and his
wife, but also her parents. Vogt (1969) reports that a husband attempt-
ing such a reconciliation may bring a bottle of rum with him. He doesn't
mention why rum is brought or who drinks it. It would be consistent
with Maya ritual that the wife's parents, especially her father, would receive the rum. Vogt, I think, is saying the reconciliation is not simply
between husband and wife. Rosenbaum (1993:110) cites an example of
a woman's mother playing an active role in the reconciliation. Her attempts to maintain her daughter's right to remain with her family of
origin, away from her abusive husband, is met by the decision of an all-
male group of indigenous political leaders that the woman should return
to her husband.

In general, such male authorities ultimately control women (Rosenbaum 1993:119). Mayan legal systems, run exclusively by men, work
on a harmony ideology much like Zapotec law (Nader 1990). Reconciliation, rather than justice, tends to be the goal. Mayan wives facing
alcalde court therefore usually return to their husbands. During my stay,
few women took their cases to *alcalde* court, or to the Belizean national
court. A recent *alcalde* court ruling that men have the right to beat their
wives (Crooks 1993) [19] probably discouraged women from arguing their
cases there. Also, few women were confident enough of their English-
language skills to take their cases to the Belizean national court. Most
settled their cases at home, with their families, often with their father
acting as judge, as in Chiapas (Nadar 1990:61–64).

If reconciliation takes place at home, the woman's family is not obligated to take the daughter's side. Indeed, when Francesca first hears of
Justina's problems with Martino's abuse, she goes to Orange Walk and
gives her adopted daughter a long lecture. As an adultress, Justina was
to blame for her beatings.

Legitimacy: Jealousy and Controlling Women's Sexuality

The sexual world of Mayan women is highly controlled. In Chamula, parents warn young women that men will try to "steal them." Young women quickly learn not to act in any way a man might consider inviting: They avoid eye contact, they never talk to men, they may even react violently when a man tries to speak with them. Young women fear rape, and they fear gossip that might suggest they are inviting or even condoning a man's advances (Rosenbaum 1993:38–39).

Young women in the village also avoid young men. Parents and godparents warn them of the possible harm that may come to their bodies and their reputations due to a man's actions. Gossip often focuses on those who talk freely with young men, especially if they speak in public. Fathers may physically reprimand young girls if they are rumored to "like boys too much."

These restrictions do not apply as harshly to high-school girls. Adults recognize that schooling requires more freedom, at least temporarily.

As fathers, and sometimes brothers, control women's sexuality before marriage, husbands control their sexuality after marriage. Jealousy seems paramount in a man's emotional makeup in the village and in other parts of the Mayan world. In Chimaltenango, husbands keep careful tabs on their wives, even when they leave the house at night to urinate (Wagley 1949:42). The village husbands may interpret the simple act of walking on the road unaccompanied as a wife's attempt to find another man (Danziger 1991:90).

Mayan men often control their wives' sexuality with violence. A jealous husband might beat his wife, even if he has only a suspicion and no proof of her infidelity. Proof of a wife's infidelity justifies violence against her. When women speak of a "jealous" husband, they often mean he is violent.

A Double Standard

No one told me of women beating their husbands for infidelities. In the United States, people under-report such abuse to protect men from embarrassment. Perhaps Maya also under-report such beatings.

Mayan women do talk about others who abuse their husbands. Some women, they say, refuse to cook for their husbands, or to perform the duties required by traditional gender roles. Some report that women sometimes verbally abuse their husbands, calling them drunkards or saying they are lazy. Others are said to slander their husbands. These are all common topics of gossip.

Women who are the focus of such gossip may find it difficult to create alliances with the women around them, since they are thought of as bad women. Forming friendships with such women may indicate support for the idea of abusing husbands in this way.

Men do not always get away with their infidelities, however. One woman in her sixties told me that she threatened her son-in-law with a machete because he "went with the next lady." He was coming home after spending several days with his mistress when his mother-in-law spotted him on the path. She ran out of her house with a machete, swinging it wildly. The man hid in the outhouse while she circled it and called for her daughter to come and laugh at him. She told me and several of her friends the story using great animation, swinging her machete around the yard. We laughed uproariously.

When women talk of their husbands' infidelities they emphasize the fact that it hurts the family financially. An adulterer brings his mistress gifts, straining the household economy of his legitimate family. In any gossip circle, you can hear statements like, "Maybe he thinks I don't need kerosene to see at night, or cloth to make clothes, but I need these things. What about his children? They need these things."

Emphasizing the financial consequences of infidelity may relieve the emotional pain of rejection, as it did for one woman I met. However, it definitely focuses discussion on the husband's refusal to provide for his family. The main reason women give for joining "women's groups," craft or corn mill cooperatives, is that sales provide them with money that goes directly into their household funds. Their husbands, they say, spend their money on alcohol or mistresses. Husbands' contributions to household finances are unreliable. Working and providing for one's family, as we saw in the previous chapter, is important in the Mayan world.

Violence, Drinking, and Jealousy

Violence is part of Mayan drunken comportment.[20] When drunk, men sometimes beat their children (Rosenbaum 1993:60, Eber 1995). In the village, drunken fathers beat their daughters for reasons similar to those they give for beating their wives: laziness and to discourage flirtations with boys. Fathers beat their sons mostly for laziness.

Drunken sons also beat fathers. Martino beat his father several times when drunk, once with a fishing pole. In fact, one of the reasons Martino and Justina went to Pomona was because Martino was afraid he might beat his father again, perhaps more severely.

For Maya, drinking seems to remove inhibitions against violence. It also seems to increase self-pity and sadness. When drunk, men, especially older men, suffer bouts of tears. Drinking makes men focus on their misfortunes and, perhaps, reminds them of the jealousy they feel in the back of their minds. In the forefront, jealousy swirls together with reduced inhibitions against violence, allowing the drinker to justify using violence to right perceived wrongs. A woman's infidelity is a wrong that Maya take seriously. When drunk, violence seems an appropriate response.

In Chamula, husbands have murdered their wives' lovers (Rosenbaum 1993:59). In Chimaltenango, every case of homicide in memory was related to adultery (Wagley 1949:43). Alcohol is prominent in such cases.

In the village, I watched a drunk man hold his brother's head down and raise a machete over his neck. He suspected his brother and wife were having an affair while he was away taking courses at Teachers College in Belize City. He halted his attempt to decapitate his brother when he was struck with the realization of what he was doing. Later, when I returned to the shop where this happened, I found him drinking, and repeating the phrases "one ma, one pa" and "I nearly kill my brother." If he was not a brother, I am sure he would have killed him.

When jealousy spurs drunken violence, however, men most often direct this violence toward their wives. The reasons may be logistical. The wife is at home when her husband returns from a night's drinking, her lover may be more difficult to find, she is usually physically weaker.

Drinking, however, does not cause violence, domestic or otherwise. Violence also occurs when people are sober. For Mayan men, however, drinking seems to reduce inhibitions against acting on jealousy. Most instances of domestic violence in the village occur when a man is drunk. Justina recognizes this and repeatedly secures a promise from Martino that he will never drink again. But he still does.

Pressures to drink come partly from Mayan ritual traditions. Maya expect alcohol, especially *chicha* and rum, to be served and consumed at any celebration following a rite of passage. It is traditional for a male member of a host family to circulate through the guests at baptism, graduation, and marriage and funeral celebrations, offering alcohol. The server's job is to meet rejection with a long ritualized speech, meant to convince the guest to drink. It is difficult, and somewhat insulting, to say no. Unlike Pedranos in Chenalho (Eber 1995), Mopan in Belize would never consider using a soft drink in such rituals.

Other pressures to drink come from peers. Accepting a drink in a shop signifies accepting another's friendship. Drinking has especially become the habit of soldiers home on leave. They "teach their brothers to drink," partying late into the night, giving advice and telling stories of their experiences outside the village.

Maya, however, consider drunkenness disrespectful (Danziger 1991). If a husband drinks and becomes violent, his wife has a legitimate reason for leaving him. No one, however, forgets or forgives her offense, if she has committed one. Still, she may elicit help, especially from older women, if they feel she is being overly punished for her wrongdoing. Justina has Francesca's support in leaving Martino in part because Francesca feels violence is wrong. Francesca and other women say violent couples live like animals, without respect. Francesca also gives Justina support because she wants to adopt Ronny.

Mayan Adoption

For Justina, like many abused women in the United States, the decision to leave her husband has economic consequences. Fear of economic hardship makes leaving Martino difficult. Justina must leave the village and find a job. If she could return home, she would take a position much like that she left upon marriage, doing whatever work Francesca might assign. She might be able to marry again, but it is unlikely that anyone from the village would solicit her due to her adultery. Returning home would be returning to a kind of immaturity made increasingly uncomfortable by Angela's growing up.

However, Mr. Coc, Justina's adoptive father, refuses to welcome her back into his home because she is an adultress. She must leave the village. Doing so, she faces the problem of what to do with Ronny.

Employment for Mayan women outside the village is limited to working as a domestic, in a factory, or in the tourist trade. Employers pay too little for employees to afford child-care and rent. None allow children on the job site.

A viable solution is to take advantage of "traditional" forms of adoption.[21] In Chan Kom, Maya recognize two forms of adoption: *regalado* and *prestada* (Elmendorf 1972:3–21). *Regalado,* in Spanish, is "given," *prestada* "loaned." While the difference is not linguistically marked in the village, adoption takes several different forms.

Francesca has adopted and raised several children: Cil, Justina, Emilio, and Angela. Cil came to stay with Mr. Coc and Francesca because his family decided to live *pach kut,* literally "behind the fence." It glosses as "out of the village." Cil's parents wanted him to continue going to school. The walk was long, and difficult for the boy. They asked his uncle, Mr. Coc, if he could stay at his house. Coc welcomed the boy, on the condition that he work for him occasionally. Cil grew close to Coc and Francesca, and today finds it difficult to visit the village because he must divide his time between his parents' house and the Cocs' house. A split in loyalties has also strained Cil's relationships somewhat. Coc complicated Cil's life when he announced Cil would inherit land from him when he dies. The difficulties between Cil, his biological family, and his adoptive family extend to his wife and children (see Chapter 6).

Justina came to stay with Coc and Francesca at the age of two, when her parents moved away from the village. Because her parents were not in the village, Justina didn't feel a strain on her loyalty or time when she was growing up, nor does she now. However, Justina resents the fact that Francesca made her work hard. She fears that her departure from the village will leave Ronny in a similar situation. There will be no one to protect Ronny from exploitation.

Emilio came to take Cil's place after he went away for police training. He returned to his parents after only a few years because he felt he was working too hard. His parents, who live *pach kut,* outside the village, gladly received him.

Angela is Cil and Michaela's first daughter. She stayed with Francesca after Cil went on his first police assignment, in Belmopan, Belize's capital. Angela was young but used to village life. Her parents and adoptive parents felt transferring the youngster to an unknown location to live an unknown lifestyle might be harmful. So she stayed with Francesca. Francesca will soon expect Angela, at age seven, to begin learning her work. During my stay, Angela would occasionally wash one of her own dresses or pat out her lunch tortillas. Francesca treats Angela lavishly, however, constantly buying her gifts and treats.

Each adoption is unique. However, there is a difference between those where the parents remain close by and those where the birth parents are not available to monitor the adoptive parents' treatment of their children. Children whose biological parents are nearby can go back home, as if the adoption were a loan. This variability may underlie the typology people in Chan Kom make.

It is clear that Justina would be giving Ronny to Francesca. If she doesn't give Ronny away, severing her claims and rights to the child, nothing can stop Martino from reclaiming her and remarrying. Justina doesn't want to give up her motherhood to an unknown woman. Making the adoption official, in Belizean law, would ensure that neither Martino nor Justina could reclaim her. Ronny must be given away outright.

Gloria, a woman with acidic wit whom I often visited, once asked me, while I was playing with her three-year-old, if I had any children. She loved to joke about the differences in power between white women, such as myself, and "Indian" women, as she called herself. She was especially excited to make such jokes in the audience of her daughters. The political undertones were not lost on me and often made me feel uncomfortable, but I liked her style.

When I told her no, I had no kids, she laughed. "Too bad," she smiled. "I thought maybe you could give me one of yours to clean my pigsty."

As in European fairy tales, Maya expect surrogate parents to be cruel. People, they feel, treat their biological children better than adopted or stepchildren. If you give your child away, you rely solely on the goodness of the guardian. Even if the guardian is a *compadre* or *comadre,* they may not live up to the agreement to be kind. Therefore, giving a child away is scary. It is, however, an available option for women who, for whatever reason, are unable to care for their own.

Running Away in Belize: A Small Country with a Large Gossip Network

Belize's improving transportation infrastructure allows women to flee their abusive husbands and return home no matter where they live in Belize. It also helps women, like Justina, who run away from the villages. However, Belize's informal communication system prevents women from running anonymously or secretly.

Belize is a small country, with a large gossip network. The network is expanding even beyond the limits of the country, with electronic mailing lists received worldwide by anyone interested in discussing Belize. Although some of the "back" villages may seem isolated, their isolation is limited (Wilk 1991). People have been leaving the villages for decades now, to find employment and seek various opportunities. Mayan teachers, police constables, agricultural workers, factory workers, politicians, and even radio personalities live throughout the country, and maintain contact with their families in the villages. Sisters, brothers, mothers, and fathers visit, bringing news from home. The population of Belize is mobile, with connections everywhere. There is a saying in Belize that everyone knows everyone else. That is not far from the truth.

This informal communication system prevents women from disappearing without a trace and facilitates their husbands' attempts to find them. Someone somewhere knows where the missing person is staying. The fact that differing opinions exist about the legitimacy of domestic violence ensures that few people remain quiet on the topic.

CHAPTER FOUR

Daughters

Felicia

I am going to make tortillas this morning. With a small plastic bucket of cooked corn tucked between my hip and forearm, I start down the hill to the Tapir grinder. Tapir is a cooperative. They charge more than the private grinder, but I grind so infrequently it doesn't really matter to me. Besides, I like being with the women who run it.

I wave to Prim as I pass his shop. He is sweeping the veranda.

"So today you grind, *ix* Laura," he yells, smiling.

"Yes, today I grind my little corn." I chuckle and hold my bucket up for him to see.

He laughs and returns to his sweeping.

Quickly and quietly I approach the mill house. Carefully, I lean against the outside wall of the building so no one inside can see me.

"*Deyoos.*" I am nearly shouting. I saw Erasma (Ma) in the mill house before I approached, and I want to tease her. Hiding and saying hello is like sneaking up on someone and covering their eyes. Young women tease each other like this all the time. Older women, too, might hide like this when visiting someone's house, but then it is usually a self-humbling. When you do it to show you are humble, you don't speak so loudly, nor do you giggle like I am doing now.

"*Deyoos, o ken, ix* Laura." Hello, come in, Miss Laura. Erasma's laughter rings out. I can never fool her. She's my Belizean mother, how can I fool her? She reminds me so much of my real mother that I liked her the minute I met her. She works constantly. Even in her quietest moments, she busies herself with new and interesting projects, and she is always ready to find the humor life brings. She is heavier than my real mom. Her plumpness and talent for loving life fit the jolly fat-lady archetype of American culture. Her laugh is like music. How can you not like Erasma?

"How can you know it's me?" I show myself by standing in the doorway.

"*Ix* Laura!" Erasma's words force their way through her laughter in puffs. "You are something else, I'm telling you!"

I smile and nod at Julia. I didn't see her before because she is quietly sitting down, sewing. I greet her by saying her name, but I sit on the bench next to Erasma. "*Bi ki lech?*" How are you? I focus on her face, enjoying how completely it expresses joy in seeing me.

"*Toh in wohl.*" Good. Her laughter still fills the small cement mill house. I realize now that she reminds me of a smiling jack-o'-lantern, eyes reduced to slits by her huge grin. Her way is so easy. She relaxes her grin somewhat, so she can speak. "You bring your little corn, *ix* Laura."

"Yes, today I want my tortilla." I nod my head with determination to Julia. A delicate smile crosses her face as she lowers her head.

"So today you will stay at home and work, instead of going all kinds of places." Erasma pauses; her eyes twinkle. I know a joke is about to follow. Erasma times it right, she knows her audience. "You know, when you make your tortillas like an Indian, you will find a husband fast."

Julia giggles, still looking away from me.

"A husband! But, Ma!" I'm an apprentice comic, but she has set me up fine. "I've told you, I already have a husband in the States!"

We all giggle for a second or two. Erasma picks it up again, in mock earnest. "But maybe he has found the next lady. How do you know?" She shakes her head with sympathy. "He is a long way away."

Julia, her head lowered further, holds her hand to her mouth. She is trying to hide the fact that she is laughing at this fictitious misfortune.

"Better you stay here and find an Indian husband." Erasma's smile stretches across her face to ensure I know she is teasing. "An Indian husband will work HARD for you, *ix* Laura."

"Yes! An Indian husband!" I widen my eyes, as if surprised by the revelation. I hold up my bucket of corn. "I have enough corn for two husbands today!"

Erasma and Julia both laugh unashamed.

"*Ix* Laura! Two husbands!" Erasma, belly still jiggling, shakes her head and waves her hand.

"But if you have two husbands, one will lash you." Julia's small voice is followed by a twinkle in her eye. The Tapir women never seem to tire of devising scenarios in which Michael beats me.

"Yes! Maybe BOTH will lash you." Erasma erupts with more giggles.

"But one is in the States, they'll never know." I stand, put the bucket of corn on the table, and remove the cover.

"Oh, *ix* Laura." Erasma, one hand on each thigh, pushes herself to a stand. Her laughter spills outside the building.

Julia picks up the sewing that was resting in her lap and puts it in her woven plastic handbag. It is nearly ten o'clock. She probably arrived around 5 a.m. to open the business. If so, it is nearly time for her lunch break. Today, like every other day, she has wash to do, and she must prepare lunch for her children. When she finishes, she will come back so Ma can take her break.

"I'll help Ma grind, Julia. You go do your work." I move toward the counter, reaching in my pocket for my change purse. Erasma has already carried my corn to the scale, measured it, and calculated what I owe. I give her ten cents.

"Thanks." Julia smiles. I notice again that she is beautiful. Unlike most women in the village, Julia looks young for her age. She is in her late thirties but looks about twenty-five. Her lavender dress accents her coloring and seems to add life to her eyes. She finishes packing up her sewing and is gone by the time Erasma and I get the machine running.

Erasma's roundness keeps her legs hidden by her *p'ik,* her full-length traditional skirt. When she walks, she looks as if she is floating on air. This apparent etherealness persists as she grabs hold of the mill's crank and begins to turn it. She starts slowly, but soon she is moving so fast that I can hardly see her. Hair, head, arms, her whole upper body are whirling into a blur making me wonder if she exists at all. Her strength is amazing, her movements polished. She reminds me of the wild ancient Indians Mr. Coc tells me about on Sunday afternoons or while a group of us are shelling the kernels off dried ears of corn or "busting" open cacao pods to strip the seeds and the sweet gooey sap from the hulls.

The wild Indians live far in the bush. Sometimes, however, they visit people in the villages. They ask for lodging, as if they were travelers. If you give them a place to sleep and a little food, they will stay another day and help you do your work. But they work fast, so fast you can hardly see them. Their hair, heads, and arms blur together in a whirl of motion. Then the work is done. When they eat, they keep their heads down and they use their hands. Again, their hands, heads, and hair blur together. The food is gone within seconds.

When it is time for the wild Indians to leave, your son might tell you he wants to marry their daughter. She works hard and she is beautiful. And it is true; you can see that the girl can work. You decide it is good to ask them if your son can marry her. When you ask, they think, they talk, and eventually they say yes. They agree to the marriage. However, they insist that the boy, your son, must come with them, to live in the bush. They won't allow their daughter to stay with your family.

Your son is too frightened to leave his family and go with these strangers. He reneges on his proposal.

After the wild Indians leave, you see their footprints in the mud. But not far from your house the footprints change to the pugmarks of jaguars.

Erasma is no jaguar, but sometimes she is wild. I spent Christmas Eve with her, plucking chickens at midnight for Christmas tamales. She was so busy with the grinder, literacy classes, and her housework, that she had no other time to make tamales.[1] At 4 a.m., around the time many were waking up, she fell asleep, her work finally finished.

Christmas morning, we went to visit Erasma's *comadre,* Filemina Choc.[2] Filemina, pleased to see I had tagged along, immediately brought me into the kitchen to feed me. She, her daughters, and her sister were cooking every dish imaginable, *caldo* and tortillas, tamales, rice and beans with stew chicken, roast *gibnut.* I choose the rice and beans, a traditional Creole dish. I have only seen it served in Mayan kitchens on special occasions, even then in only a few households.

Her *compadre,* Antonio, was celebrating Christmas with his friends, drinking rum and dancing. His cassette player, powered by a car battery, was blasting a variety of marimba, salsa, Punta, reggae, and steel-drum music. He expressed his happiness that Erasma and I came by offering rum, wine, beer, and soft drinks.

Erasma and I took a few rum drinks and a few wine drinks. Then we joined in the fun and Punta-danced. Punta is a traditional Garifuna dance.[3] To dance it you move your feet in small movements while rocking your hips back and forth. When two people dance together, Punta can look very erotic.

Drunken men, dancing, nodded their heads and exaggerated their movements to show their appreciation. Those taking a rest from the dance raised their beers or rum cups and smiled, or tapped their feet. *"Kichpan ok'ut!"* Beautiful dancing!

It is rare for Mayan women to dance; they are usually too shy. So, when the music was over, the men called for us to dance again. Everyone smiled and clapped his hands when we did. Later, Antonio came to me while I rested and to breathe a lengthy rum-soaked appreciation into my face. He was glad I was enjoying myself at his party.

For me the day was amazing. Punta dancing with a Mayan woman on Christmas Day just seemed like a wild thing to do. I may never get the chance again.

But now, back at the corn grinder, Erasma and I have just finished grinding my corn. I pick it up from the catch basin, return it to my plastic bucket, and take my place on the bench once again. The plastic cover on the bucket will allow me several hours before the *masa*, the ground corn dough, gets too dry to work with. Erasma sits and picks up the basket she is weaving.

A roaring silence fills the mill house, now that the machine is off. I lean over and peek out the door to watch some pigs root in the dirt nearby.

"See my basket." Erasma puts the small beginnings of a basket on her lap and uses her hands to outline the basket she intends to make. "I want to make a big big basket." The imaginary basket is clearly ten times bigger than any basket I have seen in the village. "They say you have to make different kinds of baskets for them to sell. Maybe someone will buy a big one."

I pick up her basket and examine it. "You make such nice tight stitches. It's gonna be strong."

"Maybe." As she says this, Rosenda, Anna, and Evadio, my neighbor's children, step into the building. Rosenda is ten. She is learning her work as a woman. She is carrying Evadio, who is three. Anna, eight years old, carries a bucket of corn.

"Deyoos." Rosenda nearly whispers. She and Evadio stay by the door, while Anna comes forward and puts the bucket on the table. She retreats quickly to the door and stands behind her sister.

"Deyoos." I respond. Then I say Anna's name so she doesn't disappear completely.

She peeks out at me from behind her sister and covers her giggle. Her smile contrasts with Rosenda's down-to-business attitude, making her seem happy-go-lucky. She is too young yet to begin her work as a woman. Since she has an older sister, she may be saved from the heaviest burdens of work in her mother's house.

Erasma and I move in harmony. I turn the crank to get the machine rolling as she feeds corn into the hopper, slowly dripping water into the *masa* from a spigoted bucket that hangs above. Water helps the mill grind the corn and softens the *masa*, making it easier to pat into tortillas.

The grinder's diesel motor makes the loudest noise in the village. You can hear it from far away, like a giant mad jaguar or a million howler monkeys all yelling at once. When I first started to come to the grinder, I got headaches from the sound. But now the noise doesn't bother me. It's a quiet time, now. It is the only time people can't talk. In the days when I was struggling with the language, it was a blessing.

Now it is making a shrill cry since the corn just entered the grinding mechanism. It is beginning to drop *masa* into the large catch basin beneath. The sound gets lower in pitch until Erasma nods to me to stop the engine. Rosenda's *masa* is finished. Erasma puts it into the bucket and collects seventy-two cents.

Rosenda, Anna, and Evadio quickly depart. I watch them walk up the hill to Prim's shop. They have a busy day helping their mother prepare dinner and meeting the needs of the family. I sit quietly on the bench next to Erasma. The roar of silence pushes the diesel engine's grumblings outside to be heard only as an echo, somewhere else. We sit, enjoying each other's presence in silence. I am sewing, and Erasma resumes work on her basket.

Erasma catches my eye. "A man come to engage Felicia."

"Really? Who?" I am excited. Felicia is nearly twenty, almost too old for marriage. Dionesia, the chairlady of the Tapir group, once told me that if Felicia didn't marry soon, her womb would dry up and she would be sterile her whole life. She would never get to be a mother.

"It's not the first time. She has three boys come since she is fifteen. Now she is nineteen and another one comes." Erasma giggles; the jack-o'-lantern face returns to replace her own. "When the last one come, she get vexed. 'I am not your girlfriend,' she yelled." Erasma's belly jiggles, "Yes, she yelled until her brother come outside and tell the boy to leave." Erasma's face continues to beam. She shakes her head. "Yes, that Felicia, you know, sometimes we think she is quiet, but she says it. She says what is on her mind. She doesn't take anything."

I laugh along with her, "For true. I've seen. When was that? When did the boy come to engage her?"

"That one was a long time now. But this boy from Pueblo Viejo, he come two nights ago. But she don't want him. He say he wants to take her to Pueblo, but she don't want." Her face is still aglow with a smile.

"To Pueblo? You have another daughter there, not true?"

"Yes, Aledora is there. It is her husband's brother who comes for Felicia."

"But what will she say? Will she go with him?"

"Only God knows, *ix* Laura. Only God knows." Erasma silently looks back down at her basket. Her smile is gone. "If Felicia leaves, I don't know what. There is so much work at my house."

"For true. Felicia does a lot of work for her mother." This is especially true now that Sabrina, her younger sister, has started high school in Punta Gorda and stays in town with her godmother. I sit quietly.

Oh Sweet Jesus
Our Savior
Our Lord

Erasma's singing voice rings out. The first time I heard her sing was shortly after I arrived in the village. Catholic hymns came from the darkness, to lull me to sleep that night, before I had even met Erasma. Now, in the daylight, Erasma's hymns lull her own anxiety. They lull us both into thoughts of the future.

"I think she'll tell that boy to leave her alone. She don't want to marry. Not Felicia. She sees what happens. She sees what happens with Justina. And she sees what happens to her sister. She don't want a man." Erasma begins to chuckle. "I'm telling you, that Felicia. Sometimes we think she is quiet, but she says what she thinks."

"For true." I quietly echo our earlier round.

"She tell that one boy never to come back, she doesn't want him. She tell him he is ugly and that she doesn't think of him like a husband." She looks up at me. "My Felicia says that." Pride and laughter keep the jack-o'-lantern's candle lit. "That Felicia, she is something else, you know." Her belly jiggles as she chuckles.

"She say that to him?" I make the nasal "Hhhmmmm" that indicates amazement and approval in Belize.

"You know what she say to me, she say, 'Mommy, I don't want no man to come and engage me. I'm not ready for that.' That is what she say." Erasma looks at me, her small round eyes as big as they get. "She say she is too young and she is not looking for a husband. 'Why does he think I am looking,' she said. 'I'm not looking.' Then she say, 'A man's words are so sweet, yes, but not for me. I don't want no man to marry.' Oh, sweet Jesus, that is what she said!" Shaking her head with pride and amazement, she continues, "That Felicia is something, you know." Erasma's eyes are just slits again, her smile reclaims her face.

"She sure is." I chuckle.

"Just like me, last week a man came and ask me to marry him." A laugh slips out from her grinning mouth.

"For true, Erasma, a man come to engage you?"

"Yes, for true. You know that man who goes to Prim's yesterday. He come here to the grinder and he ask if he can come in. 'You can come in, the building is for everyone,' I say. 'Excuse me, Miss,' he say, that is how he say to me, 'excuse me, Miss. I see that you work hard. I see you work every day. You work for the grinder, you work for your children, you work for the literacy class. You work for your family.' And that man he sit down there." She points her lips to the bench on the other wall, where Julia was sitting. " 'Yes, you have many children and you work hard. I have seen you.' That is what he say. I say, 'Yes, it is true.' And it is true, you know, I have fourteen *pickney* and I raise them all good."

"Yes, all your children are good. Sabrina is in school, Tommy is BDF,[4] Alejandro is BDF, Anselmo has his business, Adolfo has his rice fields, Felicia works hard. They are all good."

"Yes, it is true. I am a mother." She points her index finger in the air. "It is a mother that is good."

"And you are smart, and you work hard."

She smiles, embarrassed by my compliments.

"Yes, it is true, I have plenty of work. But this man, he want me to come and live with him. He want me to be his wife."

"What? But you have your children."

"Yes, that is what I say." She looks indignant. "But you know, that man, he follow me home. He come to my house." Seriousness wards away any teasing I might attempt. "I don't ask him to come, but he comes to my house and he say . . ." Erasma stages the conversation between herself and her suitor. She signals that he is speaking by mimicking him, bowing her head as he did. He was humble. She always turns to the left and uses her left hand to accompany his words. She turns to the right to quote her replies.

"Excuse me, Miss, but I have plenty *pickney,* too." Erasma turns to her right. "Yes, I know it's true." Lowering her head even further, turning to her left, "But their mother, she die, long time now, and I raise my *pickney.* Now, excuse me, Miss, but maybe you can come with me and be my wife. To raise my children. That is what he say."

"What? He come inna you place and say dem tings?" My Mayan Creole a bit shaky, I continue with a question I know any woman in the village would ask. "Were you scared?"

"No, I am not scared of that man. I tell him if my son comes home he will fight him." Her laughter returns, bursting into the room, seeming as loud as the grinder. "It is true, you know, that is what I tell him."

"What?" I join her laughter.

When it subsides into giggles, she says, "And it's true, my son, he starts to come home!"

"What?" My laugh stops dead.

Erasma manages to force her words through her giggles. "Yes, Adolfo, he starts to come home. He walks right into the house."

I raise my eyebrows and turn my head slightly. I am still looking at her out of the corner of my eye. I wave my hand in front of my face. I am making Mayan movements to express polite disbelief.

She is serious again. "It is true, and when Adolfo come home, the man, he runs." She slaps her hands together making one pass the other after the clap. "Yes, he run right out the back door." Her body begins to jiggle even before the laughter comes out. "And Adolfo ask, 'Who is that man?'"

Gasping for breath between giggles, I say "Oh, Ma, YOU are something else."

"It's true, you know." She laughs. "I don't want to marry that old man."

When Julia comes back, Erasma invites me to make my tortillas at her house. When we arrive, I stand next to her as she reaches into her blouse and pulls out a key. When she opens the front door, Innocente, her youngest child, is sitting on the dirt floor with one foot squarely on the floor, so that his knee is nearly level with his head. His other foot is neatly tucked under his bottom. He holds his elbow high, so that his forearm is parallel to the floor. His wrist is in his mouth; most of his forearm is wet with saliva. As soon as Erasma has opened the door completely, he rocks back and forth, making a loud barking sound. Cente is physically and mentally handicapped.

Yukie, Erasma's dog, pushes past him, his tail wagging in Cente's face. Cente doesn't seem to mind. He makes a huge smile and begins to shake his head jerkily but rhythmically from side to side. Cente is excited. Yukie runs outside, and Cente barks again.

When we are in the house Cente pulls himself up to a standing position and hugs his mother.

"Oh, Innocente, you are something else." Erasma hugs him back. He sits back down on the floor with another excited bark.

Erasma opens the side door, goes into the kitchen, opens the back door and the kitchen window. Then she begins the work of cooking her twelve o'clock meal.

As I enter, I pat Cente on the head. He smiles and moves his head rhythmically again, occasionally pausing to peer up at me, one eye wandering on its own accord. He makes a sound, raising and lowering his pitch. I interpret it as pleasure. I go into the kitchen and sit down.

Cente follows, moving himself along the floor, foot first, then rump. Erasma has already put the hammock down for me to sit in, while she starts the cook fire. Cente sits at my feet and puts my hand on his head. Ever since he got his hair cut, he likes to have his head caressed. I pat his head again. He puts his lips on my knee, leaving a wet spot.

A scolding burst comes from Erasma. Cente quickly scoots over to his mother and makes a sudden sharp sound. "You see, he understands. He wanted to kiss you, but I tell him to leave you alone." She pauses to blow on the embers of the morning fire. "Sometimes he can get away with what many men want." She chuckles and the flame catches the wood she has just gently placed in the hearth.

I smile.

Cente makes the rising and falling sound I think indicates pleasure and twirls his head.

"It's true, you see. But, he don't even know. That Innocente, he's rude sometimes." She laughs as she put more wood into the fire under the *comal*. "Now you can make your tortilla, *ix* Laura. Your little *wa*."

"*Boticex*." Thanks. I stand and put my little bucket on her dinner table. I wash my hands in the low plastic washbasin that rests on an awkward extension of that table. I move her short round tortilla table closer to the grill and find a *banco* to sit on. Stuffed under a pot, on the food prep table, I find a round sheet of plastic that I pat out my tortillas on. I remove the *masa* from the bucket and set it on a small plate onto the tortilla table.

"Is it good?" Erasma asks.

I pinch off a clump of *masa* and roll it in my hands. It's soft and cool. "Yes, it is good. Soft. Nice."

I place the clump in the center of the plastic cutout and begin to pat it into shape. One, two, THREE, turn, one, two, THREE, turn, one, two, THREE, turn, one, two, THREE. I round the edges. One, two, THREE, turn, one, two, THREE, turn, one, two, THREE. I flatten the shape again. One, two, THREE, turn, one, two, THREE, turn, one, two, THREE. I pick it up and pull the tortilla off the plastic cutout. I place it on the grill and start to form the next one.

Erasma busies herself by cutting *ku'la,* an edible shoot which tastes much like mushrooms. "Maybe we have eggs, too." She steps out of the house. I can see her skirt moving toward the chicken coop. She returns with two eggs. "And *culantro?*" Cilantro makes the simplest meal exceptional. So I smile when she lifts the lid off a small pot on the prep table and says, "Yes. *Culantro.*"

"We can make a good lunch, Ma!" I reach over and muss Cente's hair. He barks. Erasma and I giggle.

"Oh, that Cente, he's something else, I tell you." Erasma puts about an eighth of a cup of lard into a fry pan and balances it above the flames between a length of rebar and a thick slat of metal that looks like part of a car spring. When the lard melts, Erasma adds the *ku'la,* and then the eggs, cilantro, and salt.

I continue to pat out tortillas, carefully placing them on the grill. I burn my finger flipping one, but ignore it. There is no time to baby myself. The burn's not too bad anyway.

Cente pulls himself closer to me and rolls his head. He starts to bark, "*Wa.*" It takes me a few minutes to understand he is asking for a tortilla, a *wa.* I give him one. He moans and twirls his head quicker and with greater energy.

"You see, that Innocente, he knows what he wants." Erasma smiles and looks up, first at me, then at Cente. She is stirring the *ku'la* mixture, bending over the flames. "You know some people are afraid of Cente."

I am quiet for a moment before I ask, "Why?"

"Because he's not good." Handicapped.

"He's just a little different." I check the tortillas on the grill, turning those that are ready.

"Adolfo says I should send him to a school in Belize City." Erasma brings the fry pan to the prep table. "These eggs are ready."

I have completed ten tortillas, minus the one I gave to Cente. Erasma, Cente, and I probably won't eat more than that between us, but Erasma smiles when she sees how many I have finished. "*Ix* Laura, only that? Your husbands will starve."

I laugh as she grabs another *banco,* sits across from me and quickly makes another seven. I manage to make three more. When we finish I stand and put my *banco* back where I found it. I turn around, and Felicia is quietly standing in the kitchen, by the hammock. She has a large bucket of wet cloths in her hands.

Quickly and in a harsh tone Erasma barks, "If you don't hang those clothes, they will stink!" She doesn't even look at Felicia.

"Okay, Mommy." Felicia smiles as she acknowledges my presence, "*Ix* Laura."

"Hi, Felicia. Should I help you?"

"No, gal." She giggles. All of Felicia's giggles have the same pattern. They don't flow naturally. They seem forced, or scripted and badly acted.

I sit at the table and watch Felicia through the window as she hangs the clothes to dry. Erasma places a bowl of hot pepper soaked in oil on the table and sits across from me. Cente is to my left. The eggs and *ku'la* are delicious wrapped in tortillas, especially when you dip them in the pepper. "Eat, eat, Laura." Erasma encourages me.

Felicia reenters the house. "Eat, *ix* Laura, don't you worry. Eat. Ha ha. Ha ha."

I take another big bite. I really don't need encouraging, the food is delicious. "Felicia, you eat, you worked hard washing and hanging those clothes. Eat." I try to encourage her.

"No, gal. You eat." She uses the hammock as a chair. Cente twirls his head. He has a tortilla in his hand.

"Felicia has to rest before she eats. She just come from the river. If she cooks now she'll get pains." Erasma looks up at me. Felicia says nothing.

"Pains?"

Felicia and Erasma smile at one another. "Yes, because the water is cold. The fire is hot. It's not good. Ha ha. Ha ha. I'll get pains in my hands, gal. Ha ha. Ha ha."

"Is that true?" I stuff the rest of my tortilla in my mouth and prepare another.

"Yes, gal. Ha ha. Ha ha." Felicia giggles. "I'll get pains."

"That's what they say, gal." Erasma catches my eye.

Cente barks for another tortilla. Erasma prepares it, careful not to wrap too much *ku'la* and eggs into it. She hands it to him, he takes it and twirls his head.

"Eat, don't you worry, gal." Felicia giggles and swings her hammock.

Erasma, Cente, and I finish the eggs and *ku'la*. We have about seven tortillas left. Erasma gathers the dishes onto the work table in the kitchen, then returns to the dining table and washes her hands.

Felicia stands and takes the dishes outside. She takes a pail next door to fetch water from her Aunt Rosa's rainwater vat. When she returns, she washes our dishes on the table just outside the kitchen door.

Cente stands and carefully makes his way to the door, so he can watch her. He holds the door jam for support.

Erasma lies in the hammock. "Yes, I am thinking of sending my little boy to Belize City." She sighs, and puts her left leg on the floor and pushes herself into a swing.

"They have schools for boys like Cente?"

"Yes." She brings her leg back into the hammock.

I am afraid the question will lie flat in the air, like steam on a cold day, but I ask it anyway. "Why is Cente the way he is?"

"He had fever when he was young, gal. My poor baby, he had fever. So hot, gal. And he started to SHAKE." She trembles in her hammock. "His arms, his legs, he couldn't stop." She raises her arms and legs and shakes them hard. "His eyes went wwwwhiiite." Dramatic pause. "When he get good, he is a little bit stiff. I thought that sweet Jesus was going to take the boy from his mother. So, I prayed all day and all night, even when I did my work I prayed. That's why sweet Jesus leaves the boy with his mother, because his mother prays. The poor boy is like this now."

"Does anyone at the school in Belize speak Mopan?"

"I don't know." She pauses. "Adolfo says I should put Cente in one of those schools. But maybe I miss my baby too much. Sabrina gone, maybe Felicia will go, and maybe Cente will go too. All my babies will be gone."

Cente walks toward his mother. Carefully stepping with his right foot, he drags his left. His left forearm is still parallel to the ground, his index finger tensely points upward. For support, he holds the wall with his right hand. Then he reaches for the table extension that holds the wash-basin, and finally the table, where I am sitting. He smells. I can see a brown liquid running down his left leg. He barks.

Erasma looks at him standing next to me. "Innocente!" She stands quickly and takes him by his left arm. He barks again. Erasma takes his arm and makes him walk quickly outside. "Felicia! This boy stinks!"

I can't see what is happening outside, but I hear Cente barking loudly and Erasma scolding Felicia. Cente quiets down. Erasma reenters the house, washes her hands in the basin, and then takes the basin outside and throws the water in the grass. She returns and smiles at me. "Maybe Julia is worried that I will never come back to the grinder."

"Yes, maybe it is time to go." I stand and look in my plastic bucket. The *masa* is still on the tortilla table by the fire. "I will leave the *masa* for Felicia. She's hungry."

I peek my head out the back door. Felicia is holding Cente by his left arm and splashing water on his now bare buttocks. Her movements are quick. She looks up at me. "Felicia, I'm leaving you some *masa* to make your tortilla. It's only a little."

"Oh, thanks, gal. Ha ha. Ha ha." She takes a bar of soap in her hand.

"I am going then."

"Oh, okay, gal. Ha ha. Ha ha." She rubs the bar on Cente's bottom until it begins to lather.

"Maybe I'll circle back."

"Oh, yes. Ha ha. Ha ha." She continues her work. "Yes, gal."

I walk through to the front of house. Erasma is waiting. She has packed up her basketwork into her plastic handbag and is standing by the door. "Maybe I will work on my basket again."

"I have to drop off my little bucket at my house and then go down to the river. I will circle back to the grinder, though."

"Okay, you have your work. Be sure you stop by for tea tonight, Felicia will make something nice."[5] She smiles and heads down the hill toward the grinder. "Felicia is a good cook, you know."

I am out of laundry soap, so I stop by Coc's shop to get some on my way to the river. On a whim, I also buy two Cokes. I will bring them with me and visit Felicia before I wash. Maybe I can get her to tell me something about her suitor.

With the Cokes hidden in my laundry, I stand just outside the front door. "*Deyoos.*"

"*O ken, ix* Laura." Felicia is shelling corn. She stands to bring me a chair.

"No, no, I'll sit here and help you." I sit on a *banco* and begin to husk and shell the corn she has piled in the middle of the floor. Finishing one ear, I stand, walk over to my bucket, and pull out the two Cokes. I rifle through my backpack for my Swiss Army knife and open the bottles. "This one is for you, and this one is for me."

"*Ix* Laura!" Her laughter seems real this time. "That is good, gal." She giggles until she sips the Coke. Finishing her first sip, she reverts to her stilted laughter again. "That is good. Ha ha. Ha ha."

We shell and drink in silence. Occasionally, she looks at me and makes that staged laugh. Hearing enough giggles, I try to induce conversation, "Where's Cente?"

"He sleeps, gal. Ha ha. Ha ha."

Silence. I am direct. "Your mother tells me a boy come to engage you."

"Yes, gal, but I don't want." She looks sternly at the corn.

"Why?" I catch her eye and smile.

She smiles back and shakes her head. "It's not for me, gal." Her giggles return. "Ha ha. Ha ha."

"What do you mean?" I pick up another ear. There are only five ears left. The chick that has been walking around the room finally finds what he is looking for, shelled corn kernels. He scoots between us and grabs one.

Before he gets another one, Felicia yells. "*Shik!*" Get away! With animated motions she grabs a stick with a corn husk attached by a string. The husk's movements and Felicia's shout scare the chick away. She looks at me and giggles.

"The chick wants your food."

"Oh, yes, gal. Ha ha. Ha ha." The chick's distraction allows her to ignore my question. Silence.

I try again. "So marriage is not for you."

"No, not for me, gal. Ha ha. Ha ha." All the ears are shelled. Felicia stands and retrieves an empty sack from the corner of the room, where more corn is stacked. She begins to put the cobs in it.

I want her to talk more about her resistance to marriage, but I know she won't. She will just repeat her rejection, and giggle. That's all. Corn isn't the only thing that has husks, and chickens aren't the only ones scared away by them. I stand and pick up my bucket. "Maybe I will see you later. I have to do my wash."

"Oh, yes, gal, maybe later." Giggles. "You must go to the river and wash. Don't be lazy, gal. Ha ha. Ha ha."

I enter the riverbed just in front of the Mennonites' house. This is the path Felicia likes to take. I take it now because I am thinking about her.

The water is shallow here, so I cross, but continue to wade. The water is cool on my feet, and the moss tickles. I walk upstream until I reach my usual washing station. It is in the same area where Erasma's family and Francesca's family wash. It is deep enough to swim.

As I fill my bucket with water, I remember coming down here with Felicia once. It was when I first came to the village. She was so happy. "I have friend." She smiled. "It's good to have a friend."

When we finished our work, we played in the water, washing ourselves and splashing each other. She wanted to try my shampoo and was grateful when I let her.

She used to visit me at my house back then. That is when I lived in the cement house. I have a picture of her sitting on the veranda in a bright blue dress and a huge toothy grin. I remember one time she came to visit with some tortillas and pork. I sat down and ate them immediately, I knew they would be good. Felicia is a good cook.

I remember Felicia sat next to me at the table, and watched me eat. She refused the fruit and drink I offered. "I have a gift." She smiled.

"I know, the pig. It's good." I wiped my greasy chin with a cloth I used to wrap tortillas in.

"No, gal. Another gift, because you are my friend. Ha ha. Ha ha." She moved her hands from under the table. She was hiding it on her lap. It was a greeting card. A pretty floral design surrounded the words "For Mother." "It's pretty, not true? Ha ha. Ha ha."

"Yes." I held it. "It's pretty, Felicia." Inside it said, "A mother's love is delicate and sweet, Happy Mother's Day." Adolfo's signature was below. Felicia's brother had given it to Erasma. I smiled awkwardly, knowing I couldn't accept it. I searched for the right words. But first, I had to acknowledge the giving. I put it on the table and said, "Thank you, Felicia, it is beautiful."

"But you must not let anyone see it." She put her hand over it. "It's just for you. Ha ha. Ha ha." She smiled. "It's just for you, gal."

I put it under a stack of papers on my desk. "I will keep it here and look at it when I think of you." Maybe I could give it back to Erasma somehow.

"Yes, gal. Ha ha. Ha ha." She smiled. "Will you go to the Toledo Days?"[6]

I sat down and continued to eat the pork. "Yes, in P.G., next week. I'll go. I want to see what happens."

She began nodding her head. "Good, gal. Good. It's fun, gal. Ha ha. Ha ha." Her whole body bounced with her words. "It's fun."

"Yes, I think it'll be fun. Music, different kinds of food." I smiled, ripped a tortilla in half and dipped it into the pork juice.

Felicia raised her eyebrows. "Do you have a friend to go, too?"

"I don't know," I said. "I think I'll go alone." I shook the excess juice off the tortilla and stuffed it into my mouth.

"Maybe you can ask my mommie if I can go with you." Hope filled her eyes as she leaned into the table.

I really just wanted to go alone. A companion would mean having to negotiate every move. I wanted to be able to move about freely at the fair. I would have a lot of work to do observing the ways Garifuna, Creole, and Maya interacted. I would have to be fluid. "That would be nice." I lied. "Do you want to go?" I smiled, hoping secretly she would say no.

"Oh, yes, gal. Yes. Ha ha. Ha ha. I want to go." Her face was aglow.

"Do you want me to ask your mother?"

She began nodding again. "Oh, yes, gal. Yes. You can ask my mother."

"Sure." I smiled. "I can ask your mother."

"Oh, yes, please. You must ask her tomorrow, gal. Ask her tomorrow so she will say yes. Ha ha. Ha ha."

"Sure, I can ask her tomorrow." I finished the other half of the tortilla. "We can go together." I tried to sound as if I thought it would be fun.

"Thank you, gal. Ha ha. Ha ha. Thank you." She stood and walked to the door while she spoke. Standing in the doorway, she added, "Oh, yes, gal. It's good to go with a friend. Ha ha. Ha ha. You are my friend, *ix* Laura. Ha ha. Ha ha."

"Yes, I'm your friend, Felicia." I followed her to the door.

"I must go back to my work, gal. You will come visit. Ha ha. Ha ha. Come visit and ask my mother. Come tomorrow, gal. You won't forget."

"I won't forget," I promised, and I didn't forget. When I returned the plastic bowl Felicia had brought the pork in, I asked Erasma if Felicia could accompany me to Punta Gorda for the festival.

Now, as I rinse my T-shirt in the river, I can still see how Erasma smiled, a tense and mechanical smile, and said nothing at first. I remember she took the bowl, still smiling, and spoke. "I'm sorry, Miss Laura. I can't let Felicia go. She has too much work."

"Oh, too much work." I was relieved, but still felt I owed Felicia more. "I just thought it would be nice to have a friend to go with."

Erasma's smile was fixed, her eyes were stones. "But she has work. Her brother is breaking (harvesting) corn that day. She must cook."

I knew then I should leave it. I haven't asked Felicia to accompany me anywhere since. Especially after she came to me that night to thank me for asking. It was then she told me she had never been out of the village, except to visit her sister in Pueblo Viejo. She only stays home.

The water keeps flowing past me, as I stand here in the river washing my clothes.

My alarm clock goes off at a quarter to four. I set it thinking that fifteen minutes would be plenty of time to get dressed and walk to the grinder. It is still dark outside, so I bring my flashlight.

I am happy Dionesia has finally trusted me to work at the cooperative. With Josephina thinking of leaving, Tapir is in serious danger of closing. I am glad to fill in until Josephina straightens things out with her husband.

Francesca's dogs bark as I pass her house. I reach the grinder at five minutes to four. It is locked. I realize now I forgot to ask who would be working with me and which one of us should carry the key. I sit by the door and wait.

My watch says 4:05. I stand, stretch, and walk out into the road to look at the sky. A bright star shines above a thin rim of light on the horizon. The sun is rising. Could the star be Venus?

I sit on a rock across the street from Tapir, so I can watch the sunrise over the mountain across the small valley. Maybe a third of the people of the village live in this small valley. I see smoke seeping out of the roofs of a few houses, morning fires. I realize now I am cold and hungry. It is 4:15. I have been up for thirty minutes. My initial alertness is beginning to fade. I yawn.

In the distance, I see the figure of a woman, a stout woman. As she comes closer I can see that she doesn't walk, but floats; it is Erasma. When she gets closer, she takes the key out of her plastic handbag and unlocks the door. "How is your morning, *ix* Laura?"

"Okay." I slide inside and sit on the bench, stretching and yawning.

Erasma sits down, reaches into her bag, and pulls out several tortillas

A young woman using a small tumpline.

wrapped in a brightly colored green cloth. She offers me a few. Then she pulls out a thermos bottle, the only one I have seen in the village, and pours herself a drink. "Find your cup," she smiles. I find a cup behind the counter and she pours me some drink. We sit quietly nibbling our food and sipping our sweetened hot tea. I am glad she brought enough for two.

About a half hour later, three sisters appear just outside the door. One, maybe ten years old, has a bucket of corn in each hand. The youngest, maybe seven, has one bucket. The third, the oldest, has none. Each stares at me with wide eyes. Finally the one in the back, the middle child, says "*Ix* Laura."

"*Deyoos, o ken, tel a banco. Hay ixi'im?*" Hello. Come in, take a seat. Is there cooked corn? They giggle at my awkward wording. Maybe I should just be quiet today. I rise and take two of the buckets that they have placed near the counter. I begin to pour the contents of one into the scale. Erasma stands next to me, taking the weighed corn and pouring it back into the bucket. Each of the three buckets weighs around sixteen pounds.

The girls hide themselves. Two peek in the building through the door, the other pops her head up and looks through the window. They all giggle. After I crank the machine, I stand next to Erasma and help her put the corn in the hopper. The sound of the grinder pushes all remnants of a quiet morning far away from us.

When we finish, Erasma totals the cost, four dollars and ninety-five cents. We have just ground a lot of corn. The oldest girl takes a five-dollar bill out of the front pocket of her black plastic backpack, steps into the building, and puts it on the counter. Then she retreats outside. The others giggle.

"So, your father is working in the fields today? Or maybe there is a special party." Such a large amount of corn isn't just for breakfast.

The youngest giggles, but the middle child speaks, "Yes, my father has hired men to work."

"So you will make tortillas!" No one responds. Erasma hands the oldest her change, and then we load the *masa* into the buckets. To make their burden easier, we make sure each bucket weighs about the same. The two older girls push the youngest into the building. She giggles, grabs a bucket, and runs outside. The middle child steps forward and takes the remaining two buckets. The three are gone in a few seconds, running down the road.

Erasma and I sit in the echoing silence. I finish my drink. "So, did Felicia say if she will go?"

"She won't go. She is afraid of that boy."

"Afraid, why?"

"He is the brother of her sister's husband."

"Yes." I realize I am still holding my empty bowl. I stand and walk over to the water bucket.

"And she says she remembers what happened to her sister." Erasma looks away from me. She waves her hand. "She don't want that."

"What happened?"

"One day her husband lash her. He lash her so hard, one tooth come out. It never come back again." Erasma crosses her arms.

"Why?"

"I don't know, maybe he was jealous. You know Tommy, he was stationed in P.G. Someone came from Pueblo to tell him his sister was lashed. So he get vexed. He knows my husband never hit his children, and now his sister was being lashed by her husband. She's not used to that. It hurt him, because she was his sister. She was the only girl then. One girl and five boys. So the brothers love their sister."

"Someone went and told him?"

"Yes, and Tommy Cho get vexed and he came to the village and he found his brothers, Agapito and Marcisco, and they get drunk that night, because they were so sad to hear their sister was hurt." She turns and puts both feet on the ground. "They drink brandy then, because he learned how to drink it when he was in the BDF. So, he teach his brothers that night to drink brandy." She grips the edge of her bench with both hands.

"They didn't drink it before?"

She ignores my foolish question. "This night they drink and I hear them, right in my house. I hear them talk. I hear them make a plan to kill their sister's husband. But I don't say anything, I just pray they don't make such a sin. All night I pray to sweet Jesus, that they don't kill this man."

"They were gonna kill him?"

"Yes, that is what Tommy Cho and his brothers decide to do. In the morning, they make themselves ready. They tell me they are going into the bush, but I know they are going to kill this man." She stops for a second, straightens her back, and begins again. "So I pray again. 'Please, sweet Jesus, don't let my sons commit such a sin, please in all of your heavens, in all of your grace, only you can stop these boys from making such a sin, please, sweet Jesus talk to their hearts, talk to their souls, please, sweet Jesus make them decide not to kill this man.' That is what I prayed."

"Yes."

"And they go to Pueblo to find this man." She looks at me. "They go to their sister's house and they see, yes, it is true. She come to the door, but she can't walk so good." Erasma touches her eye gently. "Her eye is big and swollen." She moves her hand across her face. "Her face is black, and she have one tooth gone in her mouth." She pulls on her left upper incisor. "It is then that Tommy Cho cries." She nods her head. "He sees his sister this way and he gets to cry."

"Tommy Cho cried?"

"His brother Marcisco, he just gets vexed, but Tommy, because he remembers his sister when they were just babies, he cries. But Marcisco wants to know where is this man who hurt his sister so badly."

"Was he there?" I mirror her, holding the edge of the bench, looking her in the eye.

"No, his sister tell him that the man is in Guatemala to sell beans.[7] Because they have a lot of beans that are ready, fresh beans, so he goes to Guatemala to sell these beans." She shakes her head. "Lucky for that man that he was away, because my sons were ready to commit a big sin."

"So the man is not there?" I lean back.

"That is what she told her brothers. So the brothers, they come home. And I said, 'Thank you, sweet Jesus, my sons don't kill this man.' I am happy because they don't commit such a sin." She nods.

"How long after the wedding did this happen?"

"Maybe two years. Maybe my daughter is used to the place by then. She don't want to leave him." She looks at me and smiles. "She say, 'Better I stay with my husband, like I promised.' That is what she says. But maybe she worried that maybe her brothers wouldn't take care of the babies she had then. Maybe because they belonged to that man, they wouldn't take care of them."

"Tommy wanted her to come back here?" I look at my feet. Erasma reaches over to her handbag.

"Yes, but she's already used to her place in Pueblo. So she say, 'He will just come for me again, when the bruises are gone, that's all. Better I die with him than be separated. Better I live like I promised. I'm used to my house and my children.' That is what she tell her brothers then." Erasma pulls out her basket that she has been working on.

"She tell them, 'Maybe one day he will be a good man.' That is what she say."

"Did she go to the police?"

"No, no. My sons, they try to tell me to go to the police here, because he is the same police for Pueblo. They tell me their sister nearly died. But I don't go to the police. I just pray for my daughter. Like she said, maybe one day he will be a good man." Erasma pushes her needle into the basket and begins to sew.

I am quiet. I watch her take several stitches. After each stitch she pulls tight to make the basket strong. Then she pierces it again with another stitch. I watch until I find myself asking, "Is he a good man?"

"Yes, today it seems he is good. He is a hard-working man, and even Tommy Cho loves him. Everyone love him. He is a good man. Sometimes he brings me money from the beans he sells, or corn. He remembers his mother-in-law. He is a good man. He says to me, 'You are a blessed mother, because you never take me to court.'" She looks at me, pausing from her work. "And it is true, I never have him arrested. He is grateful today, that I was able to forgive him."

Erasma is working on her basket, piercing the body, and pulling the next layer of *jippyjoppa* tight, just as she has built her life, pulling each event tighter, closer, so her family can remain strong.

"So he never beats her now?"

"No, not now. She suffered and now he is good. But I think maybe she was too young when she gets married."

"When did she get married?"

"It's a long time now. She was fourteen years and eleven months when she was married. So close to her birthday, so we had a big party for her fifteenth birthday." She smiles and gently sways her head to and fro. "Now she tells Felicia, she tells her sister, not to marry so young. She says, 'Enjoy your youth with your mother, don't marry too young.' She tell that to Felicia last month when Felicia went to go visit her sister."

"How often do you get to see your daughter in Pueblo?"

"Not so much. I have too much work."

"Do you think she would tell you if she ever was beaten badly again?"

"No, she doesn't want to burden her mother with her own troubles." With a determined nod, she adds, "She's a good daughter."

"She doesn't want to make you worry."

Erasma aligns the new piece along the rim of the basket. "No." She pierces the basket and wraps the thread of *jippyjoppa* around the new bunch. "It's not good to worry. You get sick."

A long silence sits between us as we both work. "Did your husband ever beat you, Ma?"

"No, not my husband." She pauses, holds her basket out at arm's length to see if it is even. "But my second husband, the man I go with when Vitalio died, it is true he beat me. That is why I left him. But to this day, I never tell my children that he lashed me. I don't want to give them headache." Pierce and pull.

"What happened?"

"That man was a jealous man. He wants me to keep the door closed while he is away. So, I keep the door closed. But his daughter, she don't like the door closed at all, so she opens it. Then that man he come home and see that door open, and he get vexed. He decides to lash me."

"What did you do?"

"I took the lashing, what else can I do? But then, because he doesn't take care of my children, I decide to leave him. It was something his own daughter do, but I don't tell him that, I took the lashing." Pull and pierce.

"He didn't care for your children?"

"No, but I tried to treat his as my own. But he, he would get vexed that my children had new clothes and plenty to eat. He likes to get vexed too much, so I decide, better I leave this man. I was thinking of my children first." Pull and pierce.

"Yes. How old is Felicia now?"

"She is nineteen. She says she's not ready yet for marriage. She says she sees her classmates. Some are married and have a good life, and some suffer, but she is just the same. Better to be the same than suffer." Erasma rests her basket on her lap, then she puts it on the bench and stands. She leans on the window frame. "She is seeing more, experiencing more before she gets married."

"Yes." I keep my eye on my sewing.

The sun is fully up now and the whole village is awake. "But maybe one day, one boy will make a problem for Felicia." Erasma looks out the window. "Sometimes, they like to go to a bush doctor (a traditional healer) and cause problems."

"What kind of problems?"

She whispers loudly, "They like to *obeah*[8] too much."

"*Obeah!*" Erasma's fear is serious. I met a girl in Punta Gorda who once lived in the village. We talk almost every time I go to P.G. Recently, she told me that her mother had fallen ill. She whispered to me that she thought the illness was caused by a man who recently approached her parents asking to marry her. The girl asked my help in contacting her godmother, a former Peace Corps worker, in the States. She wanted her godmother to send money to hire a bush doctor to do a healing. I helped her write the letter, but feared the address she had was no good. Americans, I told her, move around a lot.

"Do they hire a bush doctor for that?" I whisper.

"Sometimes yes, sometimes they do it themselves." Erasma shakes her head and closes her eyes. She leaves the window and sits close to me.

"How?" I put my sewing down.

"I don't know."

"What happens?"

She turns her head toward me and whispers again. "You know the lady Josephina's husband goes to?"

I shake my head. "No, I don't know her."

"Her husband died three years ago because he was *obeahed*." She nods her head. "It's true."

"How?"

"He was chopping in the bush and a snake bit him." She frowns. "He dies soon. It was the *obeah* that made that snake bite him."

"Really?"

"Yes, and that is also why that woman has red on her face." Erasma has given up whispering.

"Red?"

"Yes, when you see her, she has red all over her face. But that doesn't stop her from talking to so many men." Erasma sits down, crosses her arms, and rests them on her belly.

"She has more than Josephina's husband?"

"Yyyyeeeessss." She makes this little word last a long time.

"She's a busy lady!" I chuckle.

Erasma wipes her eye and laughs. "Oh, *ix* Laura, you are something else."

"She's never been to P.G. but now she's going to fly away from us in an airplane." Rosa, Antonia, and I laugh as we pat out tortillas on the small round tortilla table. "Yes, who knew it could happen?" Rosa continues with a chuckle.

Antonia holds her hand to her face as she giggles, tossing a tortilla over to Rosa to put on the grill.

"And such a big plane, too." Rosa is in one of her talking moods. "Such a big plane. It's one of those cargo planes." She laughs. "Who knew it could happen?"

Adolfo hands Antonia and me a Coke. Rosa shakes her head, "You don't have one Sprite? Please, one Sprite for your auntie?"

"No, Auntie, only Coke." Adolfo still holds the Coke out in his hand.

"Well, okay, then. If you don't have Sprite, I have to drink Coke." She takes the soft drink in her hand and takes a big sip. "Yes, she's going to fly away from us here in the village. Fly away, just like a bird. Our Felicia is just like a little bird." She puts her own tortilla on the grill. "When he brings her back from Pueblo, she'll go far away again."

"Who is he?" I toss Rosa a tortilla to grill.

She flips a few already on the grill and makes room for mine. "He's a BDF, gal. Yes, he lives in a big house in Ladyville." Rosa flips another tortilla. "He's a BDF, gal."

"BDF? And he has babies?" I sip my Coke.

"Yes, gal." Rosa laughs. "We think she's far away now, but she's only in Pueblo. Soon she will be in Ladyville. Our Felicia." She raises her eyebrows and looks at me. "We will miss her, you know."

"Yes, we will miss Felicia." Antonia makes a short breathy contribution to the conversation.

Rosa takes a tortilla off the grill and places it in the calabash with the other finished ones.

"Yes. It's true. I know that I'll miss her." I sip my Coke and pull a clump of *masa* and roll it in on my plastic tortilla-making form. "Ladyville is far. She has to go all that way to do her work."

"Yes, far, gal." Rosa reaffirms. "And plenty of work. That man got three *pickney*."

Just as she says this, a jeep pulls up close to the house. I can hear Erasma's laugh. They must be back from Pueblo Viejo. Rosa leans forward trying to peek between the slats of the wall. "They come back," she announces.

Felicia, her face aglow, is the first to enter the house. She has a flashy green dress on. The material catches the light and glimmers. Erasma floats in behind her, her jack-o'-lantern face beaming. "That jeep is something else, you know."

Cente quickly scoots on the floor to meet Felicia, barking and twirling his head.

"Yes, ha ha. Yes, Mommie. Ha ha. Ha ha." Felicia pats Cente on the head as she rushes to the mirror in the living room and tames her hair.

Cente follows.

"Soon my Felicia will be gone." Erasma smiles. "She will leave her mother."

"Yes. Ha ha. Oh, yes. Ha ha." Felicia reenters the kitchen. "I will leave my mommie." She squeaks out a more genuine sounding laugh. "My mommie will be all alone. Ha ha. Ha ha."

"Yes, Felicia has found her work in Ladyville. She can't work for her mother again." Erasma smiles and shakes her head. She caresses Felicia's hair. "Who knows when she will see her mother again?"

Cente, supporting himself by holding the kitchen table, barks loudly.

"Yes," Rosa chimes in, "who knows when we will see Felicia?"

I can hear Adolfo and the man from Ladyville talking outside. I don't know what they are saying, but they seem to be enjoying each other's company. "So, how much will he pay her?"

Rosa responds immediately; she is the one who set up the deal. Her son told her his friend was looking for someone. "Fifteen a week, gal. That's good."

"Fifteen a week?" That is seven and a half U.S. dollars. I try not to sound too shocked at how inexpensive that is for a live-in maid.

"Yes, and she gets her room, her food, everything." Rosa reminds me.

"Fifteen a week, that's good," I try to convince myself as I toss another tortilla toward Rosa.

ANALYSIS: RAISING DAUGHTERS

One benefit of narrative ethnography is that it can convey the ways common patterns knit together to shape individual lives. In this narrative set, several themes repeat from the first two sets. Like Risa, Felicia resists marriage. Like Justina, Erasma and her daughter Aledora fear for their children's future. Like Justina, Felicia seeks employment outside of the village. However, these women's lives differ. The themes I have identified manifest themselves differently, and they mean different things for each woman. To abstract these themes out of individual lives to fit them into generalizations means losing some understanding of how Maya live and thus of how Maya respond to domestic violence.

Therefore, this analysis section repeats some of the same themes from previous chapters, but puts them in specific reference to Erasma and her daughters, Felicia and Aledora. It also takes up two new themes: economic development and the importance of forgiveness.

Development and Its Problems

Erasma loves her daughter Felicia. She is proud of her sensible rejection of suitors and her attempts to stand up for herself. This section analyzes why this might be so.

Belize has included women's projects as part of its "development" almost since the first days of independence from Great Britain in 1981. This inclusiveness is due to the hard work of women like Cynthia Ellis, the first Minister of Women's Affairs. Such women have made great efforts to assure women's rights in Belize. They fought hard to make domestic violence and rape severely punishable crimes. They have also instituted organizations like BOWAND (Belize Organization for Women and Development) and BRWA (Belize Rural Women's Association) which facilitate dialogues between women.

One of BRWA's long-standing efforts to promote women's economic development has been to establish "women's groups," cooperatives which support women's efforts to make cash by making and selling crafts. These efforts have benefitted women in the village greatly.

Along with economic development, BRWA, BOWAND, and other women-centered agencies promote a feminist ideology. However, the women who developed these organizations were educated outside of Belize, and none of them are Maya. As a result, the feminism they promote sometimes translates awkwardly in Belize's rural villages (Ellis 1997).

Erasma is involved in several women's groups and is participating as a student and a teacher in the Literacy Council's efforts to teach women to read and write. She is one of the most outspoken women in the village on women's rights. She benefits greatly through her involvement both economically and psychologically. She has gained a sense of self-worth consistent with government feminism.

For Erasma, like any other woman in the village, involvement in these activities is contingent on her ability to meet household obligations. Because she is a widow, Erasma's involvement does not create marital tensions like those that develop in Chenalho (Eber 1995, Eber and Rosenbaum 1993). She has no husband to become jealous, or for whom to work, although Innocente's mental and physical handicaps require her to give him close attention.

As is traditional in Mayan households, Erasma expects her eldest daughter living at home, Felicia, to perform many of the household duties necessary to living, including taking care of Cente. By promoting Felicia's resistance to marriage and her naivete, Erasma can continue to count on her support within the household. Erasma's freedom depends on Felicia's servitude. Without Felicia, Erasma cannot participate freely in the women's activities available in the village.

The "feminism" promoted by the Belizean government includes support for delaying marriage and resistance to arranged marriages in rural Mayan areas. This ideology construes early marriages and arranged marriages as mechanisms of women's oppression.

Popular culture also supports these feminist ideas. Everywhere in Belize radios blare Chico Ramos' "I Want Marry To Ah," a Punta Rock classic about a family's dislike of a young woman's boyfriend. The song encourages parents to allow their children the freedom to marry whom they wish. Mohobo's "Sticky Starchy," another Punta Rock song, encourages young adults to seek education instead of sexual activity which may lead to pregnancy and early marriage.

Add to these influences the stories of spouse abuse told by a young woman's classmates, neighbors, sisters, and mothers, and a woman like Felicia has reason to want to remain unmarried. Erasma delights in Felicia's exposure to stories of domestic abuse, especially the stories of Aledora's and Justina's abuse, since she is close to both. These stories help to reinforce Felicia's decision to stay home.

Felicia is not alone. Stories of abuse, the messages of popular music, and a growing feminist rhetoric contribute to young women's fear of marriage. While many mothers help their daughters overcome these fears, Erasma has motives to encourage her daughter to resist marriage. These social messages justify using her daughter's labor to allow her own freedom to participate in women's activities available in the village, activities meant to better the lives of all women, not only widows with grown daughters.

What Will Happen to the Children?

Erasma's fear of what will happen to Cente if she puts him in a home for mentally disabled children encourages her to exploit Felicia. She understands clearly that the abilities Cente has are due to her loving guidance, which she can't expect of anyone not bound by kinship.

Her fears are similar to those Aledora feels when her brothers gave her the opportunity to leave her abusive husband. Justina also faces these fears when she decides to let Francesca adopt Ronny. Erasma took action against these fears once before, when she left her second husband. No matter how close a woman is with her child's surrogate parents (brother, husband, or adoptive mother), it is difficult for her to give up custody. Doing so is giving up her motherhood.

Both Erasma and the son who suggests sending Cente away understand that Cente is a burden on Felicia. Cente's handicap extends his childhood beyond the typical time a parent must care for a child. He will need help long after Erasma's death. Therefore, she tries to extend Felicia's unmarried state for as long as possible.

Time for Change

It is difficult for Mayan women who do not marry or have children to achieve adult status. Maya do not base status on chronological age but on life events. An unmarried woman may be "locked in the category of childhood" (Beyene 1989:84). Women in the village, like Dionesia, feel a woman can lose her ability to have children if she doesn't do it when she is young.

It is for this reason, and because she tires of caring for her brother, that Felicia yearns for a life outside the village. Leaving the village to find work lets young women achieve adult status without bearing children. By working, she supports herself economically and may even send money to her family remaining in the village. Working outside the village creates a new status system for women. This system is flexible and seems to be burgeoning as more women opt to give it a try.

Although there are few employment opportunities for women leaving the village, professional non-Mayan women outside the village want Mayan nannies and live-in maids. People wishing to hire such domestics often look to friends and acquaintances in the villages for leads on women who might be interested in employment. People in Belize recognize Mayan women's competence and know most are satisfied with low wages.

Belize's minimum wage in 1994 was $5.00 BZ an hour, but few employers pay that much. Many expect Maya to work for a pittance because they believe Maya have little need for cash. This assessment is correct insofar as rural life for Maya almost ensures a parcel of land and therefore access to subsistence. Those who recognize that living outside the village requires that Maya buy food and pay rent often justify low wages by offering free room and board as perquisites of employment.

Adding to employers' comfort in paying low wages is the idea that Maya women "are still down." Belizean feminists believe that Mayan culture oppresses women and that, therefore, hiring them helps to free them from their economic oppression.

Some village Maya, like Felicia, are gullible in this respect. Any amount of money may seem like a lot when you have none. Women like Felicia who have had few experiences outside the village and have never had to think about how to survive in a money-based economy are especially susceptible. Others are fully aware of the differences in village and town economies and are competent maneuvering in both.

Felicia returned to the village just after I left the field site. She worked for the Belize Defense Force officer for two months. A mutual friend wrote to me soon after I returned to the United States that Felicia returned because she "missed her mother too much" and "couldn't get used to being left alone with the children." I don't know what she is doing now or if she ever grew to understand the degree to which her employer took advantage of her.

Forgiveness and Health: Erasma and Aledora

Aledora's story is embedded in Felicia's. This section examines why Aledora never left her abusive husband, and why Erasma never encouraged her to do so.

Faith, Forgiveness, and Getting Older

> You have learned that they were told, "Eye for eye, tooth for tooth." But what I tell you is this: Do not set yourself against the man who wrongs you. If someone slaps you on the right cheek, turn and offer him your left . . .   (Matthew 5:38–39)

> There must be no limit to your goodness, as your heavenly Father's goodness knows no bounds.   (Matthew 5:48)

Like Matthew, Maya often equate forgiveness and goodness. It is in efforts to be "good" that Mayan women forgive their abusive husbands and continue to live with them. Forgiveness and goodness can also justify a mother's failure to encourage her daughter to leave an abusive relationship.

At the root of forgiveness is faith that an abusive husband will one day change. Indeed, abusive husbands in the village apparently "stop feeling jealous" as they get older and subsequently stop hitting their wives. Those who drank may continue to spend long periods of time and great amounts of money drinking, but they tend to become less violent. While the reasons men become less violent as they age may be numerous, I focus on only one. Women gain status as they get older. This change in status makes women inappropriate targets.

When first married, Maya don't consider women fully grown (Danziger 1991:89). Their parents, in-laws, and husbands therefore must teach them responsibility and how to maintain a household. This instruction is what Risa is experiencing now, and it puts her in danger of being beaten.

After several years of marriage, however, women gain adult status and authority over their household. The birth of a woman's first child often signals her adulthood (Cosminsky and Scrimshaw 1980). Justina is at this stage of her life cycle and is therefore responsible for her actions, including her infidelities. This contributes to her adoptive father's refusal to help her when her husband becomes abusive.

In the Mopan gender hierarchy, a mother is still inferior to her husband (Danziger 1991:90). The gap narrows as women enter yet another stage of their life cycle. In some societies, this later status increase occurs at menopause (Flint 1975, Griffen 1977, 1982). For Maya, however, the rise seems related to other factors, especially an adult son's marriage. In fact, a son's marriage may precede menopause by nearly a decade (Beyene 1989).

Women display, create, and exercise their new level of authority in the household, where they teach their daughters-in-law to "do their work as wives." At this time Maya fully recognize a woman's knowledge, competence, and consequent authority. People outside the household also recognize changes in older women and no longer expect them to be as shy and withdrawn as younger women. Instead, people consider older women to be strong, experienced, and practical. I have often heard women in their fifties or older say, "He may think I'm foolish, but I'm not a young girl anymore," when complaining about their husband's attempts to take a new lover, or to mistreat his family in some way.

Erasma recognizes that these changes in women's status come with age, and therefore time. She has faith that one day her daughter, Aledora, will no longer suffer beatings, since she will rise in status and her husband will become less violent. Perhaps Aledora has such faith and understanding, too. Neither encourages the posse of sons or brothers to confront Aledora's husband. Instead, they prefer to forgive, and wait.

While Aledora's waiting and suffering through her husband's violence allows her the eventual status increase that comes with age, it also benefits her mother. Erasma, by not calling in the authorities, and by having faith in the eventual change in Aledora's husband, can exhibit her goodness and maturity. Forgiving and having faith are signs of a good woman. They also obligate her son-in-law to her, allowing her to receive an occasional sack of corn or cash when she needs it. These are important resources for Erasma, a widow with fourteen children.

Goodness, Harmony, and Health

Erasma's sense of goodness and forgiveness is accompanied by a strong belief in maintaining harmony. This is why she doesn't tell her children about the abuse she suffered at the hands of her second husband. It is also why she considers Aledora a good daughter. Aledora maintains harmony by not complaining to her family about the abuse she suffers, by not pressing charges against her husband, and by being willing to wait out the suffering. Maintaining such harmony means not giving family members reason to worry. Maya often feel that worry and strong emotions, such as anger, are not good for your health.

Maya believe that strong emotions, like anger and worry, cause imbalance and reduce people's resistant to illness (Cosminsky 1977a, 1977b). Making one's parents worry by reporting abuse may make them susceptible to illness. Maintaining harmony by shielding parents from worry and keeping one's woes to oneself maintains their health.

Maya also suspect that people can cause illness by manipulating spiritual powers or entities. Women sometimes suspect their husbands will hire a "bush doctor" or shaman to make them ill. In Chuchexic, Maria, a woman who left her husband because he beat her, suspected him of making her and her son sick because both illnesses developed the day after she left him (Cosminsky 1977a).

Fears and suspicion of *obeah* are fairly common in the village. In fact, Erasma fears that a spurned suitor may cause Felicia and her family health problems. Again, Mayan "witchcraft" beliefs probably predate their contact with Garifuna, even though they use the Garifuna word *obeah* to discuss such ideas. The use of Garifuna language may signal an overlap in Maya and non-Maya ideology. Such an overlap could help rationalize, justify, and enhance *obeah* beliefs in both communities.

Although no one reported fear of *obeah* as reason for staying with an abusive husband, it may have that effect. Ideas of health by harmony do contribute to some women's choices of staying with their husbands, forgiving them for their violence, and not bothering others with their problems.

CHAPTER FIVE

"When We Go to High School, We Change"

Homework

I am walking home from the river, thirsty. The sun is hot. The air is humid. Sabrina is walking in my direction. She has her pail of laundry in hand and her baby, Santos, in a tumpline sling on her back. She smiles as we meet.

"From where do you come?"

I stop and put my bucket down and use my hand to shield my eyes from the sun. "Oh, the river. I did my laundry."

"The sun is hot, gal." She puts her pail down, too, bending her knees so as not to upset the balance of her tumpline and drop Santos.

"For true, the sun is very hot." The river was refreshing, but now the walk back home is making me hot and sweaty again. We stand smiling at each other with nothing else to say.

"Okay, then." She bends her knees again, lifts her pail, and continues toward the river.

"Okay." I pick up my bucket and watch her leave. I can hear Lucky Dube's "Prisoner" recording in the distance. It gets louder as I approach Erasma's house. I remember she said that her son will soon get a short vacation from the BDF. He likes his music loud.

Nobody knows what is right
Nobody knows what is wrong

I hum as I continue home. Maybe I will stop and get a Coke from Mr. Coc. I try not to drink too much of the sticky sweet stuff. It is sweeter here in Belize than it is in the States, and it rarely quenches my thirst. Lime juice always works, but I don't feel like squeezing. I am hot and tired and right now can't convince myself that I will ever feel any different. The luxury of a Coke seems worth it.

The village is quiet now; it feels strange. Nobody is here but Sabrina and I. There are three pigs digging up the football field, and Chiac's nasty old horse is tied up and standing by the community pump. The pump that never works, the pump that can't quench my thirst.

As I reach the top of the hill, at the crossroads, I see that Coc's shop is closed. I'll have to continue on to Prim's if I really want a Coke. It's not really that much further. Maybe Sprite would be more cooling. I could get a Sprite and a gingerbread cookie at Prim's. I can talk to Prim for a while, and see what's new. His shop is always cool.

I don't see anyone behind the counter. "*Deyoos*," I say anyway, as I timidly enter.

"*Deyoos, ix* Laura." Leona, Prim's wife, is sitting in a chair in the private part of the shop. A wall hides her from view. I have never been in that section. That is where Prim sleeps at night if he stays too late or drinks too much to walk home. Leona likes to sit there when she is alone, especially if men are drinking at the shop.

"Leona, how are you? I haven't seen you in a long time."

"Oh yes, my husband, he's working at the plantation today, so I mind the shop." Her broad smile seems toothless. Her eyes twinkle as she giggles.

"I think maybe nobody is left in the village. I don't see anyone today." I put my bucket down and lean on the counter.

"The sun's too hot, that's why. Everybody stays inside." She sits on the stool behind the counter. "Ai! The sun makes the people lazy, *ix* Laura!"

"Yes, it's true. I don't see anybody today. Only pigs."

"Oh, *ix* Laura." She giggles.

"Maybe, can I have one Sprite?"

"I think I have one cold. I just put new ones in so they're not so cold yet." She gets up and moves around to the cooler. A blast of frosty mist stays low around the cooler opening, and surrounds her hand and head as she reaches in. "Yes, one cold Sprite." She pulls it out.

"Maybe you want a soft drink, too? I can buy one for you."

"Oh, no, Miss Laura. I don't want one now, maybe later." She walks back over to me and opens the bottle. She picks up the dollar bill and the twenty-five-cent piece I have put on the counter. She walks over to the money box and brings back fifteen cents change.

I stand straight, with my hand on my hip, and consume half the bottle in one gulp. The glass is cold in my hand. I am tempted to rub it on my forehead and neck, but it's sticky. My stomach reminds me that I want a gingerbread, too. "Maybe a gingerbread, too." I put another dollar on the counter as she walks over to get the cookie. I place the half-empty bottle on the counter next to the dollar.

Leona comes back; seeing the half-empty Sprite, she scolds me. "Mind you don't get sick!" She takes the money again and returns with the change. Giggling, she sits down again.

"Do you make this gingerbread?"

"No. Another lady does. You know Olympia?"

"I don't think so." I take a few more bites, "They're good, though."

We visit in silence for a while. I eat my gingerbread and finish my Sprite.

"So Justina is gone." [1] Her voice is a whisper.

"Yes, she gone already." I put the empty pint bottle on the counter.

"Maybe that's good."

"Yes, I think it is. He knocked her hard. She had blood coming from her ear." I touch my left ear, the same side she was bleeding from. "He kicked her on her side." I touch my left side, the same side where Justina was bruised. "And on her hip." My hand follows my body down to my hip. "And she nearly can't walk. She thinks that maybe one day he will kill her." I hope I am not telling Leona more than she already knows.

"Maybe it's best she's gone." She holds her left arm across her body, her left hand resting in the inner notch of her right elbow. Her right hand is in her lap.

"I think so."

We say it again.

"Maybe it's best she's gone." She raises her right hand to her face.

"I think so." I lean on the counter, near the chair where Leona is sitting.

Leona breaks our chant, without hesitation, without shame. "My husband used to lash me, you know."

I am silent. She must have been married before Prim.

Maybe she recognizes my confusion, because she continues with ease. "Yes," she waves her hand in the air. "He used to lash me hard."

I am still silent. What should I say? Like a fool, I ask, "Does he beat you now?" Maybe I am trying to clear his name, in a sense. Prim is one of my best friends.

"No, no more. Juana, our daughter, goes to high school, and one day they tell dem highschoolers that if your mother and father fight, you have to go and bring police to make dey stop."

"Really?"

"Yes, it's true. They say 'You are in school now, and you have to study. If your mother and father are fighting, then you can't study. You go to the police and make dey stop.'"

"They said that at the school?" I cock my head to the left.

"Yes, it's true. And my husband hear that and he stop. He don't lash me again."

I shake my head. "But why did he beat you?"

"Because he's jealous, that's why." She snaps these words out quickly. I have never seen Leona so indignant.

"Jealous?"

"Yes. But I stay home, I do my work." She nods her head, hard, to emphasize her clear understanding of herself. She is not lazy. She is not "loose."

"Yes, it's true. I know, you work hard." I pause for a moment and continue. "Did you ever leave him?"

"No, Miss Laura, I never go. I stay with Prim all the time." She shakes her head as she speaks.

"Why do you stay?"

"You know my father?"

"Santiago Chun?"

She nods. "Yes, Santiago Chun. He is a poor man. How can I leave my husband? I can never go back with my father again. He is too poor. He has nothing. You don't see he drinks here with my husband?"

"It's true. He is a poor man." Our eyes meet. "So you stay with Prim?"

"Yes, I can't find my way alone. And what about my children? Who will care for my children if I go?"

"But *now* he doesn't hit you?" As I ask this, a young woman enters the shop with her plastic woven handbag. She steps up to the counter several feet away from me. She leans on the counter and plays with the few dollar bills she has in her hand. I don't think she heard me.

Leona says *"Deyoos"* as she turns to the girl. She takes my bottle away and wipes away the condensation it left on the counter. I stand quiet while the girl says what she needs. I will wait. When another girl enters the shop, I realize my bottle is gone, my crumbs are gone, and our conversation is over.

Love Child

Francesca, Evarista (Francesca's mother), and Damiana (Evarista's sister) are huddled together on the veranda. They are sitting low to the ground on *bancos,* shelling corn. Damiana wears a tattered green *p'ik* and a traditional *camesa;* its decorative embroidery is faded. Evarista is topless, her shriveled breasts dangling above her maroon *p'ik.* Occasionally she fans herself with a clutch of turkey feathers tied together with a dried vine. The heat is incredible today.

I am sitting on the car seat, behind Francesca, quietly watching until I understand exactly how to help. It doesn't take long to figure out the mechanics of shelling corn. It is a simple task. I pull up a *banco,* between Francesca and Damiana, and join in. Evarista and Damiana look at each other and giggle.

"My mommy and auntie like to see you work." Francesca giggles, too.

I smile. "I like to work." Mastering Mopan women's work is important to me.

I pick up two ears of dried corn and rub one against the other as the two old women do. The kernels come off the cob easily and fall onto the cement floor. Damiana smiles and nods.

"My auntie thinks you learn quickly." Francesca laughs and smiles.

I pick up another ear, but I can't seem to budge the kernels off the cob. I rub the two cobs together with little luck. I abandon one cob and simply apply pressure to the other with my thumb. Finally, I break through. A few kernels drop off onto the concrete. With these kernels off, the whole cob easily strips clean. I toss the empty cob onto the pile to my right and grab the next.

I realize now that some cobs are half rotten, others are not. The rotting ones are easier to shell. Some are so rotten, however, that the cob disintegrates as soon as you pick it up, leaving a fine itchy dust on your hands and forearms. Often, you can see a weevil or two fall from the cob and scramble to take cover under the shelled kernels or discarded cobs. Weevils live in almost all the grain and beans in the village, especially those that have been sitting around for awhile. That is why we wash our grains before we cook them.

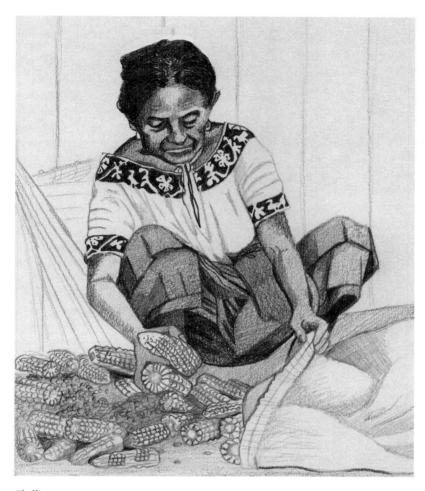

Shelling corn.

We shell in silence. I start to hum the only work song that comes to mind, "Pick A Bale of Cotton." I can hear Leadbelly singing in my mind. The old women giggle. My arms start to itch. A rash of fine red dots covers my hands.

A young woman approaches the gate between the house and the shop. She is very thin, wearing shorts and a T-shirt. Her long dark hair is in a braid; the braid is twisted into a bun. She has a clipboard in her hand. "*Deyoos,*" she says, as she nears the gate.

Francesca rises to meet her. They talk for a moment, then Francesca lets her in and motions for her to take the seat I just abandoned.

She smiles and says "hello" to me, and *na'chiin* to both Damiana and Evarista. Francesca goes in the house and squeezes lime juice into a pitcher of water and sugar.

"Hi." I continue to shell corn, watching the young woman adjust her clipboard as she sits. She has bad skin, but doesn't seem to be sweating even though the heat is unbearable. I introduce myself, but I just give her my name. I say nothing about why I am here shelling corn with old women.

She smiles a big, horsey smile and says she is Olive Tzir.

Tzir is a Mayan name. I think maybe she is "mixed," with a Mayan father. It usually goes the other way, though, Creole men and Mayan women. I am puzzled.

"What are you doing?" I feel awkward asking.

She smiles again and nods, "Oh, it's a survey."

"Oh." I smile, pushing my thumb against another cob and wait for her to offer more information. She doesn't seem shy, like a Mayan woman. She seems assertive, like a Creole. Assertive, but quiet.

"What for?" I prompt.

"For the Literacy Office." She clasps the clipboard in her lap.

"Oh." I toss my empty cob onto the pile and grab the next one. Evarista and Damiana are quiet.

Francesca returns with a glass of lime juice for Olive and one for me, nothing for Evarista or Damiana. She usually uses plastic cups for drinks. I am impressed with the glass, but don't say anything. Francesca has reasons for doing whatever she does. She sits in the chair on the other side of the doorway from Olive.

Olive finishes her juice quickly, then addresses Francesca in what seems to be flawless Mopan. She has to be Maya, I haven't met any Creole who would take the time to learn Mopan so well. But I haven't met any Maya women here who would wear shorts and go door to door alone to ask questions, either. I listen to the survey.

"Well, first they want to know if anyone, either you or anyone else in the household, like these old ladies," Olive motions to them with a nod, "might want to take literacy classes."

"How much are these classes?"

"Oh, nothing. The Literacy Council will provide the books." Olive's lips pout slightly. "Only your exercise book, you need."

Francesca laughs and claps her hands together. "Only that?" Free stuff always excites her. "But when am I supposed to take these classes? I have too much work." Francesca motions to us, shelling corn.

"What would be the best time for you to participate?" Olive awaits her answer, pen poised.

"I don't know." Francesca sits quiet.

We are all silent. I scratch my arms. They are tingly, the red spots are all the way up to my elbows. My sweat seems to aggravate it. Maybe I am allergic. Evarista watches me scratch and smiles, showing me that her arms are splotchy, too. Damiana nods and says something to Evarista, but it is too quiet for me to hear. The pile of corn to shell is getting low.

"Maybe in the morning," Olive sighs.

"Maybe. But sometimes I have to run the shop." Francesca is resistant.

"But you might be interested if the time is good?"

"Yes. I would be interested." Francesca frowns and nods.

"How about your mother?"

Francesca makes her high-pitched, double-breath laugh that she reserves for the ridiculous. "Maybe she wants to go to school and read some books." Her laughter evens out into chuckles.

Olive ignores the ridicule. "How about Mr. Coc?"

Francesca raises her eyebrows. "You have to ask the men?"

"Yes. Men and women. Everyone should learn to read and write." Olive smiles.

"No," Francesca shakes her head. "He knows how."

"How about your auntie?"

Francesca looks over to Auntie and asks her in Mopan, "Do you want to learn how to read?"

Damiana laughs a high-pitched squeal, like Francesca's "this is ridiculous" laugh. "Maybe I can be a teacher," she snorts in Mopan. Francesca and Evarista join her laughter. Damiana continues to laugh after everyone else has finished. Then she looks at Olive and whispers in Mopan, "But I don't even know how to speak English, how can I learn to read?"

Olive writes this down on her clipboard, then rests it on her lap and watches us work.

Damiana slowly stands and walks over to the baskets sitting in a pile to our left. She chooses one and returns with it. Evarista stands, too, so I do the same. Evarista walks into the house and returns with an empty sack.

Damiana and I scoop up the shelled corn with our hands and toss

it into the basket. Olive watches as we track down and pick up individual kernels that we missed earlier. Damiana uses Evarista's clutch of
feathers to sweep stray kernels into a pile. Weevils run and try to hide
under pieces of corn silk. Damiana lightly blows on these piles of corn
silk and cob dust revealing the weevils and more stray kernels.

When we have collected all the kernels, Damiana gets another basket
and slowly pours the kernels from one basket to the other. Occasionally,
she raises and lowers the basket while pouring the corn, sometimes lifting it way over her head. As she does this, the wind catches the bits and
pieces of cob and silk that we collected with the corn and blows them
away.

As she winnows the corn, I help Evarista with another task, stuffing
the old dried corncobs into the sack. I hold the bag open while she stuffs.
Although we have never done this together before, our movements seem
perfectly choreographed.

When we finish, Evarista goes back into the house and returns, drag-
ging another full sack of corn that needs to be shelled. I help her dump
it onto the cement veranda. We start all over.

Olive stands slowly, tucks her clipboard under her arm. She needs to
go on to the next house. "*Boticex. Bin ka.*" Thanks. I am going. She turns
to me, "Maybe I will see you again."

I nod and smile. "Maybe. I'll be here for a while, maybe a year."

Olive's horsey smile returns. She walks back down to the gate and
heads to the next house.

"Who is she?" I ask when I know she is out of earshot.

Francesca joins the work crew again. "That is the daughter of Dionesia Sho."

"Dionesia from the grinder?"

"Yes. That's her mother. She lives that side." Francesca moves her
hand in the direction where Olive lives. In the same gesture, she motions
the curves in the road you need to take to get there.

"So she is Mopan."

"Yes, gal!" Francesca laughs her "this is ridiculous" laugh again. "She
just come back to her mommy from Cayo." She catches my eye and
smiles. "Maybe she miss her mother too much."

"Cayo." My thumb is sore; it is developing a blister already. "What
did she do there?"

"I don't know, gal."

We sit in silence again for a moment, shelling corn.

"But, they say she likes the boys too much." Francesca turns her head away from me and looks out over the veranda onto the street.

I pick up the next cob, continue to shell, and watch as Olive enters the next house.

The multipurpose building is dark, but the windows and doors are open. I look at my watch as I approach the bright yellow building. It is 8:45; Erasma told me the literacy class ends at 9:00.

As I get closer, I can hear the familiar sound of women's gentle laughter. I peek in the window. Erasma, Leona, Jesusita, Eladia, Julia, and two younger women I have never met are sitting around a table. Each one wears either *camesa* and *p'ik* or a new-style Mayan dress. Olive Tzir is wearing bright red shorts and white T-shirt with a toucan embroidered on the left breast. She stands in front of the wheeled blackboard.

"It looks like we have another student," Leona whispers loudly to Erasma, then covers her giggles with her hand.

Everyone turns to see me at the window. I am a disruption already, so I enter the building and sit on a bench, hoping Olive won't get angry.

"Maybe *ix* Laura wants to learn English." Erasma's belly jiggles with laughter. Everyone laughs and stares at me.

"Yes, I have to learn English." I smile, looking at Olive. "I hear Olive is a good teacher." A little butter never hurt anyone. Everyone laughs, to my relief, even Olive.

"So write those sentences from the workbook into your exercise books, and underline all the nouns. Also, don't forget to write out the numbers from twenty to thirty." Olive announces the homework assignments in a crisp authoritative voice, almost like the voice I have heard government officials use with Maya. Hers, however, is mellowed by words of respect and an air of camaraderie.

The students organize their exercise books, small, thin, paper-covered bundles of lined paper with a staple binding. Most have the word *CUADERNO* (notebook) printed across them, like a title. They cost twenty-five cents in the shops; school children use the same ones. Each student also has a workbook, larger, thicker, glossy cardboard-covered books with sewn bindings. These have "The Literacy Council of Belize" stamped on the covers. All the supplies go into their plastic woven handbags, with their sewing and their shopping. One of the women, whom I don't know, has a small baby. Her handbag probably also contains a clean cloth for a diaper change and a tiny brightly colored dress.

I chat briefly with Erasma and Leona before they leave, then I help Olive close up. We pull the hinged windows in and secure the slip locks. Some of the windows are warped, making it difficult to throw the lock. "Olive, I was wondering if I could ask you a few questions about the literacy class, and about your experiences in school. I'm doing research here in the village about women. It's about their lives, their work, and the changes they are facing."

She laughs nasally. "That's what I hear." Then she shrugs her shoulders, "Sure, no problem." The sun seems extremely bright as we step outside. With the windows closed the multipurpose room is almost completely dark. Olive swings the door closed, locking the darkness inside. "What do you want to know?"

"Well, I was wondering if you could come over to my house. I'd like to record you. Just so I can listen to it later and be sure I understand exactly what you say." I always feel awkward asking if I can tape someone's words.

"Do you want to do it now?"

"Sure." I am surprised she has suggested that. I had planned on just making an appointment. "If you'd like."

Olive opens her umbrella as we walk up the steep part of the hill. We pass Erasma's house, and walk toward mine. She uses the umbrella as a parasol, the way I have seen many Creole women do in Punta Gorda and Belize City. Her long thick braid swings back and forth as we walk. The braid falls around the small of her back. Unbraided her hair must be below her buttocks.

As we pass the schoolhouse we can hear the schoolchildren chanting. I picture their teacher standing in front of the blackboard, leading them in the familiar yet surreal rhyme. It is a math lesson.

> One little, two little, three little Indians
> Four little, five little, six little Indians
> Seven little, eight little, nine little Indians
> Ten little Indian boys

The chanting then becomes less musical, more mundane. The math lesson continues.

> One is less than two,
> Two is less than three,

Three is less than four,
Four is less than five—

All the way up to ten, then back down again:

Nine is less than ten,
Eight is less then nine,
Seven is less then eight,
Six is less than seven—

"So, you know how to shell corn?" Olive queries.

"Yes, I do." I feel somewhat awkward. "Do you shell corn?"

"No, it's too itchy. It makes my skin crawl, especially with the bugs." She wiggles and pretends to itch. Her laugh invites friendship. "And my hands get all raw."

I look at my hands. A callus has started to grow on my thumb, just below the knuckle. "Yeah. I get blisters and red spots on my arms when I do it. But then I go to the river and bathe. That seems to stop the itch."

"So, you wash at the river. You don't have a shower?" She twirls her umbrella as she walks.

"Well, I did when I stayed in the cement house." We pass my old house as we walk. As we round the corner, I motion to her my current residence. "But now I live in that thatch house and there is no shower." When we reach my house she smiles again. "Well," she laughs as she speaks, "this is your house."

"Yes, this is my little house, dirt floor, bugs in the roof and all my stuff." I walk her through, a mini tour of a tiny space. She laughs, sits in the hammock, and I on the bed.

"Remind me to go to the phone when we finish. I have to call P.G. and see if they have my paycheck."

"Is it late?"

A familiar sarcastic burst of laughter reminds me that this is Dionesia's daughter. "Yes, it's always late. I haven't got one yet!"

"Not one?"

"They said they would pay me," she smirks, "but now they don't know how much the hourly rate is going to be." She speaks clearly, with humor in her voice. "So they pay me nothing." A chuckle reaffirms her easy attitude.

"That's a problem! How can they expect teachers to teach, if they don't pay?"

"Well, you know, it's not so much of a problem for me," her big smile turns into a frown, "because I don't have anything else to do in the village. I like to have a job to do. I don't like to sit around all day and do sewing or feed chickens." She nods, as her frown turns to a smirk. "But, my helpers, yes, they like to get paid. They want the money, you know."

"You have helpers?"

"Oh, yes." Big eyes open even bigger. " 'Facilitators.' Erasma, Jesusita, and Asteria. They are all level-three learners, but they help me teach level one."

"Ah, I see, and they are all supposed to get paid."

Her big eyes are bright. "In the beginning, I had seven, including the men. But now only three. One dropped out last week. Each one is supposed to get a little stipend, you know."

"They dropped out already?"

"Yes, because it's been two months now. The last one, she couldn't continue without money. She dropped to find her money somewhere else." She pauses, "I told the others that maybe they should drop, too, but they said that as long as I'm doing it they will stick with it."

"Yeah?" I am proud of their devotion.

She smiles, tilts her head shyly. "So I will be doing that for them. I'll be fighting for their pay."

"You said you had men helping, too?"

"Well, yes, but only one really wanted to stick with it, you know. But I had to tell him he can't help." She stretches her neck.

"Why?"

"Well, them ladies. They're not used to it." She glimpses my confused face and explains. "The men, they weren't really that interested in literacy class." She shakes her head mournfully. "So a lot of them dropped. I only had the helper who wanted to continue. So I told the ladies that he would be in charge sometimes"—her big eyes catch mine—"if I wasn't around."

I nod, I am following.

She turns her head and continues, in a tone of disgust. "But they all said no, they wouldn't come if he was there. They don't like it."

"Why?"

"Yes, they said if I ever do that, no one will come to class."

"But why?"

"Well, sometimes, people start to say different things about others. Even if it's not true. They will say this,"—she waves her hand to the left, and then to the right—"or that."

Looking up to meet my eye, she continues, "Especially if it's a young girl." I know what she is hinting at, but I need her to say it. I pretend confusion. "You know what they will say."

"What?"

"That they are boyfriend and girlfriend." She breathes it out, like I am an imbecile, and laughs. "And, you know, I do get a lot of dropouts because he stayed in the class. For me it was nothing, because I am already used to that, but for the ladies, no."

"I went to my bosses, and we decided I have to ask that man to leave. Even though he wanted to help and to learn, I had to tell him he couldn't come. Yes! They didn't like that young man there. I had to drop him out." She smirks. "It's sad, but there is nothing I can do." Her voice doesn't sound sad, nor does it sound angry. She sounds smug.

"What did you mean when you said you were used to it?"

"Well, in school, high school especially, the teacher tells you to sit here or there, and you have to do it. You can't tell the teachers anything, because it is not their culture. They don't know that in the village, if a young boy sits next to a girl . . . ," she waves her hand in front of her face, "they move themselves away." She pauses and nods, her voice changes slightly, turning a little preachy. "But now it is beginning to change a little. At first, though . . ." Rather than say, she hums loudly, nasally. "Hhmmmmm." Then she begins to nod, with her whole body.

"If you go to high school, you change. Yes, that's the main thing. You change. The culture will be gone one day." She shows no regret.

"Why do you say that?"

"The answer to that is: When we go to high school, we change. In the past, girls would only go to primary school. Sometimes, they wouldn't even complete primary school. They would drop out and follow their mothers. Wherever their mothers went, they went. They would never walk alone."

I nod my understanding, thinking of the many girls I know in the village who act that way.

"And if a boy comes to engage them," she shrugs, "they will say okay. But now," she smirks, "because we attend high school, and the young boys, too, they see how others are doing it. Not everyone gets married right away."

I continue nodding.

"That's the main thing, the marriage. They won't just get engaged to a person who they don't love. They like to choose their own. You can't," she makes a fist, "force them any longer. You can't just give them like that." She delicately opens her hand and says, "Like here, here is a pretty mango, just take it away." A burst of nasal laughter, then, nodding her head, she continues. "At first it was like that." Slowly shaking her head, no. "Now, you won't see that again."

"No?"

"Now young girls and boys are talking to each other. They should be talking. Not like before, when girls married boys they have never even seen before."

"So the culture is dying."

"Yes," Olive barks with her crisp, authoritative voice. "Because, here, our culture is hard. Yes, that's why I have so many dropouts. When I did the survey, I had thirty-five people sign up. Many of them have found excuses not to come. So, now, I only have a few." Her big eyes look at me directly, "BUT, they come all the time. They're the regulars. It's just a little bit sad to see so many drop out."

"But, I don't understand why they dropped out. What kind of excuses did they make?" My words sound whiny to me.

"Well, you see, it's the culture." Olive is patient, bringing me back to step one. "It's the culture. It's a hard culture. When the husbands are at home, the ladies can't go anywhere. They have to be there to make their husbands' lunch on time, do the washing, grind the corn, sweep the house. That's the main thing. The women are tied down when their husbands are home." She pauses. "Only a few really get the opportunity to go, you see? It's not for everybody." She makes a small, timid smile.

It's not for everybody. I have never heard those words refer to opportunity before, only to ability and desire. So, only those with no husband or with a husband who thinks his wife's education is important get to go to the literacy classes. A quick survey runs through my head: Erasma is a widow, Eladia never married, Asteria and Jesusita not married yet. Who knows about the two girls I had never seen before. Leona is married to Prim. One of Prim's favorite topics is the importance of education and how he is upset that his kids aren't doing better in school. I never met Julia's husband. Sounds about right.

"Why do you think the regulars keep coming?"

"Oh, yes, that's a good one." Olive smiles. "I think everyone has their own reason. But when I did the survey, most people said they wanted to learn so they could help their children in school."

"To help their children." I say it softly as I rock gently back and forth.

"Yes, because sometimes, the children come home from school with homework and the parents don't know how to help them. That's the main thing." She's so matter-of-fact. "Yes, that and many of the women are making crafts, and selling crafts."

"Ahh," I nod.

"They want to know how to make change. It's important because sometimes the buyers want to take advantage of the ladies." She says each word with delicacy, putting a little cotton candy around each of her crisp authoritative words. "Yes, especially if they go to Belize to sell, or Cayo. The shopkeepers are not very honest sometimes."

All I can do is look at her. I can't think of another question except, "So, are you married?"

"Yes, and I have five kids." She laughs. "No, I'm not married, not yet. I'm not engaged, either. That's why I can be here. If I was married, I'd be tied down." She pauses. "But sometimes, I think about it, but then I say, let me enjoy my freedom while I have it."

I smile. "Yeah, freedom." I look down at the ground between us, where the tape recorder should be. "You know what, Olive?"

"What?"

I look up at her, a smile cocked to one side of my face. "I forgot to tape this."

"Aiy, *ix* Laura," she laughs, clapping her hands together. "Maybe we'll have to talk again sometime, but now I have to make a phone call before they close the office." She stands and picks up her umbrella. "Maybe you can come to see me at my mother's house."

"Oh, yes. I'd like that, Olive." I keep my eye on her, smiling, feeling comfortable with her. I watch her as she leaves through the gate and crosses over to the telephone.

Sitting next to Dionesia in the mill house, I pull my yellow legal pad out of my backpack. Fingering the edges, I ask, "Dionesia, can you help me to learn a little Maya?"

"Yesss, I can help you." She keeps her eyes on her sewing.

"Thanks."

"But you have to ask me, I didn't hear you yet." She looks up with a wry smile.

I smile back. Slowly, unsure, I say, *"Ka' kaanseen ti'i tz'eekak aj Maya."*
Teach me a little Maya.

She nods and goes back to her sewing.

"I don't know how to talk about marriage." Holding my pen above
my paper, trying to think where exactly to start.

Dionesia knows where the lesson should go. "If someone asks you,
Tzo' a ka'an wa abeel? Are you married? You say, *Ja'ja, tzo' ka'an inbeel.*
Yes, I am married. Because you are married, right?"

I thought I told this to Dionesia before. "Well, yes, I have a husband;
a *ve'cham*. But we weren't married in a church. We just live together."

Still looking at her sewing. "So, you have to say *Ma' xtoj tzo k'ok inbeel.* I am not married yet."

"But it's like we are married. Legally, in New York state, we are 'domestic partners'; it's kind of like a common-law marriage."

Dionesia smiles, still focusing on her sewing. *"Tuba ka'a ve'chem?*
Where is your husband?"

"He's in the States," I answer quickly, dropping the Maya.

She drops it, too; our conversation is too important to allow miscom-
munication. "How do you know he doesn't have the next lady already?"
She chuckles. "You know how men go."

"Well," I chuckle, "if he did, and she leaves when I come back, that's
okay. But if she stays, then there's a problem."

With a loud burst of nasal laughter, Dionesia has finally looked up
from her sewing. Still laughing, she continues, "You have to beat her
until she leaves." Then with one eyebrow raised, "Or you can come back
here and find an Indian husband."

I join in the laughter. "Or I can just forget about Michael and find a
husband here now."

"Oh, *ix* Laura." Shaking her head, still chuckling, "But why do you
want a husband? For me, I like my freedom. I'm glad I never married."
Dionesia's eyes find her sewing again, she works her needle diligently.
"My sisters all have trouble with their husbands, but not me. Yeeesss,
sometimes I live a hard life, but I thank God every day."

"You never married?"

"No, no, not for me." She frowns. "I told Olive her father was dead,
until it was time for her confirmation. That's when I told her who her
father was. She asked me, she wanted to know. So, I told her and I gave
her the ring he gave me. She wears it now."

"What happened when you got pregnant?"

"Oh, nothing. I was working in Punta Gorda at the time, doing cleaning. When I come home to tell my ma and my pa, well, my pa he just didn't say anything. He never lashed me."

"Wasn't he angry?"

"Yeesss, he was angry. But, he was just angry because of who the man was, not that I was pregnant. My father is a good man." She pauses. "My pa don't like that man. He said that man is lazy; he only likes making babies, not feeding them. My pa say, he is a jealous man, so he won't let me stay with him."

"No?"

"No." She pauses a second. "He lives there," motioning down the road with her chin, "by the river."

I look down the road but can't see anything, just trees. "Was it hard for you?"

"Yeeesss. I only had one dress, but I worked. I worked hard so my daughter can have things, go to school. I did my best for my daughter. A mother has to do everything she can for her baby, and that's what I did. But then, it's up to her baby to take what her mother has given and make a life for herself."

"Do you think it's easier for girls who get pregnant now?"

"I don't know. But for me, yes, it was hard. It's up to my baby now to make a life of her own. I just hope she thinks of God. And her family. But what can a mother do? It's up to her to do what is right."

I am standing outside the multipurpose building. It is nine o'clock. I am worried that Olive might be angry with me. We had planned to get together yesterday, but when I made those plans I forgot I had a prior commitment. The only students today are Eladia, Leona, and Jesusita. I know Erasma's not feeling well, but I wonder what's up with the others. I stand outside, next to the doorway, so no one will see me. Shifting my weight from left to right, I can hear the schoolchildren chanting "more than" and "less than" again, like numerical scales.

Chatting briefly with her students before they begin their journeys back home, Olive closes the windows. When she closes the door, I smile at her. "Sorry I didn't come the other day. I forgot I was asked to make tortillas with Rita. Her husband was planting corn that day."

"So, you know how to make tortillas."

I can't read her, she's less animated than before, but I don't think she is angry with me. "Yes, I do okay."

She looks at me, silently, shielding her eyes from the sun. "You can come today?"

"Yeah, if that's okay." I notice a ring on her hand. A silver heart-shaped ring. Carved out of the center is a peace sign.

"Yeesss, *ix* Laura, it's okay." Olive yawns as we begin our walk, in silence, up the hill.

I follow her as we cut off the road, single file, onto a footpath. It looks as though the footpath just leads to a thatch house, but as you follow it, you can see it really goes between two houses, at the crest of the hill. A shortcut.

The silence is making me uncomfortable. I need to talk. "Olive, what made you go into teaching?"

"I'm not really a teacher, you know. Actually, I didn't finish high school. I got sick." I am grateful that she has paused. I need to catch my breath.

"Sick? Oh, that's too bad." I wipe the sweat from my brow, looking down the path the way we came.

"Yes. It happened when I was in second form. When I got better, they told me I should go again, but I lost interest in school." She smiles at me, "Aiy, *ix* Laura, if you live with the Indians, you have to learn to climb steep hills."

I begin walking again, even though I need more rest. "Yes, I guess so."

"But I learned that even if you are a dropout, you can still take the teaching exams. So I'm taking them now. Why waste money at school if you don't need to?"

"Oh, yes. That's a good idea." Ashamed, I try to stifle the breathlessness in my voice. "Did you get paid yet?"

"No. My mother is starting to worry that I'll go back to Cayo. I worked in Cayo as a receptionist, until my mother got sick. That's why I came back. She was sick." Olive climbs effortlessly. "Then the Literacy Council came and asked if I could help with the survey. So I did. Now, I teach."

"Oh, you're doing well." I stop for two seconds, then hurry to catch up.

When we reach the crest, a calabash falls from a tree. I watch it roll in front of Olive as we walk single file down the hill to the river. The calabash takes a sharp right at the fork in the path; we take the left, down a steep muddy cliff.

"At first, I told them no, I'm not for teaching. But they said they thought I could do it. So, I said, I can try. All I can do is try my best. So, I took the training. Then I said yes, I can do this. I can help my community. I will put my mind to it and now I enjoy it."

The cliff flattens out at the riverbed. I struggle to keep my balance and take my sneakers off. We need to ford the river. Olive easily slips off her sandals, giggling at me as I pull my socks off because I almost fall. The mud feels warm between my toes at the bank, but cold in the water.

On the other side, Olive slips her sandals back on and begins the ascent out of the riverbed. I am left with wet feet and a handful of socks and sneakers. I stuff them in my backpack and climb. When I see an apple tree, I know we have reached Olive's house.

I stay two steps behind Olive as we approach the house. It is made of wood. The trim is painted yellow, but the siding is stained. It sits on a cement pad, with a sizable veranda. Dionesia and an older woman are sitting on green, painted wooden chairs. Dionesia is sewing. The older woman has Dionesia's smile.

"So, you come to see me at my house." Dionesia is wearing a brown dress with a plain bodice. It is in the style middle-aged and younger Mayan women wear, by far the most popular style in Toledo. Most, however, are brightly colored with lacy bodices.

Another woman leans out of a big window. There is no glass or screen on the window. "Who is this?"

Dionesia answers, "This is Laura. She wants to learn about the women here in the village."

Olive smiles. She returns from the kitchen with two kitchen chairs and motions for me to sit.

The woman from the kitchen comes outside. She has already poured lime juice into a glass for me. Olive continues the introductions. "This is my Auntie Theofila, my grandmother Eugenia, and you know my mother."

"Yes, good to meet you all." I sip my lime juice. "What are you sewing, Dionesia?"

"Oh, this is for a Maya blouse, you know, the border around the top and the sleeves." She holds it out for me to see. The design is geometric, triangles. She is sewing it in three colors, black, orange, and green. I have never seen this design before.

"I like it." I sip some more juice.

Dionesia smooths it onto her lap, so I can see it better. "It's *pach caan.* Snake skin."

Olive's face twists into an awkward sarcastic smile. "The old heads say, if you wear this, you must wear it three times. If not, a snake will bite you." Her smile changes to laughter.

Dionesia echoes with a chuckle. "That's what they say."

Eugenia is silent.

"Yeesss, I started this because of what happened to Mario."

Animated again, Olive explains. "Mario is one of the loggers who is staying with us. He's from Mexico." She crosses her arms and leans them on her lap. "Two days ago, he was working and a snake bit him."

"Is he okay?" I lean back on my chair, tipping it up on two legs. Uncomfortable in this new balance, I ease the front legs back down.

"Yes, we sent him to a snake doctor. A Spanish man, he lives way in the bush." Dionesia points her lips toward the road. "I think he's okay."

"Yes, and he showed me the bite." Olive smiles, then releases a rapid worried monologue. "You're not supposed to show the bite to anybody, you're supposed to cover it. And you're not supposed to be running around in the cold, like that. He shouldn't be working today."

"I sent him to the bush doctor because the doctors in P.G. can't treat snake bite." Dionesia speaks in a matter-of-fact tone, the same tone Olive often uses. "They can't help you with snake bite, instead they cut off what the snake bit." She waves her hand in disgust. "You see what happened to Marcus. He was bitten by a snake and they cut off his leg. He can't plant his corn now." She shakes her head and smooths the sewing on her lap again.

"How did the snake doctor treat Mario's bite?"

Olive shrugs her shoulders. "Oh, I don't know. Maybe he gave him some bush medicine, maybe he talked to the snake. I don't know."

"Talked to the snake? How? Why?"

Dionesia looks away, as if she was trying to make the questions follow her gaze, away, down the road, back to the bush doctor.

"I don't know," Olive responds, but I know she can't answer my questions. Dionesia might be able to, but she remains silent. Soon, we all fall silent.

It falls to me to change the subject. "Your sewing is nice, Dionesia. How do you know the designs?"

"Oh, we Maya have been sewing for many years, you know. My mother taught me. I have been sewing this design since I was a child, and my mother, too. This one is very old." Dionesia whispers to Olive, who stands and goes into the house.

I turn to Eugenia. "Do you sew?"

Dionesia's horsey smile crosses Eugenia's face, but she shakes her head. "No, no."

Olive returns with a few pieces of tattered embroidered cloth.

"How about Olive? Do you sew?"

"Well, I can sew. But I don't do things like that. I sew for myself, not to sell. Like this T-shirt." Among the tattered pieces of cloth is the T-shirt she wore the other day, with a toucan embroidered over the left breast. She must have anticipated my question of her.

"You sewed that? It's beautiful." I hold it examining the close, perfect stitches.

"Thanks. I wanted to show you the designs my mother sews." She holds out one of the tattered pieces of cloth. It has several different strips of embroidery on it. As I touch it, I can tell it is old. She holds up another one, this one stained and ripped.

Dionesia laughs. "I had those when I was young. Younger than Olive, but the pigs got them and ran." She slaps her two hands together, one sliding over the other. "I find it all ripped up, dirty. Some pieces I never found."

"But you still have it." I hold both on my lap, examining the stitches, admiring the patterns. Birds, animals, floral patterns, geometric patterns, *pach caan*.

"Your T-shirt is nice, Olive, but why don't you sew these patterns?"

She sits and scrunches up her face. "That is for my mother. Not for me."

"Yeesss, Olive doesn't like to sew the old styles." Dionesia beams and looks up at her daughter.

A young woman, Olive's age but heavier, wearing a bright yellow Maya-style dress, comes out of the house onto the veranda. Olive smiles and pulls on the skirt of the woman's dress. "Oh, this is the one you have to watch out for. This is the one that is trouble." Giggling, Olive stands up.

The woman doesn't sense my presence yet. When she finally turns and sees me, her eyes grow wide, and she runs back into the house. Everyone laughs. She bashfully comes out again, at Theofila's urging. She smiles, showing crooked teeth, and turns her giggles away from me. "This is Tomasa. My friend." Olive fills me in. "She has come to see Mario."

Tomasa, her face red, laughs, "No, you are the one that wants Mario."

A group of seven men appear in the distance, walking up the road toward the house. "Are these your loggers?"

Olive and Tomasa stand together. Tomasa is giggling. Dionesia slowly turns to look. "Yeesss, these are our loggers. They are coming for lunch."

Eugenia goes to the kitchen and begins to pat out some tortillas. Theofila sets the table.

"Where are they logging?" I watch the men approach, laughing and joking amongst themselves. One trails behind the rest. He is the youngest, maybe in his early twenties, maybe younger. He is tall and muscular.

"Along the road to P.G. You don't see it on the bus?" Dionesia smiles. "There is Mario, the one in the back. He's walking by himself."

The men have reached the footpath that leads behind Theofila's chicken coops to a small cement house, a hundred yards from the veranda. Each man waves and says "Hello" as he passes. Mario still trails.

Olive calls to him. "So you are fine today, but still you come from work soon." She turns to Tomasa and continues, loud enough for him to hear, "I told you that boy is lazy." Tomasa and Olive laugh. Dionesia joins in.

The men file into the small cement house. We all stare at the house, until they begin to emerge and head up the small hill to the veranda, where we sit. They nod and smile as they pass and enter the kitchen. Mario still trails. He smiles at Olive, just before he takes his place at the table.

Olive stands at the window looking in. "So, Mario, any more snake bites today?"

Tomasa and Dionesia giggle.

"What?" He looks confused. She repeats her question making her hand a snake, biting her arm.

"Oh, yes." He nods.

Olive and Tomasa laugh.

"*No problema.*"

Olive and Tomasa laugh again.

Dionesia turns to me, "Mario is learning to speak English."

Olive returns to our group, giggling. She stands behind Dionesia, leaning on the back of her mother's chair. Occasionally, she glances at the men eating at the table and smiles.

When the men finish their meal, they file back into the cement house. It's not long before they head back out toward the road. We watch them again, like 3-D television. Mario is not with them.

"Do they come for lunch every day?"

"Oh, yeess. A truck picks them up, at the junction. Sometimes they like to take a few beers at Salam's shop while they wait." Dionesia picks up her sewing again.

Mario stands by the cement house for a few moments. Then he starts up the hill toward the veranda. "So you don't want work this afternoon?" Dionesia teases him.

He looks confused. Olive makes a sound to imply he is stupid. Then in the loud, slow voice of frustrated communication she says, "You are lazy, Mario. Not true?"

Giggles echo between Tomasa, Theofila, and Olive.

"No, I am not lazy." The slow, soft-spoken words of someone unsure. A dimple claims his cheek as he smiles. His humility in the face of English makes him attractive, but so young. He reaches over and pulls Olive's braid. She swings around and taps him with her fist on his chest.

Dionesia laughs. "Don't hurt the boy, Olive."

"Do you want lunch, *ix* Laura?" Theofila asks.

"Umm. No. No, thanks, I think I should be going. I have some work to do." I stand.

"Don't leave just because Mario smells." Olive smirks, flashing an exaggerated smile to Mario. Tomasa and Dionesia laugh. Mario looks confused again.

I smile and look at Olive from the corner of my eye. "No, no, he doesn't smell. I really have work." I gather up my backpack and realize my sneakers and socks are still inside. I will try the trails barefoot; few people wear shoes anyway. "Don't worry, I'll come again."

It is a quiet afternoon. I am relaxing at Prim's shop, sipping one of his famously cold soft drinks. Two men with survey equipment have just passed by the shop, waving to Prim during the brief moment their image crosses the doorway. "Who are those guys, Prim?"

"Why, Miss Laura, are you missing your husband?" He chuckles.

"No, Prim." I try to show disappointment with my voice. Disappointment that even Prim can't seem to avoid sexual innuendo. "I don't like those men. They're too rude. Every time I walk by all I hear is, 'chichi-chichi.' It makes me nuts, I'm gonna do that to one of them one day." I mimic a dullard, "Chichichichi, come here, baby."

"Those men are with the government, Miss Laura. They are surveying the village." Prim is serious. "They are trying to record who has what land, and what kind of house is on it."

"They're still rude. They bother all the women, 'What's your name, baby?' I never see them do work, they just want to play." I repeat the words the women at the corn mill use to talk about them. The mill is next door to the small cement government house that they stay in. The poor women have to put up with them all day.

Prim has no response.

After a few seconds, I change my approach. "Maybe that's why I see so many people pouring cement and building houses." I look out onto the street, through the doorway. "Salam, Castellanos, Chiac, Sho, everyone is building right now."

"Yes, Miss Laura. Soon, the government will make it hard to just make a house. You won't be able to just find your little lot and make a house." He sits on the stool behind the counter. "This government wants us to pay tax. They send these surveyors so they can keep records of who uses what land, and how much tax they should pay."

"Maybe it will be expensive to live here soon. Land tax and the new water system. Just like the States." I lift my eyebrows, nod, and take another sip of my Coke.

"Yes, Miss Laura." Prim nods too.

A young woman is standing on the veranda as I leave Prim's shop. She is looking over toward the mill house. Her hand covers her mouth, and her eyes are wide. I hear Olive's voice, laughing. I turn to see her coming out of the mill house. Her hair is loose. I have never seen it unbraided before and am mesmerized by its length. It is way below her buttocks, down to mid thigh. This long black cape sways back and forth as she walks past the surveyors' house, shrieking with laughter, smiling at them, flirting. The young woman, her mouth open in amazement, stares as Olive saunters down the road. The surveyors are watching, too, smiling, nudging each other, laughing that deep laugh of sexual interest.

The early morning sky is a transparent midnight-blue backdrop pulled tight across the sky. Tiny pinpricks of light shine through as stars. Occasionally, roosters crow, breaking the heavy silence. Everyone sits sleepy-eyed on the shop veranda waiting for Pablo to start the bus up and come around the corner. The 4 a.m. Saturday morning trip to Punta Gorda is sometimes just a little too early for everyone.

I find my seat, nodding, and saying hello to those already on the bus. I plop down and lean my head on the seat in front of me. A few more minutes of sleep would help a lot.

When I wake up, the sun has risen and Tomasa is sitting next to me, giggling. "So, you finally wake up." I hear Olive's voice from the seat in front of me. She's kneeling on her seat, looking at me over its back. Theofila is sitting next to her. They, of course, are both giggling.

"Yes, am I in the States yet?" I attempt a meager joke.

Olive's shrill laughter pierces my ears. "Am I in the States? I think she's still sleeping." Tomasa and Theo laugh. "No, you're not even in P.G. yet." Olive sits back down in her seat.

I wipe my eyes and say to Tomasa, "Are you gals just doing some shopping?" I notice her black plastic backpack is stuffed. "Or are you gonna catch the eleven o'clock to Belize?"

"I'm going to Ladyville," she smiles and speaks a little louder, "and Olive is trying to go back to Cayo. But she thinks she'll miss Mario too much, so maybe she'll stay." Tomasa giggles.

"Back to Cayo?" I look over the seat, tapping Olive on the head.

"Yes, I'm going back to the hotel where I worked before. I'm going to make some money." She remains seated.

"They still don't pay you?" I speak softly, trying not to let the whole bus know her business.

"No, they pay me. But, you see, it's not so much. Asteria is going to run the program now. She's good, you know." A touch of sarcasm taints her compliment.

"And you are going to Ladyville?" I turn to Tomasa again.

"Yes, I'm going to find my job there. If I can't find anything, I'll meet Olive in Cayo." Pablo swerves the bus to avoid a deep pothole, pushing Tomasa into me, giggling.

When we settle again, I ask, "Why don't you stay in the village, Tom?"

"There's no jobs there." Another pothole, unavoided, jiggles us.

"Maybe you can stay and get married?"

Olive pops up again. "She can't get married again. She was married already, no one will take her now." Olive smirks, "Just like me, no one thinks we're innocent."

"You were married, Tom? I never knew." I look at her bowed head.

"Yes, but my husband died. He had something with his . . . ," looking up, unsure, she offers, "append- . . ."

"Appendicitis?"

"Yes," she nods excitedly. "I was married only for a year when he died."

I look down, following her eyes into her lap. "Do you miss him?"

She looks up at Olive and giggles. "No, I didn't love my husband. He came to engage me when I was fourteen. Only a few months after I was married, he started to beat me because he was jealous."

"He was jealous?"

"Yes, because his sister liked to tell lies about me." She swipes her tongue over her crooked teeth. "Only when he was dying did she tell him she lied."

"So now, she wants to make her own life. She's going to find her job and see what happens." Olive smiles. "Like me."

Tomasa beams. "Only God knows what will happen. But I think I can find my job."

Olive nods. With mock boredom she says, "Yes, you can find your job."

"What kinda job do you want?"

"Maybe in a factory." She giggles and shakes her head. "I don't want cleaning. And I DON'T want to take care of babies."

Olive sits back down in her seat, disappearing from our view. "Factory jobs are good." She smiles at me. "I can make some money. I know how to sew."

We smash into each other again. Another pothole.

ANALYSIS: EDUCATION

Many young women in the village wish to delay or avoid arranged marriages. Some have found that continuing their education beyond primary school allows them this freedom. This section examines the conditions necessary for women to enroll in secondary school and the changes education brings them and others.

Who Goes to Primary School?

Creole and Garifuna education officials and government workers routinely bemoan the fact that Maya do not send their daughters to school. They often follow such comments with the suggestion that Maya try to

Graduating from primary school.

"keep women down" by denying them opportunities. Their assumptions are incorrect.

Gregory's 1969 household survey indicates that 79 percent of 122 respondents in San Antonio, a large southern Belizean Mayan village, agree that girls should receive as much education as boys (1984:106). A village-wide survey during that same year found that boys and girls attended the primary school, at equal rates (Gregory 1984:16).

Furthermore, the Belize census for 1968–1969 shows that men and women at various ages had attained equal levels of primary-school education. Boys and girls have been attending the village's primary school at equal rates for a long time. In the past, these "equal rates" have been low. That is, neither boys nor girls stayed in school very long (Gregory 1984:104–105). Today, most attend until they reach the age of fourteen, when Belizean law no longer requires them to attend. Since most turn fourteen during their tenure in Standard 6, the final grade in grammar school, both parents and students feel their education is complete.

In 1994, I examined the village's grammar school attendance records and calculated dropout rates for boys and girls for two five-year periods. From 1979 to 1984, girls had a higher dropout rate than boys, never completing grammar school. From 1985 to 1991, however, girls were dropping out at a lower rate than boys. Most, however, made it to Standard 6, the highest grade available in the village.

Maya are aware of and enthusiastic about the benefits of literacy and communication skills for economic advancement. Indeed, most parents are interested in ways to improve ALL of their children's abilities to learn, or to "make they find it easier" (Crooks 1993). The primary school, however, provides its students with the skills Maya in the village consider most important. Parents are less enthusiastic about sending their children to secondary school.

Secondary School

Between 1950 and 1977, only four girls and twenty boys sought advanced education or vocational training beyond primary school. Why so few? Primary school provides students with adequate literacy skills to participate in village life, read newspapers, albeit haltingly, and understand basic financial transactions. Many people agree that more education would be beneficial. Few, however, have seen it as a possibility.

Toledo Community College (TCC), the district-wide secondary school, is in Punta Gorda, the district capital. Only recently has a school bus been transporting students from the village to TCC daily. Prior to the availability of the daily bus, students had to find room and board in Punta Gorda. The total cost for school and board was considerable: nearly $1,550 BZ/year (Crooks 1992:94).

Apolonia Cal[2] was one of the first girls to go to TCC, with a government scholarship. Although her father has a secondary education and feels education is important, it took great energy to convince her parents to let her go. Apolonia's parents never felt girls shouldn't get an education, as Gregory (1987:16–17) has suggested. Instead, they, like most everyone in the village, felt girls shouldn't travel alone. Since two of her girlfriends would be going as well, they eventually agreed.

Boarding away from home was cause for worry. Girls who stay in the village must travel in groups to be careful to avoid sexual encounters, desired or undesired, and gossip of such encounters, real, imagined, or fictitious. Girls leaving the village to go to school had to do the same. Girls leaving the village to work sometimes became pregnant. Dionesia Sho did. There is no assurance that leaving for school wouldn't have the same outcome. Parents would thereby lose their investment in the girl's schooling and the girl would return with an extra mouth to feed and with diminished chances of finding a "good" husband.

Now that the school bus is available, many more girls attend TCC without fear of gossip, temptation, or unwanted sexual encounters. Many return to the village every evening after school, so their parents can keep a watchful eye over them. Others board in Punta Gorda during the week with *comadres* and *compadres,* people who have entered a ritual agreement vowing to act as co-parents and to advise students on moral behavior. This arrangement lessens the economic gamble, but does not even the score. During the 1994/1995 school year 37.2 percent of TCC's enrollment were girls, while 58.7 percent were boys (Belize Ministry of Education 1997).

Gregory (1987) reports that parents feel girls "turn out bad" when they leave the village for employment. He interprets such comments to mean that Maya feel the experience of gaining employment outside the village changes girls too much. He implies that parents deny their daughters independence, which, for him, is key to women's rights. He uses his data on people's beliefs and attitudes about young women leaving the village to gain employment to explain why there is a great disparity between boys and girls going to TCC.

Although going to school and seeking employment both require women to leave the village, parents and others did not equate the two. Parents secure in their ability to raise the money encourage their daughters to attend high school. They feel it allows the girls, and themselves, economic success. But parents rarely encourage their daughters to seek employment outside of the village, unless they have already married and become widowed or divorced. Such women, they feel, have little chance of remarrying and therefore face poverty if they stay in the village (see Chapter 3: Another Legitimate Beating).

It is also rare for parents to encourage their oldest daughters to continue their education. Parents tend to encourage their younger children, of both sexes, to attend school. The older children in a family, both male and female, often drop out of school because their family needs their labor at home. Once the older children are settled on their life paths, i.e. girls are married and boys are either married or employed outside the village, it is easier for parents to take the gamble of education with the younger ones. Their family is, at that time, smaller and needs less. Most of the children are also old enough to do chores, so there is less work. Also, older brothers who have joined the army, or who have found employment outside the village, may contribute funds to send younger siblings to school. Those able to attend secondary school, therefore, tend to be "extra labor," who grow up while a family faces relative prosperity.

It is easy to say that parents deny their daughters education and thereby contribute to Mopan women's oppression. This would be the interpretation that Olive or non-Maya educators might suggest, but I don't think that that is the whole picture.

Going to school is a life choice for girls who are marriageable but not yet married. Like the early years of marriage, it is a training period, where a daughter gains adult life skills. The difference is that education is expensive. The cost has been decreasing, but it is still an economic drain for most families. The drain is both in cash and labor. As the number of dependent children in a household decreases over time, due to marriages and "jobbing out," education becomes a greater option for the younger children in a family.

Education and Domestic Violence

Although women in the village feel that getting an education decreases their chance of being an abused wife, I cannot determine if this is so. The village keeps no records of reported cases of domestic violence; therefore, statistics are unavailable. I felt uncomfortable doing a household survey on the topic. All of my information about domestic violence comes from observation and from women who initiated the topic in discussion.

Few of the women I became close to were educated. The educated women I did get to know never talked to me about their own experiences with domestic violence. One woman, a primary school teacher, often remarked that her husband was not jealous, and that he was kind. Indeed, he was kind and respectful. They seemed to have a sharing, egalitarian relationship. It is hard to tell if her education has anything to do with the seeming lack of domestic violence in their home. They lived near her parents. Her father is a well-respected man in the community. It is impossible to point to any of these factors, either singly or as interconnected phenomena, and say, "That is why she is not beaten." Also, I can't be sure she is not a victim of domestic violence.

Since there is little work available in the village, many educated women leave. Some work as schoolteachers, living wherever the Ministry of Education assigns them. Others find jobs as nurses, receptionists, clerks, and so on throughout the nation. Many marry non-Maya, and their spouses refuse to live in the village. I cannot determine if such women suffer domestic violence.

A few women in the village told me stories similar to Leona's story. Her daughter's indoctrination at TCC, and her husband's hope that his daughter will succeed, has reduced the amount of violence to which Leona's husband subjects her. This is one obvious way education has reduced domestic violence.

Education has contributed to young women's ability to control their own lives. Because education is an alternative to marriage, it allows them to avoid an arranged marriage at a young age. It facilitates a woman's ability to marry later, and to marry someone of her own choosing.

Going to Punta Gorda for education has loosened prohibitions against women traveling alone. Parents and others have grown to trust that their daughters are not arranging secret meetings with lovers, but are attending school and educational events. Education is not alone in providing women more freedom to travel; development projects have also provided some women more freedom to travel.

Gender relations change for young women and men attending school. As Olive Tzir says, teachers require boys and girls to sit next to one another and to speak to each other. Educated girls are less timid around young men, and to some extent the girls' parents understand this change as necessary for the child to succeed in school.

For young Mayan women, school is not just about gaining skills or knowledge to increase economic potential. It is also about sociological changes, such as a decrease in arranged marriages, freedom to travel alone without being subject to gossip, freedom to talk to and befriend boys, and the expansion of peers beyond the kin group. Education has captured many girls' imaginations as the purveyor of freedom. This belief is also true of non-Maya in Belize and of women around the world.

It is unclear, however, whether these changes in educated women's lives will reduce domestic violence.

As mentioned above, most educated women marry non-Maya and leave the village. Therefore, there are few role models living within the village for young women to learn from. Educated women, whether or not they live in the village, do contribute to an air of change in the village, as have development projects (Gregory 1984). One mother often told me that her daughter, now just seven, will grow up and become a nurse, as Nurse Chun had done. Therefore, "brain drain," the migration of educated people from rural areas (Gould 1993:191), and subsequent loss of female role models, is not as detrimental as it may seem. The fact that some women get an education and find a career outside of the house is, at least, inspiring to others.

Women's ability to inspire others is related to their ability to maintain a "good reputation." They need to negotiate an identity acceptable to those in the village. Going to secondary school requires young women to change.

"When We Go to High School, We Change"

> *If you go to high school, you change. Yes, that's the main thing. You change. The culture will be gone one day.*
>
> Olive Tzir, above narrative, p. 185

> *Only if you are a weak person will you become Westernized. If you feel ashamed of what you are, then you change.*
>
> Irene Paquiul, interview, June 8, 1994

Schooling systems, such as Lwin experiences in Gaspar Pedro Gonzales' novel *A Mayan Life,* often degrade, demean, and deculturalize indigenous people, violating their self-esteem. In tears Lwin explains to his mother how formal education in Guatemala has attacked him, as a Mayan man, and made him more insecure than if he hadn't sought education. Furthermore, he explains, "When you come into the system, the first thing you have to do is put your values aside. It's like taking off your clothes and putting on someone else's" (Gonzales 1995:116).

Such violence to a person's being can happen in the Belizean education system as well, but it is less likely. Many educated Maya have become schoolteachers and administrators. Half of the teachers at the village's primary school are Maya, as are the principals of both the primary school and Toledo Community College. Most Maya educators are dedicated to maintaining a Maya identity and encourage their students to "remember who they are." Many belong to the Toledo Maya Cultural Council (TMCC), the Mayan rights group fighting for a Mayan homeland in the Toledo District. Education, they feel, is necessary to gain their rights as a cultural group.

But words like "identity" and "rights" are difficult to define. During Deb Crooks' field stay (1990–1991), a man beat his wife. The wife went to the *alcalde,* an educated man active in fighting for Mayan rights, and in some ways a spokesperson on the topic of Mayan culture and tradition both nationally and internationally. He answered, "It's a man's right to beat his wife" (Crooks 1993).

Women in the village confirmed Crooks' information and added that the *alcalde* eventually requested that the police constable lock the violent husband up for several nights. After the first night, however, he asked the constable to lock up the woman, too. She had refused to bring food for her husband. This *alcalde*'s actions have contributed to his somewhat unsavory reputation within the village, especially among women.

No woman I met agreed that it is a man's right to beat his wife or that a woman should cook for her violent husband. Yet most recognize that men often beat their wives. Some see it as part of their identity, in the sense that they think women from other groups (white American anthropologists, missionaries, Peace Corps Volunteers, Garifuna, Creole) don't suffer such abuse.

Olive Tzir's enthusiasm for the changes she believes education brings women, including a belief that domestic violence will disappear, couples with her conviction that Maya culture will soon die. She rejects Mayan identity, refusing to do anything she and others associate with a Mayan woman's life. She feels her culture enslaves women. She is not alone. Many young women want to continue their education because they have a conscious desire to escape their culture.

Olive, however, is more adamant and outspoken about it than most. She refuses to shell corn, bathe in the river, or embroider traditional designs. She does what she can to act in defiance of village beliefs about proper behavior for women. She openly flirts with boys and men. She takes others' gossiping about her as affirmation that she is not part of the "old ways."

As a result, she lives between the village and the rest of Belize, frequently traveling back and forth when she begins to "get bored" with village life or misses her family. She is not interested in negotiating a reputation that "old heads" would find respectful.

Irene Paquiul, a teacher at the Teachers College, is an active member of the TMCC, where she is part of an organized effort to define Maya identity. She wants to maintain a personal identity which others recognize as Mayan, but which leaves her the freedoms she gained through education. She sees educated Maya identity as a balance between what is modern and what is traditional. She says this balance is personal. Everyone faces "some things that are definitely Maya, and other things that are definitely modern. And there's a big gray area in the middle that people must decide for themselves" (interview June 8, 1994).

Negotiating such an identity requires strength, and not everyone always accepts the way you craft it. Although Irene strongly self-identifies as Maya, some criticize her and other members of her family for "changing the culture too much." Her response, uncharacteristically aggressive for a young Mayan woman, is, "Give me a damn definition of culture, and I'll tell you if I'm changing it!"

Irene also strongly self-identifies as an uncharacteristically aggressive young Mayan woman. Her assertiveness is part of the changes that have come to her through education, and she is doing her best to negotiate it into her identity as a Mayan woman. She is doing a good job of that.

CHAPTER SIX

Traveling Spirits

The Sun's Hot, Gal

Francesca and I are walking back from Mr. Coc's plantation. A load of oranges and golden plums shades my back from the sun. Under its weight, my T-shirt is drenched with sweat. Each time Francesca sees a healing herb growing along the road she points it out to me and tells me its use. Most everything is good for either stomach or skin problems, it seems.

Usually I am a diligent student and patient with her attempts to teach me, but today I just can't do it. I now realize that if I wrote down everything she told me, I would never have any peace. I know that I need to focus on the things I want to know, otherwise I will have nothing.

"Angela knows them all," she says, when I can't recall the name or use of some dark-leafed stinging weed.

A wave of resentment passes through my soul. No one in the States would ever consider comparing my intellect to that of a seven-year-old. Not without intending an insult. Francesca's comment hits close to home, however. Angela knows a lot more important things in life than I do right now. Suddenly my load of oranges seems heavy.

Despite my bad mood, Francesca is in good spirits today. Occasionally, she turns her stiff upper body toward me, straining under the weight of her tumpline, and smiles.

I continue silently up the road. Francesca is just a few steps in front of me. We have reached the long hot stretch along the football field. I want to pass it quickly and release my weak neck from the strain of the heavy fruit. A woman suddenly appears before Francesca. That's the way people appear in your line of vision when you use a tumpline, suddenly. It is hard to raise your head, impossible to turn your neck. All you can see is the road at your feet. A good thing, too, because it ensures that you won't lose your footing.

Francesca stops for a moment and talks, keeping her tumpline on. When I catch up, I take mine off. As I ease my load to the ground, the other woman disappears up a path and into a thatch house.

As I swing the tumpline onto my back, Francesca asks. "Do you know that lady?"

"No." I place the strap across my forehead and shift the load back and forth to better balance the oranges and to reposition a plantain that is poking me through the net bag.

She laughs. "Maybe she means someone else."

"What did she say?"

"She says she sees you at night at the church." Francesca giggles.

"At the church?" I make a puzzled face. "At night?"

"That's what she says." She shrugs. "But she can't see too good."

"No?" We begin to walk again.

"For true, she can't see too good. It's because of her husband."

I edge closer to Francesca. "Yes?"

"One night he likes to drink too much and so he comes home late." The weight of her load restricts her storytelling gestures.

"Yes." I imagine her facial expressions as she continues.

"So, because he is a jealous man, she locks the door at night, when he is gone."

"Yes."

"But this night, he is drunk and can't wait for his wife to open the door. He gets vexed because it takes her long time to wake up, unlock the door, let him in, . . ." She elongates the vowels to show how long it may have taken. "So when he finally gets in he is so vexed he hit her here." We stop walking and she turns to me so I can see she is touching her temple. "With a flashlight."

I draw air through my teeth to show sympathy for pain.

Francesca pauses dramatically, still looking at me from beneath her load. "Yes, it's true. And she bleeds and bleeds. When she go to the nurse, she can't see so good with that eye."

"For true?" I scrunch my face up in an exaggerated expression of pain, sympathy, and disbelief. I find myself rubbing my temple.

"Yes, gal. She still can't see so good." Francesca turns back to her chore of hauling oranges. "And she's a little bit crazy, too."

I imagine a flashlight across my temple. The flashlight in my imagination is a two-battery silver flashlight made in China, heavy with batteries, a flashlight like Mr. Coc sells in his shop.

I notice Francesca waiting for me up ahead. When I get closer she points to a tree on the hill near the church latrines. My resentment rises again. I am sure she is going to ask me what kind of tree that is and what it is good for, even though trees have never been part of her quizzing before.

When I stand next to her, she says, "That old man sat under that tree with one bottle."

I turn my body so I can see her. "Which old man?"

"The one who hits her with the flash." She stops pointing.

"Oh."

"And he drink and drink. Everybody think he just sleeping." She waves her hand in front of her face and closes her eyes. Her face is expressionless. "He looks like this." She holds her expressionless face for a few more seconds and then looks up at me. "But the poor man, he's dead." She pauses. "And nobody knows." She picks up her pace again, but stops again a few feet away.

I turn and look at her again.

She crinkles her nose. "And the sun was hot, gal."

The Funeral

Francesca is hanging clothes with quick, jerky movements. She nearly drops one of Angela's dresses onto the ground. Something is wrong. She has just come back from a wedding in San Miguel, and I can't figure what could have upset her. I greet her at the clothesline.

"*Ix* Laura. I just come back and I find Fidelia dead. I never knew. Mr. Coc never knows until Fidelia's boy comes to buy nails. The boy just tells him and then he cries." She shakes her head, her sorrowful expression gaining intensity with the soft sway of her head. Her movements are a mixture of extremes, sorrowful sways and nervous jerks. "Mr. Coc just tell me now. I never knew."

"Fidelia?" I catch her eye. I don't remember a "Fidelia."

"Yes, Fidelia Pop. Cil's mother. You know the lady, she walks in dey village every time." Another sorrowful sway, "Now we can't see her in the village again."

I still can't place the name. I have no face to go with that name, but I know the importance of Cil's mother. She is Angela's grandmother. She is family. There is silence between us, as I watch her hang one of the last few pieces of laundry. "Maybe you will go to Fidelia's funeral."

I look toward my chicken coop. "I don't know." Then I look back at her. "When is it?"

"Tonight, gal."

"Will you go?" My head motions to her as I speak.

"Yes, gal. She is Cil's mother, grandmother for Angela." She continues to watch me.

I nod. "Then I will go."

Francesca squints and smiles softly. I can see relief in her smile. Like any Mayan woman, she hates to go places alone. "We have to go all the way into dey bush. It's far, gal."

I am already committed. I am not going to back out just because it is far. "When?"

"Right now, gal. We will stay the whole night with her family—Benedicta, Emilia, all of her children." She picks up her plastic bucket.

"Will Cil come?" He lives in Orange Walk now, a full twelve-hour journey by bus.

"Yes, gal. That is his mother."

I gather the things I need for an overnight visit, my flashlight, warm clothes, soap. I pick up my camera and hold it for a few seconds, but decide not to pack it. Instead, I hide it in a plastic bag that hangs on a metal hook on my wall. Sometimes being a person is more important than being an anthropologist. Still, I pack a small notebook, telling myself it is less obtrusive. I replace my flip-flops with my hiking boots and head toward Francesca's.

Amelia, Mr. Coc's granddaughter, is already there. She will take care of Francesca's mother while we are away. I have no idea how she found out her services were needed. Francesca is packing and advising Amelia on what to prepare for dinner and what to do if her mother has any problems.

Justina also must have arrived while I was gone. She is standing on the veranda watching me put my backpack on. Ronny squirms and wiggles from her mother's arms. Justina holds tight.

"Are you going, Tina?" I want her to keep me company during this event and explain what is happening. Francesca might be too busy to spend time with me tonight.

Justina shakes her head, eyes wide. "Martino won't let me. He says it is no place for Ronny."

Soon, Francesca, Angela, and I start down the road. Amelia and Justina stand and watch us until we round the corner, making it impossible for them to see us, or for me to tell if they are still there.

As we round the corner, Sabrina, holding her son, Santo, stands in front of her thatch house watching us. Her house is on the hillside, overlooking the intersection of two roads, a good vantage point. She waves as I wave to her. I find her there often: She likes to watch village comings and goings. Soon she will be able to tell anyone whether their sister or brother has already passed by on the way to Fidelia's house.

As we walk by the football field, Francesca looks down at Angela. Angela looks up with an anxious smile. Francesca turns to me. "Fidelia has twelve babies. Twelve babies have no mommie now."

"Twelve, that's plenty."

"Yes, gal. And some are only small small." Francesca stands still for a moment. "What will happen to the babies? Who will take care of them if their mommie is gone?"

We round the turn to the road heading to the small *aquillo* just outside the village. The road follows the river for a while and climbs up a hill. The aquillo begins in the valley made between this hill and the next. We are quiet as we walk. Angela holds Francesca's hand. Angela usually giggles when we walk together. She and I like to pretend that she is a rooster and I am a hen. We walk like chickens and cluck and crow. Today she is quiet and I am not sure what kinds of questions I can ask.

The rain forest is lush. The ground is wet, muddy in spots. Francesca stops and points to the water-filled ruts in the road. "See, this is from the truck that bring her from Crooked Tree."

We stand and contemplate the ruts for a few moments. "She died in Crooked Tree?" I ask.

Francesca sets us to walking again. "Yes, gal. She was in the hospital. When they finish with her, they cut her three times. One here"—she motions along her left side, "one here"—she motions on her back, "and one more place, but I forget." Angela lets go of her hand and runs ahead of us a little.

I stay next to Francesca. "But why do they cut?"

"I don't know, gal." She hurries our pace a little.

"So, she died in the hospital?"

"No, gal. They let her go and she starts to get good. She stay with her son, Hilario. You don't know him. He's Cil's brother. He is police in Crooked Tree. But then she don't want to eat so much, and she die. They hire a truck to bring her here from Crooked Tree. It cost three hundred dollars."

"Three hundred?" I shake my head in conventional amazement.

Francesca's forehead crinkles with worry. "Yes, gal. So much. But they got to get her back home, to her babies."

The vista from the top of the hill, near Fidelia's house, is beautiful. Delicate cahone palms line a path up a small hill to the left of the main path. As I look out at that hill, I realize that path must lead to Fidelia's house. The thought makes me nervous. I don't know what to expect.

As we stand at the top of the hill, I see there are no corn or coffee fields here. The vista is beautiful, pristine. Land is plentiful here, that is why this *aquillo* was established. Land is getting scarce near the village. People are moving out into the bush, so they don't have to walk miles to get to their fields. This *aquillo* is one of the many smaller villages, with maybe eight or ten families, established in the past twenty years or so.

As we near the house, Cil's father, Juan Chiac, comes out. He is in his fifties, but looks younger. He has the same beaky nose as Cil. He shakes his head as we approach and takes Francesca by the elbow. He walks her to the front of the house. "I can't believe she is gone. Please, please come inside." He looks at me. "Thank you for coming." He turns to Francesca again. "Please go inside, Benedicta and my daughters are waiting. I have to find the *alcalde* about the burial. Please, I will return soon."

A younger man, maybe sixteen, steps out of the house carrying a flashlight. He vaguely resembles Juan. "*Na'chiin*," grandmother, he nods at Francesca, then silently he nods at me.

Juan continues. "I will return soon. We have to find the *alcalde*. I think he's back from his work today."

Juan and Francesca's voices fade as my attention is drawn inside. I step closer to the doorway and peer inside. The front room is candlelit.

In the center of the room is a platform, maybe a foot high. Light wispy cloth covers Fidelia, who is lying on her back in the middle of the platform. Her feet point to the door, her head to the kitchen. I walk closer to the entrance to the house, my gaze fixed on the shroud and the yellow candlelight. I am overcome by the solemnity of the room. The sacredness pulls me inside.

Four candles surround the body: one to her right, one to her left, one at her foot, and one at her head. Puddles of wax surround the foot of each candle. Those burning now are obviously not the first to burn. It is not dark outside yet, but the candles create their own surrounding darkness.

I am standing over her when Benedicta comes out of the kitchen and slowly moves toward her mother. She lifts the gauze for me to see Fidelia's face. Francesca comes to my side. Angela stands in front of me.

Fidelia's face is pale white, the same whiteness for which gothic punks strive. It is the beautiful color of lifelessness. Fidelia's dark hair, pulled back and plaited behind her, emphasizes her pallor. She wears a dark satiny blue dress with embossed flowers and lace trim. She has pennies on her eyes, American copper.

As I stand there, I still can't remember her in life. I can see a likeness between her and Angela, but I can't remember her alive. Of course, I remember Benedicta. I have seen her many times, on the bus to Punta Gorda, in town, and in the village. She is beautiful. Her long black hair is silky, her lips full and naturally red. Today, she has great dark circles under puffy eyes. As I stand there trying to remember her mother, I envision Benedicta as I last saw her, accompanied by another, older, much plainer woman. The woman's exact features are shadowed in my mind by Benedicta's beauty. It must have been Fidelia. I feel ashamed that I can't get a clear picture of her, alive, in my mind.

Benedicta keeps her eyes on her mother. "They brought her at four o'clock. She died at six this morning, in Crooked Tree." She replaces the shroud.

I nod. Francesca takes a box of candles from her bag and places them next to the candle at Fidelia's head. Then she maneuvers Angela into a seat along the wall. I sit next to Francesca. We are two feet from Fidelia's head. Benedicta sits across from us, maybe four feet away, but she is too far and Fidelia is too much of a barrier for us to converse.

Demacio, one of Benedicta's brothers, comes in the side door carrying a long heavy board which he uses along with two wooden crates to make a bench along the far wall. Then he leaves out the side door.

Emilia, Benedicta's sister, beckons Benedicta into the kitchen. Ben goes. Francesca goes and Angela trails close behind.

I am alone with Fidelia.

Two middle-aged women, one slim in a bright pink dress, the other larger in fluorescent green, enter the house and sit across from me on the newly made bench. I don't recognize either one. They whisper to each other.

Francesca, Angela, and Benedicta return from the kitchen. Benedicta acknowledges the newcomers, who stand as she unveils her mother again. The two women whisper and point at Fidelia. Benedicta covers her. Everyone sits down again.

Francesca calls to Demacio as he reenters the house, "Her mouth is coming open. She shouldn't lay like that." He nods and continues into the kitchen.

A small, middle-aged man enters from the front door. His sway reveals that he has been drinking. He sits down, hard, next to me. His eyes are fixed on Fidelia. He is quiet for a few minutes, then he rises, and takes two wobbly steps toward Fidelia. He reaches down and pulls back the cloth. He pulls it far back and lets it fall. Then he wobbles until he sits down.

Another pair of women enter. One is Maria Bolon, my neighbor. With her is Constance, the eleven-year-old girl who lives just a few houses over from me. Constance waves at me excitedly, I smile at her and wave back. She and Maria stand and look at Fidelia. Benedicta enters from the kitchen again. She covers her mother when they are finished looking. They all sit down next to the pair of whispering women.

The man next to me stands, stumbles over to Fidelia, and throws the cloth back to reveal most of her body. Her mouth is slightly open, but she still looks peaceful. He hovers above her.

Demacio returns through the side door with a strip of red cloth. He stands over Fidelia on the other side of the drunk man, leans over his mother, and pushes her mouth shut. When he removes his hand and stretches out the red cloth, her mouth opens again. He looks up at the drunk. The drunk takes another wobbly step so that he is standing directly in front of me. I lean into Angela so I can still see what they do. The drunk leans over, puts his left hand on top of her head and his right under her chin, holding her mouth shut. Demacio quickly wraps the cloth around her head, twice, tying a knot at the top of her head. They both stand straight. Francesca nods her head. Demacio covers his mother again. I can see the red cloth through the gauzy shroud. The knot on top of her head looks like bunny ears.

The drunk sits down. "I knew her," he slurs at me. "I would see her," drunken pause, "in the village." He takes a deep breath. "Maybe you know her. But I know her, too." He sways forward and backward as he speaks. He leans into me so I can smell the rum. "I don't know if you know this lady. But I know this lady."

"Yes, I know this lady."

He pulls away from me and opens his eyes wide. Louder, crosser, he says, "I know this lady, too."

"Yes, you know this lady." I try to calm him. "I know you know this lady." Maybe if I change the subject. "She is a good lady."

He stands and throws back the cloth once again. The whispering women quiet for a second, point at him with their lips. He leans over and takes Fidelia's hands. He holds them together over her chest, as if she were in prayer. When he lets them go, they fall to her sides again. He tries it again, but her hands refuse to stay in prayer.

The drunk stumbles out the side door. Benedicta returns from the kitchen and covers her mother. Several more people come to pay their respects. I know only a few. Andrea, the village nurse, is among them.

A young Garifuna woman, Andrea has been the public health nurse in the village for a few years now. Her six-year-old son, Antwan, is with her. When she enters she crosses the room to where Benedicta and Emilia are sitting, Antwan in tow, eyes wide, staring at Fidelia. They stand to greet her, each one saying "Nurse." Several other people in the room, including Francesca, also say "Nurse." I nod to her. Andrea hugs Benedicta, whose body stiffens with contact.

Emilia is more receptive to hugs. She takes the nurse over to her mother. "I'm glad you come. See my mother." She lifts the cloth. Andrea nods mournfully as Emilia covers Fidelia again.

Antwan watches, his fingers in his mouth, eyes wide, quiet.

The whispering women move down the bench somewhat, so Andrea can sit closer to Benedicta. A second after she and Antwan sit, the drunk returns with Demacio. Demacio has two lengths of thin rope. The drunk pulls the cloth back from Fidelia's body and holds her hands prayerfully again. Demacio ties them together, and covers his mother. Then, he pulls the cloth up from her feet, pushes her two feet together and ties her big toes together. He covers her feet again and leaves by the side door.

The candle at Fidelia's foot, now just a stub, goes out. Benedicta takes a fresh one from the box that Francesca brought and lights it with a flame from the candle on Fidelia's right as she passes. She secures the new candle in place.

Maria Bolon places another box of candles at Fidelia's head. The whispering women do the same, giggling as they sit back down. Three men enter. Two stand by the door, while the other trips into the house. He approaches Fidelia and throws back the gauze. "My sister, my sister, it's true." The house is overcome by the smell of rum. The other two men enter the house as well, stand next to their friend, and look down at Fidelia.

Fidelia's brother raises his hand to cover his eyes, then pulls it away in a wobbly but dramatic movement. He waves the other hand, which he forgets is still holding the cloth, completely uncovering Fidelia's body. He stumbles and starts to cry. "My sister will not walk with me again." He precariously leans over Fidelia and picks up her hands still tied together with rope. The knot comes loose, and her arms fall to her side again. He takes her left hand and drops it. The weight of her arm makes him stagger backwards into his friends. The three men weep together.

Fidelia's brother continues in a wail, "My sister was a beautiful woman, beautiful. She and me, we are children together. We walk together." He covers his face with his hands, and spends a few moments losing and regaining his balance while trying to stand.

One of his friends, less drunk than the others, tries to straighten the cloth over Fidelia. When he finishes covering her, he loses his balance and pulls the cloth away again. His foot knocks against Fidelia's plywood bed. No one seems to notice. I realize that I am the only one watching them. Everyone else is chatting.

Fidelia's brother points to the candle at her head, which is about to go out. Benedicta quickly moves in and lights another candle to replace it. She also replaces the one to Fidelia's left.

The brother's friend regains his balance and successfully covers Fidelia. The three men leave through the side door. I see it is dark outside.

As the smell of rum follows the men out, the smell of sausage takes its place. Maybe that is what all the work in the kitchen is about. I haven't eaten. I am relieved that a little food might be served. I sit quietly, watching the mourners visit with one another.

When Juan Chiac and his son return from the *alcalde*, Juan greets each mourner with the proper title of respect. His son quickly exits through the side door. Juan stops and smiles at me. "I'm glad that you come."

I don't know what to say, so I say nothing. He continues, "I hope you are comfortable. Maybe you would like some tea. Benedicta should have some tea."

I smile and nod. I am embarrassed by his attention and still don't know what to say. I feel rude not responding. Juan continues through the house and puts a box of nails on a table, not far to my left, then he moves toward the kitchen, running his hand through his hair.

Francesca follows him. A few minutes later, Benedicta comes from the kitchen with a bucket of hot liquid and places it on the table next to the nails. Francesca carries in some bowls, finds a place on the table for them, and sits down. Benedicta then approaches each person individually, "Please, you can have some tea."

A few people huddle around the table, pouring and drinking tea from plastic bowls. I wait until the crowd lessens and pour myself a little taste. It is a lukewarm mixture of instant coffee, powdered milk, and Milo, an Ovaltine-like Nestle product marketed as a nutritional drink. I take half a bowlful and sit down again.

The room is crowded now. The children who have been arriving with their mothers are beginning to expend what stores of energy they might have left after a long day. They visit and gossip with each other like adults, except they occasionally push each other, or jump up and play a quick game of tag. Fidelia's younger ones have appeared and join in the fun. Constance sits quietly next to Maria, occasionally looking over at me. She is a little older than the other children. Antwan is beginning to wiggle away from his mother's control.

The adults are chatting a little more loudly than before. The whispering women are giggling more. Almost everyone has stopped paying close attention to Fidelia, even though she lies before them.

Constance comes over and sits next to me. "*Ix* Laura." She takes my hand for a second, then lets it go.

"Constance. I'm glad you are here."

"Fidelia is my father's sister. I come with my auntie, Maria." She brushes a few renegade hairs from her brow, with a sigh. Then she stands behind me and plays with my hair.

"Why does she have pennies on her eyes?"

Constance leans forward and speaks next to my ear. "Oh, they keep her eyes closed. It looks like maybe she is sleeping, not true?"

I lean my head back into her belly. "Why is there a basin of water under the platform?"

"What?" She leans sideways this time, to see my face.

"That basin, why is it there?" I point to the light blue plastic basin under Fidelia. It is half full with water.

"Oh, that is for the animals, *ix* Laura." She stands straight again and loosens the tie from my ponytail.

"Why?" I whisper to her.

"Tomorrow they will bathe her chickens and pigs with this water. It's so her spirit can't call them and make them sick." She pulls tight on my hair and begins to braid it.

"What about the dog?"

"Oh, yes. The dog too, *ix* Laura." She giggles, pushing my shoulders away and pulling my hair close.

When she finishes braiding my hair, she unravels it and starts again. "Why do you come?"

"I want to see Cil's family. I feel sorry for them." I pause and turn my head to look at her. I whisper, "And I want to see what happens at a funeral."

Constance nods.

A new couple arrives through the front door. Francesca leans over to tell me this is Cil's brother, Hilario, and his wife, just arrived from Crooked Tree. Hilario stands in the front doorway for a moment and looks around at all the people here. He approaches and uncovers the corpse. He and his wife quietly begin to cry.

Constance pushes her way over to look at Fidelia again. A small band of children also gather around before Hilario gets a chance to cover his mother again. Each child is peering at Fidelia, some with big eyes, others through covered faces; they giggle.

Constance comes back over to me and sits down. "Why don't you look?"

"Maybe it's rude." I whisper.

"But you want to know what happens at a funeral." Her voice is too loud for my comfort. I am a little embarrassed.

I shrug, hoping she will drop the subject.

Constance braids my hair again. "You should look," she whispers in my ear.

I am silent, enjoying the way she is touching my hair.

Mr. Coc enters the front door. He has been drinking. He staggers toward Fidelia. Constance pokes me in the back and whispers loudly, "Go look." The band of children crowds around again.

Mr. Coc lifts the gauzy cloth. I stand with Constance still holding my hair. She pushes me forward a bit, so I can get in a good position to see. Mr. Coc nods and makes a small laugh of recognition at me. I nod at him, refusing to smile. I look down at Fidelia. Maybe this time I will remember her in life.

Her face is swollen. Her beaky nose is its normal size but her cheeks and the area around her eyes are puffy. Dark patches have started to form under her eyes. Her lips are purple. There is no way I can identify her now. She will never be in my mind's eye as she was when she was alive. She smells. She is grotesque.

From the corner of my eye, I see Benedicta rise from her seat and go into the kitchen. Just as I sit down again, she returns with a bottle of Florida water, a scented toilet water. She sprinkles it on her mother's upper body as Coc continues to hold the cloth high. Then he covers her again. Benedicta returns the bottle to the kitchen. The sweet smell of Florida water seems to enhance the sweet meaty smell I only faintly noticed before. I realize now there are no sausages.

"How does she look now?" Constance whispers in my ear.

The children begin to settle down for bed as their mothers lay plastic sacks on the ground for them. Antwan, however, is still wide awake. He sits on his mother's lap. I visit with Andrea for a bit. Talking with her will help pass the time. To get to her I have to pass close by the body. I inhale a breath of the smell as I pass.

"Andrea," I stand in front of her, "I'm glad to see you."

"Yes, Miss Laura." She smiles to indicate I should sit on the sack next to her. Antwan won't be sleeping on it anytime soon. "Did you know this lady?" She sighs and shakes her head.

"Only a little." I sigh. "She is the grandmother to little Angela." I point my chin in Angela's direction.

"Oh, yes." Andrea seems to be somewhere else. "Where is her father, Graciliano? That is Fidelia's son, right?"

"Yes, I thought he would come, but it is a long way. He lives in Orange Walk now."

"Yes, Orange Walk. That is far." She holds Antwan's leg and bounces it up and down. He giggles. "I hear he gives blood when she was in hospital."

"Oh yes? I didn't know. Do you know how she died?"

"Cancer, Miss Laura." She looks at me briefly and bounces Antwan's leg again.

"Cancer. Do you see a lot of that in the village?"

"She is the third case I know about in the village, Miss Laura. Another is the lady who lives near the Nazarene church. She is the grandmother of Mariana Sho." She looks at me for a sign of recognition.

"Yes, I know the lady. She's been sick for a while now." I nod my head and picture the old woman in my mind. I am surprised so many women have cancer. Men work with toxic chemicals, pesticides, fertilizers. I would expect them to have more cancer than women.

Andrea continues. "I knew Fidelia very well, you know. She was one of the smartest ladies I knew here in the village." She leans over to look into the kitchen. "And very kind. She would visit me often at the clinic, you know."

"Oh yes?"

As Benedicta passes us, Andrea reaches over me and touches her calf. "Ben, can I ask you something?"

Benedicta bends down and smiles, "Yes."

"Do you have a roll of multipurpose? I would like to make a wreath." Andrea's question is a demand. Her tone isn't harsh, but it is authoritative, expecting obedience. It is a tone of voice I have heard most officials in Belize use when talking to Maya.

Benedicta finishes what she was doing before the interruption and returns with a roll of toilet paper. She gives it to Andrea. "But how will you make it?"

"You will see." Andrea smiles. When Benedicta leaves, Andrea turns to me and in a low voice I don't recognize as hers says, "The last wreath I made was for my pa." Then she reaches over into her bag and pulls out a metal coat hanger and a ball of string. She bends the hanger into a circle and begins to rip off sheets from the toilet paper roll, placing one on top of the next. After she piles about ten sheets, she fan folds them and ties them with a piece of string in the middle.

As I watch her peel each layer of toilet paper from the others I remember the last time I made paper roses this way. I was five or so. I was helping my sister Karen make decorations for her friend's wedding. We were going to tape them to the wedding car. This vague memory of my sister is eerie. My sister died in a car accident when I was six. I watch Andrea's fingers work with what seems lightning speed, trying to call up other memories of Karen. The only memory as strong as the paper roses is the time I watched Karen take a nap on the couch. I remember thinking she was beautiful. I can see her there in front of me.

Another mourner enters, crosses the room to view the body. Antwan and the other children gather around again to see the decay. This time, I can't help but see; the body is directly in front of me. A waft of foul air seeps out from under the gauze. It circles my head, nearly attacking my stomach. The skin around her eyes is dark. She has swollen considerably since last I looked. The puffiness of her eyelids holds the pennies in place. Benedicta appears again, sprinkling Florida water. The mourner pulls the cloth even further back. The children cover their noses. Antwan giggles with disgust. The mourner drops the cloth over the body and wipes the tears from his eyes. He is another son from somewhere north. He exits out the side door sobbing.

I make another paper rose.

A man enters from the side door with a tape measure. He motions for another man across the body from him to stand. He stretches the tape out and hands the other man the end. He motions the man to move to where the body is widest: where the elbows stick out. The man with the tape measure nods to the other to let his end go. Then he motions for the other man to stand and take the end to the head. He moves to the foot. He nods again and the other man sits down. He exits the side door, but reenters a few minutes later. He measures the length from the head to the elbows and exits.

A minute or two later I stand and cross to the side doorway. Looking out I see a lantern burning bright. Several men are gathered around its light, measuring and cutting wood.

I step outside and notice the brightness of the stars. The scene is so beautiful I long for my camera. I stand and watch from a distance, in the dark. I doubt anyone knows I am here.

When my eyes adjust I notice four other men to my left standing in the darkness, smoking. Two others are sitting on a bench to my far right. I can hear they are both sobbing. I quietly watch the builders construct a coffin.

Hilario silently appears next to me. "Drink, *ix* Laura." He hands me a thin clear plastic cup of rum.

I swallow all of it in one swig without any attempt at refusal. I hand him back the cup. "I'm sorry for your loss."

"The doctors say she had cancer." He takes a small sip of rum. "But I thought she was getting better. It all happened so fast." A bigger sip empties his cup.

"She stayed with you?"

"Yes, when they release her from hospital. And now we build her this box." He wipes his lip, then pours another drink and hands it to me. "Do you have your parents?"

I take this shot of rum slower than the first. I didn't expect another so soon. "No. My father died several years ago. So, I just have my ma." I empty the cup and hand it back to him.

"It's hard when you only have one." He looks straight ahead at the builders.

"Yes, it is hard." I remember my father.

"Why don't you bring your camera, Miss Laura?"

"I didn't think you would want me to take pictures." I worry that he is annoyed that I am here, but his actions don't suggest hostility.

"Oh, yes. With pictures I can remember my mother." He lights a cigarette. "You should have brought your camera."

"I'm sorry. I wish I knew."

I have been inside for about an hour when five men bring the coffin into the house. They have painted it with white lime. They shoo everyone off the newly constructed bench. The drunk who played with Antwan leaves through the side door. Andrea, Antwan, and several of the women retreat into the kitchen. I push my way toward the kitchen doorway, so I can see what they do. I rest one leg on the bed, the other on the floor, so I can lean far enough to poke my head through the doorway.

The men remove the bench and place the coffin on the ground. Emilia brings a sack of Fidelia's belongings into the room from the kitchen. She and Francesca line the coffin with some of her clothing.

Then, two men, one at the body's head, the other at her feet, position themselves to lift her. Two more maneuver themselves to pick up the weight in the middle. Together, all four gracefully lift. The two in the middle step backward into the coffin, then in unison they step out the other side. They carefully lay her inside, still wrapped in the gauzy cloth.

Moving her makes the sweet rotten meaty smell worse. A few people cover their mouths and noses. Nauseated, I turn my face into the kitchen and take a deep breath, then look into the front room again. Constance, who was sleeping on the bed, stands up and leans out the doorway with me.

The men then lift the coffin onto the platform. The one who lifted her middle leaves the room and returns with the cover. Benedicta wedges a calabash between the body and its arm.

"She should have money," Maria suggests, searching through her bag. She puts a few coins in the calabash.

Constance tugs on my shirt. When I look at her she says, "They are giving Fidelia the things she needed when she was alive."

Christina puts a gold plastic hair clip in the bowl. Benedicta puts her hands on Christina's shoulders and draws her close. Emilia sprinkles more Florida water in the coffin. Juan places jewelry into the calabash, two gold rings.

The men place the lid on the coffin and nail it shut. There is a hole in the lid at chest level. I turn to Constance, who I just realize is holding my hand. "Why is there a hole in the top?"

"That's to let her spirit go." She shakes her head, unhappy with her answer. "I mean so it won't stay with her body." We continue to lean together and watch the men reassemble the bench.

People resume their seats. Constance lets go of my hand and finds her place on the bed again.

As I take my seat next to Francesca, I see a fly enter the hole where the spirit comes out.

A battery-powered clock chimes midnight. I am still lying on the wire bedsprings Juan suggested for a nap. I lean over to open the curtain that covers the bedroom door so I can see what is happening. Mothers are waking their children. The men are coming inside, leaving the rum behind. Everyone is standing around the coffin. I stand, walk through the curtain, and take a place next to Hilario. Children, some cranky, rub the sleep from their eyes.

Juan leads us in saying the rosary. Our voices fill the room with chant. The sound is overwhelming, the rhythm of our speech resonates throughout my body. When we finish, our bodies still hum.

Then he reads the eulogy he wrote. I am weeping. Hilario is weeping. The woman standing next to me is weeping. I wonder if anyone can see clearly.

I take a break from the foul stuffy air of the small thatch house and stand by a tree outside. The moon is beautiful. I am brought back to the four years that took six lives from my family. I wipe a tear from my eye as I remember the ambulance taking Uncle Paul away from the church service for Aunt Diane. He didn't even make it to the cemetery to see his sister put in the ground. It was as if a plague was passing through our family, a plague of cancer, heart disease, and cirrhosis that swept through, leaving a few of us behind to struggle with depression, loneliness, and confusion. It left my sister's children without a mother. Their father had long since left, after a nasty divorce that they were too young to remember.

I remember Francesca's words as we traveled to this house. "Who will care for the children?" I stretch my neck high and scrunch my eyes shut to prevent a flood of tears.

A young man stands before me with a clear plastic cup in his hand. I take it, swallow its contents, and hand it back. Wordless, he moves on to the next mourner.

I stay outside with the drinkers until I am sure I can control my tears.

We say the rosary again at two. Again, our bodies resonate. When we finish, I go outside again to drink.

The battery-powered wall clock chimes four. The body has been here twelve hours. I have been here ten. The smell turns my stomach. I have always had sleep to separate drunkenness from sobriety. Now I am slipping from drunk to sober without that hiatus. My stomach turns again. I need to get away from the stench. I retreat to the kitchen. If I go outside someone may hand me that plastic cup again.

Benedicta, Emilia, Francesca, and Andrea are in the kitchen. Benedicta and Francesca are mixing flour, water, and lard in an orange bowl. Emilia is tending a fire. Andrea sits waiting at the tortilla table; she has a small plastic plate in front of her.

I take a place at the tortilla table. Maybe making tortillas will make me feel normal again. Francesca places the finished dough in the middle of the tortilla table and finds an extra *banco* to sit on. Benedicta asks Francesca in Maya if I can make tortillas.

"Oh, yes, *ix* Laura makes beautiful tortillas." She responds in English and beams proudly. She has taught me well.

I smile and pinch off a piece of dough. One, two, THREE, turn, one, two, THREE, turn, one, two, THREE. Flour dough is stretchier than *masa*. It constantly snaps back unless you are rough with it.

One, two, THREE, turn, one, two, THREE, turn, one, two, THREE. I shape the tortilla as if I am shaping my life. I let the dough snap back only briefly before I push it back into the shape I want it to be in. The shape is one of tradition. It has been set out long before I came here. It is normality.

Benedicta and Francesca have already made two tortillas each by the time I hand mine to Emilia to cook. Normality comes to them quicker and easier. They recognize 4 a.m. as another day, maybe as a fresh start. I still see it as the middle of the night.

When we finish working all the dough and baking the tortillas, Benedicta offers some to the women who cooked, then places the rest in a bucket. The thought of eating turns my stomach again, but I take one because I know I need food. I go to the furthest corner of the house, as far away from the coffin as I can get. I can only stomach a few bites; the nauseating smell is here, too.

Benedicta takes the rest of the tortillas to the mourners in the other room. She returns with an empty bucket.

The sun is blazing. More mourners come. The *alcalde* and several more men come to dig the grave. Juan takes them to where they should dig. Some of my closest friends arrive, but I don't want to talk to them. They seem too far away from my recent experiences. I feel closer to the strangers I met here. We have cried together, chanted together, drunk together, and sobered up together: over thirteen hours together. I feel a calm rhythm in my soul that I am sure they share. A rhythm I don't think the newcomers understand.

The house is so filled with fetor I cannot go inside. I stand near the doorway. It is one of the only places out of the blazing sun. Why is it so hot this morning?

New mourners continue to arrive. Occasionally, in a quiet voice, someone will mention the smell. No one who has been here since yesterday mentions the smell. We all recognize that the nauseating meaty smell has darkened. It is rotting flesh. The sun is hot; the house is packed; the shady areas outside are packed, but we have no need to state it.

I can't wait to get the corpse into the ground and be done with it.

Benedicta, Emilia, Francesca, and Maria make tortillas again. They have to feed the grave diggers.

When the grave is dug the men enter the kitchen one by one, covering their noses with their sweaty T-shirts. They take their food outside to eat.

It is eleven o'clock. Laurencio, a catechist at the church, has arrived with the Mass book. Everyone reenters the house. There must be over a hundred people here. I have found a place in the kitchen doorway. Some people hold their breath as long as they can, trying not to breathe. Others hold handkerchiefs to their noses. Still others, including Laurencio, simply breathe as if there was no smell of death. We all pray; the words, spoken in perfect unison, nevertheless seem to whirl around the room as loose phrases.

In the name of the Father, the Son, and the Holy Spirit. Holy Mary, Mother of God, pray for us sinners. For thine is the kingdom, the power, and the glory. Lead us not into temptation. Mother of God, fruit of thy womb. As we forgive those. Deliver us from evil. Now and at the hour of our death. Now and at the hour of our death. Now and at the hour of our death. Now and at the hour of our death. Deliver us from evil. Amen.

Hilario, Honario, Juan, and the rum distributor each take a corner of the coffin. The crowd makes way for them. They bring their load outside and place it on the ground. Another man hands Juan two long branches, which he puts through the small holes in the sides of the coffin. They lift the coffin by these poles and follow a path into the forest.

We follow. Constance nearly slips as we cross the stream. Maria helps an ancient woman up the hill. A young boy pushes ahead. Angela is still sleepy, rubbing her eyes. One grave digger uses his shovel to keep his balance on the hill. The mud is slippery, I nearly fall. Emilia catches me, I smile at her, she smiles back. We keep walking. The thorns cut through the skin on my calves. I reach down and wipe the blood away. The cuts sting. Francesca passes without a word.

We reach a small clearing on top of the hill. The pallbearers are careful not to lose their balance and tip their load. They rest the coffin next to the hole. Juan slides the poles out. The others lift the coffin so he can loop a length of rope at the head, another at the foot. They lift the coffin with these ropes and lower it into the ground.

Dry-eyed, Juan throws a handful of dirt onto the casket. One by one, we each take a handful of dirt and toss it into the hole. Some people stand around and wait. A few men are standing off to the side sharing a bottle of rum. Some people retreat down the hill, back to the house. Francesca stands next to me for a few moments, Angela holding her hand. When they head back to the house, I follow. There we collect our things and begin down the path toward home.

As we leave, I see a billow of smoke rising from the area of the grave. "What's that?" I whisper to Francesca.

"They are burning her things, gal." Her response is amiable, but I can tell she is tired.

Exhausted, I reach my house, open the door, and immediately collect what I need to wash. My soap, my bucket, my scrub brush, a change of clothes.

The river is quiet. Alone, I wash everything I had with me last night. The stink of death is trapped in my clothing, my hair, my skin. I wash it all, my backpack, the extra clothes I never changed into, the clothes I was wearing, my hair, my body. I submerge myself in the deep, cool, dark parts of the river. I try to stay under as long as I can. When I come up for air, I wash myself again. I sit in the shallow parts of the river letting the river flow over my legs, my feet, my body. I wash myself again and again.

When I return home, I sleep.

Traveling Spirits

"I'm going to Orange Walk, gal." Francesca is standing in my doorway. It is about 8 p.m. We are making end-of-the-day small talk. Her statement is a hint that she would like me to come with her.

"When will you go?" Each time I go to Orange Walk with Francesca, she drags me around in the hot sun carrying her purchases of plastic cups, material for Angela's dresses, and sweet rolls. I don't know if I am interested. The ride is long, costly, and exhausting.

"Wednesday, gal. Mr. Coc will take me to catch the five o'clock." She smiles, her eyes study me for an indication that I will go.

"That's the day after tomorrow." I stare off into my chicken coop.

"Yes, gal." She smiles.

I am quiet. Lately, I enjoy making her wonder what I will do. Finally, I nod my head. "Maybe I will go. But I need someone to care for my chickens."

"Yes. They need food, water . . ." She trails off as if the chickens might need a million other things.

Now we are playing the game. I have slipped into it unconsciously. As I made her wonder whether I would go with her, she is making me wonder whether her mother might feed my birds while we are gone. She is trying to get me to ask. It is a chess game. The king, the piece you protect the most, is your lack of obligation.

She is much better at the game than I am. Before I even know we are playing, she has mated me. If I want to go with her, I have to ask her mother to care for my chickens. I could ask someone else, but they might not do it. Her mother feeds her own birds twice a day. Her coop is next to mine. She would be right there to feed mine. I am indebted to Francesca for arranging this for me, even though I am doing her a favor by going.

Calculated favors. Balanced reciprocity with carefully kept mental records and an unspoken stigma surrounding being on the receiving end, but only if you have actually asked for the favor. Favors provided for the unasking don't count. They are part of a generalized reciprocity. Favors you request, though, the ones you have "begged for," those are different.

I might as well surrender. "Maybe your mother can care for my chickens when I go."

She nods her head smugly. "Yes, my mother can feed your chickens."

"Then I'll go to Orange Walk with you." I should have let her ask me to go. Then I would still have a chance in the game. We would almost be even then.

"Rosa will come with me tomorrow to plantation. We'll pull *k'ula,* and green *kuku* (cacao) for Cil. Maybe we have *ma'buoy* for Mik. They can't get these foods in Orange Walk, you know." She sticks her lower lip out in a frown and shakes her head.

"I know." I understand these are the foods I will carry to Orange Walk. I still haven't been able to put these tasks into play. It is like not knowing how to use the knight. I can't get a woman nearly my mother's age to ask me to carry something for her. It is part of my "niceness" repertoire. It is unnatural to make her ask, but until she asks, this niceness doesn't really count. Somehow it disappears, leaving me with no "good deeds done," unable to demonstrate how "nice" I am being. "Maybe I will come, too. When will you go?"

"In the morning, gal." She smiles. That would be around 8 a.m., after Mr. Coc is fed and Angela is off to school.

After a little more small talk, she retreats to her house and I return to the dull white glow of my laptop to finish my notes about Fidelia's funeral.

Rosa, Francesca, and I, carrying net bags and swinging machetes, head off down the path toward Francesca's land. In the distance we can see Emilia Chiac carrying a small child. When we get to the soccer field, we can see the child is her little sister, Maclovia, the youngest survivor of Fidelia Pop. Emilia's eyes are teary; she is a little frantic. "The ground mole bit this baby." Her voice is shaky.

Rosa draws in air, "Aiy." She grabs the child's leg and looks at the wound.

Francesca does the same. "Maybe the nurse is in another village today."

"The poor baby." Rosa lets go of the child's leg and pushes a few hairs from the baby's face.

Maclovia makes a tearful face but doesn't cry.

"My brother, he catch a ground mole in a trap. He brought it to the house to kill it, but the baby got too close and it grabbed her." Emilia takes a quick breath. "The baby screams and I never knew what was wrong. I went to her, and I see she has this bite, and my brother tell me the ground mole bit she. I never knew that animal would bite she." She shifts the weight of the child on her hip.

"Aiy. A ground mole." Francesca's eyes get wide as she lets go of the child's leg.

The child draws the leg close to her, and makes another tearful pout.

"Go, gal. Find the nurse." Francesca motions with her hand in the direction of the nurse's station. "If she's not there you can wait with my mother."

Emilia hurries her pace. We stand and look at each other for a few seconds. Rosa speaks, "Maybe it's the child's mother."

I make a puzzled face.

Francesca looks at Rosa and then at me. "Yes, gal. Sometimes the spirit of the mother will call for that child. It's because she misses that child."

"It's true, gal." Rosa continues. "The spirit of that child might go to its mother." She continues in her matter-of-fact voice, the one she uses to distance herself from the "superstitions" that all her friends believe. "That's what the people think." She nods, but then twists her neck and says, "But it's true. That child could die."

We are silent as we continue on our way to the plantation, until Rosa finds something to laugh about again. She loves to laugh.

Francesca, Angela, and I got the last seats on the bus to Belize City, the first leg of our journey to Orange Walk. Francesca smiled and giggled, her eyes wide, and said, half giggling, "We got seats, gal."

"Yeah, we got seats." I smiled back. A few moments later I put my head down and cradled it in my arm leaning on the seat in front of me and fell asleep despite Angela's incessant wiggling.

Now, I lift my head; it is maybe an hour later. Francesca is looking out the window and Angela is sleeping. Her head rests on my shoulder. I lift it for a second as I shift my position, and place it back down. The true miracle of childhood is sound sleep.

"She's pretty when she sleeps." I whisper a giggle to Francesca.

"Yes, gal." Francesca smiles back. "Angela can sleep through anything, gal. Just like Cil when he was small. Sometimes, in the day, when I had to tend the shop or go to plantation, I had no one to watch Cil. I would tie him to the table leg and go do my work. Your work doesn't wait for when you have time, you know."

"For true." I smile at her.

"Sometimes, when I come home, Cil, he falls asleep right there, under that table." Her shrill laugh punctuates her tale. "He could sleep anywhere, gal."

I laugh. "How did Cil come to live with you and Mr. Coc?"

"His father and his mother, they live in the village at first, you know. They live close to we, and all the time I would help Fidelia and she would help me. It was good."

I nod to encourage her story.

"But then, Cil's father decides he doesn't want to walk so far to plantation. His land is far far. It's too far to walk every time." She shakes her head. "So they build their house and begin the next village, where we went to see Fidelia." She nods. "But they want Cil to go to school. They want him to learn to read, they want him to learn to write. They leave the boy with his uncle, so he can go to school, because it is so close for us. It's only a short walk. So when he gets a little older we send him to the school and he learns good. He helps Mr. Coc with the shop and he loves his auntie."

"Yes, because you raise him like a son."

"Yes, he is like our son, because we have no babies. That is why we take Cil, because we have no babies." Her eyes twinkle. "We help him find a wife."

"Michaela?"

"Yes, Michaela, and we made a big big engagement party for he. So big, gal." She smiles with the memory. "We made tents for the people to stay out of the sun, and we had soft drinks and *caldo* and bread and coffee. All kinds of food."

I smile.

"Maybe that was a long time ago."

"Angela is seven, maybe it was eight years now." She turns her head to look out the window. "But you know, Fidelia, she never like Michaela."

"No? But she's a good wife." It is really more of an inquiry, I don't know Michaela that well. "Why doesn't she like her?"

"I don't know, gal." She looks from the window back to me. "But Mik say, when she goes to visit, Fidelia don't treat her good." She frowns. "They talk about her and make faces. They are only good when Cil is there. When he goes," she gestures his departure with her hand, "they tease she, make fun of she." She looks me in the eye, "They laugh at she."

"But why?"

"I don't know, gal." She shakes her head. "Fidelia make she sleep on the floor with all the fleas, gal." Her voice turns to a whine. "Michaela say she can't sleep because she itch too much."

"I never knew she don't like Mik. Maybe that's why Cil don't come to the funeral."

She raises her eyebrows, as if she had never thought of it. "Maybe, gal. I don't know."

I wait a few seconds before I probe for the rest of the family history. "So how did Angela come to stay with you?"

"When Cil go for training for the police, Mik stay with me."

"Oh, I see." I play with the cuff of my shorts.

"When he comes back he wants to stay with he ma and he pa. But Michaela is pregnant. She was going to have Angela, and she don't want to stay on the ground with the fleas." She shakes her head and continues, "Cil gets vexed because he wants she to stay with he ma."

"Oh."

"He gets vexed because Michaela wants to stay with me. She stay with me and she was working. She was washing the dishes and he comes and hauls her back to he ma house. He want she to stay with he ma. But, that night, he try to choke Mik. He go like this," she takes her hands and puts them around her neck. "He choke she, so she will learn to love he ma. And he haul Mik to he ma house and he make she stay with he ma. But the next day she run again." She slaps her hands together, one passing the other to show motion and laughs. "She comes back to the village with me."

"She didn't go to her own ma." Michaela's family lives on the road between the village and the *aquillo*. I thought it would be a natural place to go.

"No, gal. She don't want to leave Cil, just he ma. Only he ma and he sisters, they like to tease she too much." She nods. "Cil was vexed. He say he wants divorce because she can't learn to love he ma. But she doesn't consent because she love he. She problem only with he ma." She pauses. "So, she comes to me and my mother help she give birth to Angela."

"Oh, yes?" I smile with the thought of Francesca's mother acting as midwife for Angela. Angela and the old woman are very close.

"Yes, gal." She frowns and shakes her head. "But then he gets stationed at Belmopan, and they have to leave Angela with me."

"They don't take Angela to Belmopan?" Belmopan is the nation's capital. It is a clean city with some of the best educational opportunities in Belize. I am perplexed why they chose not to raise Angela there.

"No, gal, she's just too small." She frowns. "They leave she with me."

I nod sympathetically, still not understanding exactly why they couldn't raise Angela wherever they went. "Did he stay in Belmopan long?"

"Not too long, but then he goes to Crooked Tree, to Cayo, all kinds of places. It gets so he can't come to see his baby." She shakes her head pitifully. "She stay with me." A pause. "One time Cil's ma and pa send for me. They tell me they want to give me two turkeys. So I go all that way." She frowns and shakes her head. "But when I reach, Cil is there."

I make wide eyes.

"Yes, gal. And he say he want Angela." She nods with each of the last three words.

"What happened?" I gasp.

"Angela don't want to go, gal. She gets used to me already. She don't want she pa." Francesca smiles wide. "I buy her dresses, I buy her clips, I give she sweets, anything she wants."

"So now she stays with you." I smile and touch Angela's hand.

"Yes, gal." She smiles and focuses on Angela for a moment also.

"She's happy." I look down at her again, the little princess.

"And Michaela has Sylvia." Francesca nods her head. "And now Hilaria." Our last visit two months ago was to see the new baby.

We are quiet for a long time.

"Why didn't Cil come to see his ma?" I ask.

"I don't know, gal." She looks away.

"I hope we find him."

"Me, too, gal." She breathes the words out quickly, as if she has been afraid to mention this thought for a long time. "I never call him," She looks at me. "Chen say the phone never gets fixed." She laughs anxiously. "He says he had to send its heart to Belize." She laughs again with ease. "Its heart, gal." How strange to describe an inanimate object, a piece of a phone, as a heart.

The bus ride takes us through Stann Creek District, where the road twists and turns through beautiful lush valleys before it passes rows and rows of citrus trees. The rows and rows of citrus trees are echoed by rows and rows of small wooden shacks, the homes of citrus workers. We are in the heart of Belize's citrus industry.

As we pass Pomona, a company town, schoolchildren play in the yard of the municipal building. They are on recess. I think of Justina living here with her husband and child not too long ago. I try to imagine what she did with herself. She is a bright girl; what did she do all day in one of these tiny shacks?

In the village, she tends her livestock, gathers foods in the rain forest, plays in the river. She works and talks with friends and relatives. She could join a women's craft group, if she wanted. What did she have to do in Pomona where sadness and poverty ooze up from the soil? What kind of recess did she have?

When we reached Orange Walk, I left Francesca, Angela, and all of our luggage on a bright pink bench in Central Park. Angela looked tired, but not too tired to try to convince Francesca that it would be okay for her to play on the slide. I am sure when I get back, she will be having fun with the other little girls wearing frilly dresses and patent-leather shoes.

I am on my way to the police station, to find Cil. The music shop is blaring a Mexican ballad, *muy romántico*. My footsteps fall to its rhythm. I am waiting to hear the one phrase that is always in a Mexican ballad, *mi corazón*, my heart. I can just hear it as the music fades under the roar of a sugarcane truck.

I turn my neck to watch the truck continue down the street. I can see the street is covered with escapee stalks of cane crushed flat under the weight of the next truck.

Pickup trucks and Ford Broncos race down the street after the cane trucks; decorative fringes above their windshields and crosses strapped to their rearview mirrors flutter, exaggerating their speed.

Two women are walking in front of me. One thin, wears a satiny skirt-and-blouse set. The other has a large shapely bottom under a tight, red, knee-length dress. Both balance gracefully on shiny black high heels. Their constant stream of Spanish is broken only by their laughter.

A dark-skinned man stands in the doorway of a shoe shop. His straight hair is greased back. He watches the women in front of me pass. His protruding belly is exaggerated because he is leaning on the door frame with his shoulders slumped. He seems to be made of rubber. He wears a white button-down shirt and dress pants. As I pass the shop I can see a woman wearing a bright orange sari behind the counter.

I am careful when I cross the street to the police station. Traffic seems ruthless here.

Two police constables are standing behind the desk. One is looking at some paperwork, the other is talking on the phone. They both look to be in their twenties. It seems like ten minutes before either one looks up at me. The one on the phone smiles and winks, the other speaks.

"Can I help you?"

"Yes," I smile. "I hope so. I'm looking for Constable Graciliano Chiac."

The one on the phone stops smiling and motions with his thumb to the back room. My eyes follow, and I can see Cil walk past the door.

The speaking constable slowly walks into the back room. A second later, Cil appears.

"Cil." I smile. "Francesca and Angela are in the park."

He makes a big, familiar, playful smile and nods. "Did you come on the bus?"

"Yes." I smile back comfortably. I like Cil, he always puts me at ease.

"Wait." He smiles again, his eyes are bright as he hands me his police hat. He goes into the back room and returns with a pink ten-speed bicycle, a nice ride, different from the one I borrowed from him a few months ago. As he wheels it past the desk, he turns to the man on the phone. "I'm off duty now, my family just come."

The phone man nods and smiles at me again and waves good-bye. I smile back, awkwardly.

Cil walks his bike as we retrace my footsteps back to the park. "I'm glad I found you, I was worried you might not be there and I don't know where your house is now. Every time I come to see you, you have a different house." Police get transferred a lot.

He laughs. "Yes, it's true."

We are silent as we walk. I take the silence to think about what to say about his mother. I had all day to think of something, but now it seems too hard to say anything at all. I don't know where to start.

"We couldn't call to let you know when we were coming. The phone is broken. Chen says it needs a new heart."

"*Un nuevo corazón,*" he laughs.

I smile and look down at my feet. "Your Spanish is getting good?" I look up and catch his eyes as I finish the question.

He looks at me, too. "Yes. You can't just speak Mopan or Creole here."

We laugh together, walking silently again, enjoying each other's company.

Feeling a little more comfortable, I make an effort. "Cil, I'm sorry about your mother." I look at my feet again. "I was at the funeral."

"Yes, my mother is gone now. Look, there is Angela." He points toward the slide. Angela is waiting in line at the top. She sits, tucks the skirt of her dress under her bottom, and gives herself a good push. She forgets to put her feet on the ground when she gets to the bottom and falls directly on her butt. Cil laughs, I chuckle with him. Angela looks as though she might cry.

"Angela!" Francesca jumps up and quickly makes her way to where Angela has fallen. She grabs her by the arm and pulls her over to the bench. At the bench she wipes Angela's now streaming tears away with the palm of her hand. Rapidly, in Mopan, she warns her not to endanger herself again.

As we approach, Cil's laugh has reduced to a chuckle, but he enhances it by shaking his shoulders and covering his mouth. I moan a sympathetic sound and play with Angela's braids. Angela gasps a few breaths of air and reduces her bawling to a sob.

Cil takes the heaviest of our luggage and balances it on the bicycle seat. I take up the rest, and we slowly walk a few blocks to his new house.

This house is a bright orange cement box. Unlike his last house in Orange Walk, this one is not on stilts. A swinging love seat fills the front lawn. As Cil opens the gate I can see Michaela through the doorway. She is wearing a green young-Mayan–style dress, with stains down the front. She is wrestling with wet clothes, transferring them from one side of a small semiautomatic washing machine to the other.

I had a machine just like this one when I was in college. One side you fill with water and soap, and a small agitator swishes your clothes around; the other side spins the excess water out of them. You have to wrestle the clothes from one side to the other, then out into a basket so you can hang them to dry. It takes a lot of strength.

Sylvia, Cil's four-year-old middle child, has heard the gate open and runs to greet her father. She is wearing a pair of red shorts and a striped T-shirt. She carries a red plastic dump truck with big blue wheels.

Sylvia and Michaela see us at the same moment and identical smiles cross their faces. Sylvia's is perhaps a bit more animated and definitely longer lasting. When we finish greeting each other, Sylvia takes Angela by the hand and leads her to the back of the house: sisters together again.

Hilaria, Michaela's newborn, is taking her morning nap in the hammock in the living room. Angela and Sylvia are still playing outside. Cil sits on an overturned plastic five-gallon bucket. Francesca sits on a short stool, the skirt of her dress stretched between her legs and tucked under her bottom. Michaela sits in the same fashion on another plastic bucket. I sit on a chair, my legs to one side because my skirt is too short to stuff under me the way we do in the village.

We are in a circle in the living room. A pile of dark *ma'buoy* pods sits in the middle. We are pushing our thumbs through the weak part of the *ma'buoy* pod, separating its three sections and freeing the bright orange pulp and black seeds. We guide the pulp's descent into small plastic buckets at our feet. The shells themselves we discard into smaller heaps. The *ma'buoy* juice is dyeing my thumb a beautiful bright magenta. It also seems to be numbing it.

"Yes, and her face," Francesca holds her hand in front of her own face, "it was black black." She grimaces. "And puff."

I nod, uncomfortable telling Cil about the physical decay of his mother.

"It was a long time before they come to bury her. Long time." Francesca shakes her head. "Maybe not until eleven."

I nod. "Yes, I think we didn't get home," I find myself in midsentence feeling awkward and insensitive, but I continue, "until one or two. I think Laurencio came at twelve to say the rosary."

"Laurencio?" Cil tilts his head toward Francesca. "Why doesn't Candido come?"

"He was in his fields. He don't hear until it's too late." Francesca makes his excuses. "He lives far."

Cil and Michaela nod at each other, accepting Francesca's reasoning.

"But so many people come." Francesca's eyes are wide.

"Yes, maybe over a hundred." I want to give Cil the positive information. His mother was loved and will be missed by many.

"Yes," Francesca looks at me, "maybe a hundred."

We are quiet for a little while. Then Cil quietly begins. "I tried to come, but I thought she was at Crooked Tree with my brother. When I reach, they gone already." His small bucket of pulp is overflowing. He pours it into Michaela's larger bucket. "By that time, it's too late, I can't get transport to the village. No buses, and I can't find anyone going."

"They don't wait for Cil." Michaela looks into my eyes. "His brother don't wait, they take the old lady away already."

We are silent again.

"She never get stiff." Francesca turns to Michaela.

Michaela makes her eyes wide and sucks in a breath of air. "Aiy." She looks at Cil.

"We have to tie her hands like so," Francesca demonstrates with her own hands. "And we tie her mouth, because it don't want to stay shut."

Hilaria wakes with a thunderous wail.

This afternoon, we shop. Michaela stays home with Hilaria, to cook *ma'buoy caldo*. Cil, Francesca, Angela, Sylvia, and I are walking the streets of Orange Walk in the blazing hot sun to find Francesca a tea-kettle.

Ever since we left the "clothing by the pound" store, Sylvia has been whining. Her delicate little moans and grumbles are rapidly increasing in frequency and volume. Her face has been in a pout for at least an hour. She is still adorable.

I stop, and put the packages of cloth, plastic cups, and baked goods I have been carrying for Francesca on the ground. I lean down and whisper, "What's wrong, little one? Maybe we can stop at the park and take a rest."

Sylvia's pout deepens with the attention.

I pat her head and try to wipe the pout away from her face. "This baby is hot!" I turn to Francesca.

Francesca looks at me, then at the child. She puts her hand to Sylvia's forehead. "Maybe it's fever, gal." Francesca clenches her teeth together and grimaces.

I stoop down to Sylvia's level and put my hand on her forehead, too. I look at Francesca, "She's really hot." I ask Sylvia if she wants me to carry her.

She slowly and quietly nods her head, still pouting.

I pick her up and rest her on my hip, and gather Francesca's packages again. Sylvia tucks her head under my chin and leans in close to my body. She feels sweaty and hot against my own sweaty body.

We continue on to the jewelry store by the park to buy Angela's earrings. We haven't found a teakettle that Francesca likes yet.

I can hear the neighbor lady yell as Francesca tries to scrape the leftovers onto the ground again. Francesca retreats back into the house, her brow crinkled. She turns to Michaela, "What can I do? Where can I throw the bones?"

Michaela's eyes are wide. With a crooked smile, she shakes her head. "I don't know."

Francesca laughs and shrugs her shoulders. "Maybe she doesn't throw the bones, gal. Maybe she eats them."

Michaela smiles and shrugs. "I don't know, maybe."

"Maybe that's why her dog is so *maga* (sickly)." I laugh at my own joke and twinkle at Michaela. We laugh together as Francesca scrapes the leftovers onto a single plate.

Michaela takes the wash and rinse basins outside and dumps them down the communal sink, but, like Francesca's sink in the village, there is no complicated sewage drain. The water spills onto the ground below and travels along a shallow ditch into the street.

Cil returns from the driveway-turned-patio. He had brought a bowl of *ma'buoy caldo* to his neighbor friend. His friend only ate a few spoonfuls of the bright orange soup. Like Francesca, he doesn't know where to dump the rest. He stands in the middle of the room giggling.

"Give it to their *maga* dog." Michaela smiles and looks at me.

Cil giggles and takes it to the communal sink outside. The skinny sickly dog waits under the drain. Francesca, Michaela, and I gather at the door, pointing and laughing at the dog trying to gobble up the broth.

"I HATE that dog." Cil whispers. Then he barks at Michaela and chases her into the kitchen, where he playfully spanks her bottom. Michaela's small dark eyes shine and her pale skin flushes. She turns her head to hide. Cil continues his antics chasing Michaela around the house, while she gently tries to bat him away.

"He's crazy." Michaela looks at me, when they are finished.

Sylvia wakes from her nap and stands groggy at my feet rubbing her eyes. I sit on the five-gallon bucket and put her on my lap. She looks at me with her watery black eyes and in a small high-pitched, singsong voice says, "Wa ta."

"What's that, baby?" I smile at her.

She hums and repeats "wa ta."

I stand her on the floor and pour her a glass of water from the water bucket. She takes a sip and wanders off into the living room, rubbing her eyes again. Francesca follows her with a cookie she bought earlier at the bakery.

Francesca comes back with her backpack, sits on another bucket, and pulls out a greenware censer. Michaela searches for paper and cardboard, ripping what she finds into small pieces and placing them in the censer.

"What's that for?" I look at Francesca.

"Nothing, gal." She doesn't even look at me; she is digging in her backpack for something else.

Cil calls me into the living room. "She can't say. Better you ask later. She can fill you in tomorrow." Then he goes outside and visits with his friend again.

I return to the kitchen, afraid I will miss something. Francesca pulls a small bundle tightly wrapped with banana leaves from her pack. She loosens the vine that holds it together and carefully opens it to reveal small, dark green pine needles. She pinches a few into the censer and places it on the stove.

Michaela takes a head of garlic from one of her many cardboard boxes and peels off a few cloves. "Angela," she calls. There is no answer. "Angela!" she tries again, this time mumbling "*chicha pul*" under her breath.

Angela appears through the side door with half a peeled orange in each of her hands, a gift from the neighbors.

"Aiy, look at Angela." Michaela giggles, "That gal like to eat too much." Her tiny eyes glimmer. "She'll get fat."

Francesca laughs as Michaela takes the orange pieces from her daughter and replaces them with the garlic cloves. Then she nudges Angela toward Francesca, wrinkling her nose. "That stuff stink too much."

Francesca lifts the collar of Angela's dress to reveal a dried-up piece of garlic. She unfastens the safety pin that holds it in place, and replaces it with one of the fresh cloves from Angela's hand. She puts the rest of the garlic in her lap. I want to ask about the garlic, but decide to wait until tomorrow, as Cil suggested.

Michaela gives Angela back her orange halves and nudges her back outside. Then she takes a garlic clove from Francesca's lap, wrinkles her nose again, and rubs it on Hilaria's forehead, wrists, and feet. Finally, she pins it onto Hilaria's shirt, near the collar.

Francesca takes the last clove and steps into the living room. She returns with Sylvia's cup. We finish cleaning up the kitchen.

The sun set about an hour ago, but the house is still hot. Cil closed the doors and windows after he sprayed the house with insecticide. I have been reading the stories and editorials in the *Belize Times* about how bad the mosquitos are in Orange Walk this year. Two people came down with dengue fever. Insecticide lingers in the air.

We are all watching the Mexican game show on TV. A large-breasted woman in a bright red tutu-like skirt and a matching, tight, low-cut, long-sleeved top is dancing and lip-syncing a song. Every other word seems to be *corazón*. The camera angle makes it look as though one of her shiny black high heels will kick through the television screen.

My attention wanders to other things in the room. There are two things on the wall. A calendar from People's store shows a large-breasted, dark-haired woman, her bright red lips slightly parted. Her eyes are closed and her head tilts back.

Next to that is a print of a young woman. It is hard to tell her age. She looks like a child, but the intensity of her blue eyes is echoed with eye shadow. Her blond hair flows down her shoulders, nearly concealing a kitten. She is holding the kitten to her chest, but she has no interest in it. Instead, she looks off to the left, at the calendar girl.

Hilaria kicks and squirms, smiles and mews as Michaela changes her diaper. Michaela then hands her to Cil, who stands and puts her in the hammock. Quietly, he opens the front door and leaves, leaving it ajar. Angela sits leaning over Hilaria in the hammock.

I stand in the open doorway watching Cil lift the mosquito net that the neighbors have draped over the carport. I stay in the doorway so I can see what is happening outside and inside.

Francesca comes from the kitchen with the censer and grabs a pack of Toucan matches from the entertainment center. Hilaria and Angela are looking at each other, smiling, playing.

"Where's Sylvia?" Michaela giggles at the thought of losing her.

"The gal sleep." Francesca smiles.

"Aiy. The gal sleep too much." Michaela stands in the doorway of the bedroom and looks at her daughter for a moment. Then she shakes her to wake her up. Sylvia sits up and rubs her eyes.

Francesca lights the paper in the censer and adds more pine needles. She blows on the paper to get it to catch. Soon billows of smoke rise from the censer. Francesca begins to wave the greenware pot. The slight wind from its movement keeps the smoke billowing. Francesca begins to speak, just under her breath. She mumbles and waves the censer toward Hilaria. The baby smiles and mews. Francesca waves the censer under the hammock. The child watches Angela and smiles. Francesca waves the censer over the hammock, the baby squints and blinks. Francesca waves the censer to the child's left and to her right all the time mumbling, smoke billowing. Hilaria makes a stern face but remains silent.

The woody pine-forest smell of the burning paper and incense replaces the sharp tingly smell of insecticide. Francesca repeats the same passes. Under, over, left, and right. Her voice, too low to understand, continues in a stream. She pauses only to take a small breath. Under, over, left, and right.

Still standing in the doorway I turn my head to watch Cil and the neighbors. They are laughing and joking. I turn my head back to watch Francesca, now waving the rising smoke toward Hilaria with her hand. I watch Cil again. Francesca is sitting down, adding more pine needles. I look back at Cil. Francesca lights the needles, blowing on the paper to get it to burn. Cil is laughing, his head thrown back. It must have been a good joke.

Suddenly, Hilaria screams, and I feel as though someone just slapped my face. Startled I put my hand to the pain in my cheek, and step from the doorway. Hilaria's cry calls my attention inside. Michaela is holding the baby, bouncing her to get her to stop crying. Sylvia is still standing in the doorway of the bedroom, rubbing her eyes. Francesca is in the kitchen. Angela is staring at me.

"Ha," Michaela laughs, "the door hit you." She covers her mouth to hide her laugh. Hilaria's square weepy face softens to a pout and a few sobs.

At 3:30 in the morning I can hear Cil walking around and Francesca trying to wake Angela. I step out of bed and put on the shorts and T-shirt that I laid out the night before. I stand in the doorway of my room trying to get my mind to remember what I might be forgetting.

"I can walk you to the park. You can catch the bus there." Cil talks. I can't seem to formulate a response.

"It comes soon." Francesca is worried again. She and Michaela are gathering up Francesca's purchases and belongings. I will carry these things back to the village for her.

Angela stands in the kitchen doorway blinking, mirroring me, trying to get her mind to work. Michaela hands her a cup of liquid. She sips it.

I move next to her, hoping I will get a drink as well. I am beginning to wake up. "Where's Sylvia? I can't leave without saying good-bye to her."

"She's lazy, gal." Michaela points her lips into the other bedroom.

Sylvia is lying down with her butt way up in the air. I lean over her and wipe her sleeping forehead. She is burning hot. I squat in front of her and notice a cold sore forming on her lip. "Poor baby," I mumble to myself.

In the kitchen, Michaela hands me a cup of lukewarm liquid, a sweet mixture of coffee and tea.

"Ten minutes," Cil rushes us.

We reach the park just as the bus pulls up. Cil takes our luggage to the back of the bus and hands it to the conductor. Francesca and Angela sit together next to a thin attractive Mestizo girl. I sit next to a tall blonde Mennonite farmer in plaid shirt and suspenders. I wave to Cil out the window. He smiles wide and waves back. I lower my head into the cradle of my arms, leaning on the seat in front of us, and I fall asleep.

"Sylvia was hot this morning when I touched her." We are somewhere in that flat boring stretch between Belize City and Belmopan.

"Yes, gal. She got fever again."

"She gets sick a lot." I look out the window anticipating the mountain range.

"Yes, gal." Francesca puffs concern.

I wait for an explanation, but Francesca offers none. "Cil said you could tell me what happened last night."

"Nothing, gal." Francesca wrinkles her nose and shakes her head.

"I got hit with the door." I rub my face recalling the pain.

Francesca laughs. "I just asked Fidelia to leave the children alone."

"Maybe she went out that door." I smile.

"Maybe, gal."

"What did you say last night?" I persist.

"Nothing." She looks away, then back again. "Just to leave the children, especially Hilaria, alone. I say that she had her life, she walked with us and did her work, but that she should let the children do that now." She nods her head to punctuate her statement.

"Anything else?"

"I tell she that Cil and Mik did all they could when she was dying. Cil went to the hospital, he gave blood for her, and Mik never complained when Cil bought his mother the things she needed in the hospital, nightgown, soap, everything. She never complained. She did what she could, she respected her mother-in-law." She pauses, takes a breath, and looks at Angela. "I tell her to leave the children, don't come looking to take the children with she."

I turn my head tilting it slightly, mimicking the motions Mayan women make to show concern. "She could take the children?"

"Yes, gal. She can make they spirit come with she." Francesca nods seriously. "Just like Rosa say. It's true. The garlic, it helps to protect them. That's why I put garlic on Angela. It helps Angela to be strong."

"How long will she wear the garlic?"

"Only a month, gal."

I look out the window to see the giant mountains in the distance. Then I return my gaze to Francesca. "What did you burn with the paper last night?"

"Oh, that's *romero*. You can burn it any time you don't feel good." She smiles. "It smells good, not true?"

"Yeah, like pine trees." I smile back at her. "But why did you burn it for Hilaria and not Sylvia?"

"It's only for the babies. Only if they cry a lot and for no reason. It might be the spirit that makes them cry." Francesca pauses for a second or two. "And maybe Fidelia is vexed because Michaela never come to see her in the hospital."

Eyes wide, I ask, "She never went to see her?"

A *child in a hammock.*

"No, gal. It's too far." She looks out the window. "How could Michaela know she was going to die? Mik never complain when Cil brought he ma what she needs. She never stop him from giving to he ma, never."

"No, Mik is good." I pause. "How long will Hilaria be in danger?" I follow Francesca's gaze out the window.

"Only a week, gal. Two weeks pass already."

"After that she will be okay? Right?"

"I don't know, gal. Maybe Fidelia misses the babies too much. Sometimes they miss the babies too much."

ANALYSIS: LOVE, RESPECT, AND REVENGE

Fidelia's death may not seem to have much to do with domestic violence. I have no evidence that Juan, her husband, ever caused her physical or mental harm. His devotion to Fidelia is one reason I chose to tell her story. When focusing on violence, we sometimes forget that love binds couples together, even while others and sometimes these same couples abuse one another.

This last narrative chapter and its analysis section examine *tsik,* "respect," as a foundation for binding relationships. While *tsik* can help to prevent human violence, a husband can use a wife's violations of *tsik* to justify his violence against her. Violations of *tsik* can also justify a spirit's revenge. Vengeful spirits are usually souls dislodged from people who have died. They are what some people might call a ghost, spirits of the known dead. To understand the relationship between *tsik,* souls/spirits, revenge, and domestic violence, we must first look at Mayan respect.

Tsik *and* Naab'l: *Mopan Respect and Mam Soul*

Tsik is a Mopan Maya word which glosses as "respect" or "honor." (The following explanation of *tsik* comes primarily from Danziger 1991.) It is the glue that holds the universe together; it prevents chaos both in the natural world and in the social world. Lack of *tsik* can evoke chaos in social relations and in the universe.

In the social world, *tsik* illuminates human interconnectedness, the fact that people cannot survive in isolation but need help from others. Knowing this humbles Maya and requires them to show their respect for others. To treat someone with *tsik* is to be polite and cooperative. To mock others, or trick them, is counter to *tsik.*

Maya make *tsik* greetings — set, formal, deferential greetings — in order to reinforce, create, and recognize cooperative relationships with people. Although usually people reserve *tsik* greetings for biological and fictive kin, most greet others who have served or are serving the community, like past and present *alcaldes* or community nurses, with respect. Young people also honor older people with a *tsik* greeting.

People make the most deferential and formal *tsik* greeting to fictive kin, *comadres* and *compadres.* Although these fictive kin may share a biological relationship with the greeter, they usually do not. Their relationship is agreed upon as cooperative and supportive through a ceremony that coincides with religious rites of passage: *ts'ah tsik.* When a child is baptized, confirmed as a member of the Catholic Church, or married, its parents request that a woman and a man act as *comadre* and *compadre.* Their role is to act as moral guides helping the child live responsibly, respectfully, and honorably. Sometimes parents choose *comadres* or *compadres* who can look after the child economically. For this reason, some non-Maya currently act as fictive kin. *Ts'ah tsik* is a ceremony marked by formal speechmaking, *kichpan t'an,* "beautiful speech," by both those undergoing the rite and for their fictive kin. These speeches may have a particular rhythm, or possibly rhyming couplets, but the subject matter is always a promise of service and *tsik*. *Ts'ah tsik* is the first time either partner in the respectful pact offers the other a *tsik* greeting. In this way, *tsik* greetings create respect relationships rather than reflecting them (Danziger 1991:125, 221).

Service is integral to *tsik*. Villagers say that people who serve their community, such as those who engage in the *compadrazgo* system, or, in the past, those participating in the civil-religious cargo system, have *tsik*. In this way, *tsik* can be a characteristic that someone possesses. However, *tsik* must be maintained by acting morally and maintaining an attitude of respect. Without such maintenance, *tsik* is lost. For the most part, people acquire *tsik* as they grow older, secure a stronger place in the community through service, and demonstrate a persistent moral lifestyle.

People in the village say *tsik* distinguishes Mopan from other ethnic groups and from animals. To lack *tsik* is to be like an animal, to ignore humanity's interdependency. In the village, some human actions, like incest or murder, are counter to *tsik* and can cause floods and other natural disasters (Danziger 1991). In this way, human actions affect the universe.

In many ways, *tsik* resembles the Mam notion of *naab'l* (Watanabe 1992). *Naab'l* is the awareness of the human community that a child develops as he grows up. Like *tsik*, a person must maintain *naab'l* by acting morally and refraining from destructive behavior. *Naab'l* distinguishes Mam from other ethnic groups and animals.

Watanabe (1992:89–92) suggests *naab'l* is like African American concepts of soul described by Charles Keil (1966). Both refer to a "shared way of being" rather than an essential characteristic. As with *tsik*, it is important to demonstrate *naab'l* rather than assume its existence.

Demonstrating and maintaining *naab'l* and *tsik* requires acting properly or morally. Maintaining *naab'l* conflicts with selfish ambition (Watanabe 1992:101–103), as maintaining *tsik* reins in violence, divisiveness, and self-seeking among Mopan (Danziger 1991:219).

Given the similarities between the Maya ideas of *tsik* and *naab'l,* it is possible that *tsik* greetings recognize and demonstrate respect for a connection between people's souls rather than the people themselves (Gregory 1975) or the relationship between them (Danziger 1991:216). Mopan *tsik* may have a greater supernatural component than anthropologists have previously recognized. The bonds created by *tsik* greetings may continue beyond death, at least for a short time after one of them has died.

Tsik *and a Daughter-in-Law's Love*

The lack of a formal *tsik* relationship between Michaela and Fidelia contributes to Cil's frustration and anger towards his wife. As Fidelia's biological son, bonds of *tsik* prevent him from showing his anger to her. Instead, he directs it, violently, toward his wife, trying to force her to "love" his mother. She refuses to show his biological mother respect.

Cil's violence to Michaela is similar to the violence Risa may suffer. It is based on her refusal to accept her role as a wife. Unlike Risa, Michaela happily participates in the exchange of work central to Mayan marriages. She works for her husband, and he works for her. She doesn't, however, "love" his mother.

Long-standing relationships, including some marked by *tsik,* often have a strong emotional component. In the village, people express these emotions by saying that they have "got used to" the other person. People most often refer to this comfortable feeling when talking about their spouse (Danziger 1991:93). It is this same emotion that Michaela fails to develop for Fidelia. It is what Cil, and some anthropologists (Eber 1995:195), choose to call "love."

Contributing to Michaela's lack of love for her mother-in-law, and Cil's violent reaction to her refusal even to try, is the ambiguity of her relationship to Fidelia. Cil is adopted, and therefore has two sets of parents. As is customary, he recognizes both, maintains *tsik* with both, and uses the proper *tsik* greeting when he sees any of them (Danziger 1991:75).

Michaela, however, has a *tsik* relationship only with his adoptive parents. They arranged her wedding and, more importantly, participated in the *ts'ah tsik* ceremony at the "engagement party," when the bride's father and the groom's father introduce their new daughter-in-law or son-in-law to their new affines. During this ceremony daughters-in-law and mothers-in-law make formal promises to treat each other well.

Since Cil's biological parents did not agree to the wedding, they did not participate in the *ts'ah tsik* ceremony. Michaela therefore only recognizes Cil's adoptive parents, Francesca and Mr. Coc, as her in-laws, and treats only them with respect. She stays at their house and works for them. Polite and cooperative, she is an ideal daughter-in-law. Likewise,

Francesca and Mr. Coc cooperate with and respect her. Importantly, Francesca treats Michaela kindly; she is not harsh in her criticisms, nor especially demanding. She is the ideal mother-in-law. They are bound together by *tsik*.

Cil's birth parents, Juan and Fidelia, do not treat Michaela with respect, *tsik*. Fidelia and Cil's sisters express their disrespect for Michaela when she tries to play the role of daughter-in-law in their home. They mock and tease her. Therefore, Michaela has difficulty developing a comfortable or loving relationship with Cil's biological kin.

When Cil beats Michaela to encourage her to love his mother, he is not forcing her to develop a formal *tsik* relationship. He simply wants her to try to "get used" to his parents, as a daughter-in-law should. However, she is not their daughter-in-law. Without a formal *tsik* relationship, they can easily reject her. Besides, she is forming a strong bond with Francesca, her mother-in-law, as she is supposed to do. The family politics surrounding the marriage arrangement makes a long-standing "loving" relationship with Cil's parents nearly impossible. The ambiguity of their relationship, as Cil's parents but not Michaela's in-laws, almost prevents it.

While Michaela's situation is somewhat peculiar, elements of her story are typical in any relationship between a woman and her husband's mother. The transformation of *tsik* into "love" is difficult to achieve for any set of in-laws.

After young men and their parents approach young women and their families to negotiate a marriage, the potential bride's family may discuss the suitor's mother and her relationships with her other daughters-in-law at length. If the young woman's family feels that her potential mother-in-law is too harsh, they will refuse the marriage offer. If they simply don't know what to think of her, they may accept the offer, but worry about how the two will get along, hoping *tsik* will turn to "love." As in Risa's case, a mother-in-law can cause problems between husband and wife. People often feel the daughter-in-law is at fault for being disrespectful. Her supposed disrespect justifies violence against her.

Lonely and Vengeful Spirits

Some husbands justify violence to wives for reasons beyond human respect and love. They feel their violence can prevent a spirit's more severe violence, since vengeful spirits can kill the disrespectful. Spirits can also kill children, because children have not yet developed respect for those around them. A spirit may be motivated to kill a child either through love or as revenge on its parents. A husband's violence can therefore protect the lives of both his disrespectful wife and vulnerable children.

Funerals and the treatment of dead bodies in the village resemble those of other Mayan groups: Chorti (Wisdom 1940:303–304), Quiche' (Burgos-DeBray 1984:201–202), Tzeltal (Nash 1970:131–135), and, to a lesser extent, Mam (Wagley 1949:46, Oakes 1969:44–50), Tzotzil (Guiteras-Holmes 1961:141), and Yucatec (Redfield and Villa Rojas 1934:200). Whether or not the funerary rites are similar, the survivors often perform activities to ensure that the spirit leaves the body and does not cause harm to the living (Guiteras-Holmes 1961:142–143, Redfield and Villa Rojas 1934:200, Redfield 1941:126, Vogt 1969:218, Wagley 1949:46, Nash 1970:132).

Spirits of the dead often want to take people they are close to with them into the spirit realm (Vogt 1969:218). In the village, people say such spirits try to "call" living spirits to go with them. They take great care to prevent such spirit loss. Ritual baths protect animals; garlic protects children. Even with these precautions, a spirit may sometimes cause an accident or create a fatal illness.

Children are the most susceptible to such accidents and illnesses because their souls are somewhat "loose" (Vogt 1969:184, 370, Eber 1995: 74, Watanabe 1992:87). Children's souls are often jiggled free when they fall, are startled, or suffer a fright (see Chapter 3: Another Legitimate Beating). For this reason, Justina does not take Ronny to the funeral. Fidelia's spirit may be searching for someone to accompany her. More importantly, it is why Maclovia gets bitten by a ground mole and why Hilaria frequently cries. Fidelia's spirit is calling to them, she is trying to loosen their souls and take them with her.

Francesca believes that spirits call to their children and others because they are lonely and desire company. Others have suggested that a mother's spirit wants to continue to care for its children. If my suggestion that *tsik* and *naab'l*/soul are connected is true, it may be easier to call the spirit of one's own children because the child's soul is loose and already linked to her parents. Indeed, while most people worry that any child may lose its soul during this time, those related to the deceased are in the greatest danger.

Spirits also call souls away in revenge. For Mam, a wife's spirit may seek revenge because she suspects her husband killed her in order to marry someone else (Wagley 1949:46). For Quiche', a murder victim may seek out the murderer (Nash 1970:132). For Tzotzil, the deceased may cause *"bik'tal 'ontonal* of the dead," a fatal illness which befalls both people with whom the deceased is angry at the time of death and children whose parents act immorally (Guiteras-Holmes 1961:136).

Similarly, Hilaria's soul is in danger of following Fidelia. Hilaria's bouts of sudden violent crying are evidence that her soul is in danger. Like the Mam widower who has found a new wife, Michaela needs to assure Fidelia that she did not facilitate her death. Furthermore, as Tzotzil would also say, someone must convince Fidelia not to be angry with Michaela. Francesca speaks on behalf of Michaela to explain to Fidelia that Michaela did not prevent her son from meeting his mother's needs. She must also tell Fidelia that Michaela acted respectfully, with *tsik,* even though the two did not have a formal *tsik* relationship. Michaela has *tsik.* If Fidelia is not convinced, Hilaria might die.

Mopan understand the complicated relationship between souls/spirits and the power of *tsik* to prevent vengeful violence to one's children. Therefore, wives know that it is dangerous not to demonstrate *tsik* to their mothers-in-law. They also try to develop a close, comfortable relationship with her beyond the formal *tsik* relationship. Without such a secure relationship a mother-in-law's spirit may seek revenge and kill her daughter-in-law or her grandchildren when she dies. Husbands also recognize the importance of fostering *tsik* and comfort between the mother and wife. If a husband sees problems arising he may, out of fear of his mother's vengeful spirit, beat his wife. Such a beating, he thinks, may encourage his wife to respect his mother.

Death, Responsibility, and Respect

> *He say he gonna stab me, but he didn't. I don't care. I'm not afraid for my life. I don't cry for my life. I don't care if I live.*
>
> "Justina" interview June 8, 1994

> *He tried to chop my foot with a machete, but I told him, "You can do that if you want. I don't care, it is you who will suffer. You can kill me if you want, I don't care."*
>
> "Erasma" interview September 2, 1994

Speaking of death, Rigoberta Menchu (Burgos-Debray 1984:201) says, "It's not something unknown that happens . . . ." Mopan in Belize also recognize death as part of life and speak of it matter-of-factly (Danziger

1991:95). This is not to say they care little if those around them live or die. Death is no trouble for those who die, but it makes life harder for those who survive them.

A woman's death is especially hard. Her children become motherless and her husband a widower. Widowers may be able to find another wife to complete the economic partnership that marriage entails. Children can never find another mother. No other woman whom her husband marries is obligated through *tsik* relationships to care for his children as she would care for her own. Without formal *tsik* relationships, mothers feel their children will almost inevitably suffer abuse.[1]

Women forced to give up children through adoption have these same fears (see Chapter 3: Another Legitimate Beating and Chapter 4: Daughters). It is fear of one's own death that causes mothers to encourage their children to "learn their work" early in life. At least then, they will be able to feed themselves (Danziger 1991:110,130).

Although women are fearful of what will happen to their children if they die, they speak of death often. They especially refer to their own death when speaking of their experiences with domestic violence. Quotes like those that open this section are common. In the United States, ambivalence toward one's own death signals desperation and severe depression. But that doesn't seem to be true for the women I met in the village, where people have a close understanding of the decay death brings and speak of it matter-of-factly.

Here, ambivalent comments about death have a different meaning. First, they act as reminders of the hardships of survival a man and his children will face if he kills his wife. Secondly, they point to the fact that he will be responsible for her murder. In this way, "I don't care" means "My death is your decision. It is your action." It is a reminder of the prevailing sense of individuality in the village that holds everyone accountable for their own deeds. It may also be a way to tell him that he is acting against *tsik*. Murder is quintessential non-*tsik* behavior (Danziger 1991:67). Talk of a wife's death at the hands of her husband emphasizes his lack of *tsik,* and the fact that his relationship to the rest of the village would be affected. It may also be a threat, a statement that her spirit could justifiably seek revenge. In this way, such statements warn violent husbands not to take violence too far.

Summary and Discussion

> *In these stories I'm trying to create spaces in which people are invited to enter into experiential relationships with events through which they themselves did not live. Through such spaces people may gain access to a range of processual, sensually immersed knowledges, knowledges which it would be difficult to acquire by purely cognitive means.* (Landesberg 1997:66)

These narratives allow an empathic or emotional understanding of domestic violence. They also provide a sense of the complexity that domestic violence entails. Each story tells of one or more women whose lives are touched by domestic violence. Each story presents a different understanding of the issues involved, the problems faced, and the solutions women create to endure, leave, or avoid abusive relationships altogether. These stories demonstrate that women's lives vary, even within a small village in southern Belize.

Yet, there are patterns to women's experiences. The analysis sections after each of the narratives placed the narrative's events into a Mayan context and expanded the reader's understanding of the issues involved. The conclusion now will grind the stories down, pull the data together, and describe the broad patterns of domestic violence among Mopan Maya in southern Belize. The summary occasionally discusses domestic violence elsewhere. The goal here is to reveal patterns, not to suggest universals.

Patterns of Mayan Domestic Violence

Mayan lifeways, like many others, allow for acts of domestic violence. As elsewhere, Mopan men rationalize their actions. In the village, the most common justification for wife beating is punishment for one or more of three offenses: laziness, infidelity, or disrespect for the husband's parents. Most Mayan acts of domestic violence, like domestic violence elsewhere, are a "physical reprimand" (Whiting as quoted in Brown 1992:2).

It is important to remember that these rationalizations are not based on fact, merely on suspicion or perception. In southern Belize, wives need not have committed these offenses for husbands to punish them. Instead, husbands abuse wives for offenses that they, or sometimes their mothers, perceive. Such perceptions may stem from actions only marginally akin to the alleged offense. For example, a husband may interpret a wife's walk alone through the village as a sign of adultery; or a mother-in-law may interpret a new bride's resistance to marriage as laziness, even though the bride works hard. Mayan husbands do not need solid proof of an offense to beat their wives.

Escape and Support: Newlyweds

The help available for women to escape abusive husbands varies. The greatest help is available to newly married women. Maya do not consider newlyweds as full adults. (This is one reason that parents feel it is important to arrange marriages.) The first few years after marriage are a training period: A woman learns to become a wife and a man learns to become a husband. The husband's parents and (to a lesser extent) the bride's parents monitor and guide the couple. Others, bound by fictive kinship (*compadrazgo*) and relationships of respect (*tsik*) may also keep an eye on the bride and groom. These fictive kin have a duty to the married couple and to the community to act as moral guides, explaining and demonstrating "what is good, and what is not good."

If a husband abuses his new bride, several people, including the bride's family, have a legitimate voice in determining whether she has committed an offense, and whether beating is the appropriate punishment. These monitors are likely to condemn excessive violence and condemn husbands who are drunk often, ignore the advice of others, or fail to discuss their wive's offenses with their families. Inappropriate or excessive violence is, for Maya, an offense in itself. The husband's wrongdoing allows the wife to garner support.

A husband-in-training may overlook his wife's offenses. He may not notice, for example, that she is lazy. His mother, however, as an adult responsible for teaching the bride her duties, is likely to notice. She may coax him into punishing his wife. First, however, she will negotiate with the bride's family and fictive kin. If they agree that she is at fault, they may first coax her to change her ways. In the end, they may legitimize violence against her.

Beatings at a mother-in-law's request are common in anthropological literature, especially in societies anthropologists consider patriarchal (Gallin 1992, Hegland 1992:213, Miller 1992:178–179, Wolf 1975). This pattern may fit within a general pattern of violence against women by women in patriarchy (Daly 1979:163–167, Campbell 1992:235). Such acts may increase a mother-in-law's prestige. Indeed, Mayan women legitimize their authority when they instigate violence against their daughters-in-law.

The situation may be more complicated, however. Chinese and Taiwanese forms of patriarchy provide women little security in their old age. Many feel they must secure a place for themselves within their son's household when they get old (Gallin 1992, Wolf 1975, 1985). As a daughter-in-law gains more power in the household, she may reject the old woman, reserving scarce resources for herself and her children. When a mother-in-law fights with her daughter-in-law and urges her son to beat his wife over issues of household duties, the mother reminds her son that she has cared for him well his whole life. Her care for him obligates him to care for her in her old age, whether or not the daughter-in-law agrees.

This same concern appears evident with some Mayan mothers-in-law. Older people fear that their children will "forget" them and fail to care for them in their old age. They also fear that daughters-in-law will divert resources they were relying on for their old age. Ensuring obligations by playing familial politics is common in the village. Beliefs about vengeful spirits add to people's worries. Many Maya feel that a mother-in-law's spirit can cause misfortune after her death, especially if, in life, she felt her son or daughter-in-law disrespected her or did not provide for her in her times of need.

The Mayan age hierarchy makes it difficult to garner support when the mother-in-law instigates beatings. *Comadres* and *compadres* may try to appeal to her to give the bride more time to "learn her work." However, the decision is hers. She is an adult responsible for her own actions, her own *tsik,* and her own reputation. Some women are reputed to be particularly cold-hearted mothers-in-law. Parents take this reputation into consideration when arranging marriages for their daughters. Building a marriage is building social alliances and obligations. Most parents hope to connect themselves and their daughters to people with *tsik,* people who work toward maintaining a cohesive society. If a bride's parents feel a mother-in-law is incorrigibly abusive, they may, on rare occasions, cancel the marriage altogether.

Abused wives have a hard time leaving husbands, even temporarily, if their family of origin feels they lack means to support her, for example if a woman's father has passed away, drinks excessively, is sick, or if her mother has never married. In these cases, the daughter's marriage often permits her family to gain some economic support or at least lessen their burden. Such families are a little less concerned with the *tsik* of those to whom the marriage ties them. Young brides in this situation are unlikely to gain support for leaving an abusive husband or mother-in-law.

Support for Mothers

As a marriage ages and the couple begins to have children, people begin to think of the two as adults. The couple may move out of the groom's parents' house and into a house nearby. Parents and fictive kin are now less likely to give advice or participate in negotiations about legitimacy of violence. Even if they do, the husband, now an adult, is less obliged to listen. Mayan adults are responsible for their own actions and should know "what is good, and what is not good." Adults are moral; they must build and maintain *tsik.* Ideally, both husband and wife should fully engage in the mutual service and respect that is marriage. It is their business if they don't.

In many societies women are less likely to be beaten if they are considered autonomous adults (Brown 1992:11). However, for Maya there is a transitional period that is the most difficult time for women suffering abuse. A newlywed woman is not a full adult, but she is under the protective eye of her in-laws, parents, and *comadre/compadre.* During this time many people will intervene if she suffers abuse. Later, when she has "learned her work as a wife" and has had her first child, her community recognizes her adulthood. However, she loses the protection she once had, partially because she moves into her own home, away from witnesses. She is young, with few *tsik* relationships, few connections in the community with people obligated to help her. She also has less authority than an older woman. Adulthood, for women, creates a level of isolation that newlywed "youngsters" do not have.

Although fewer people are likely to help her, some will. Aledora's brothers encouraged her to leave her husband and wanted to retaliate for the violence she suffered. Likewise, Francesca encouraged Justina to leave Martino. People respond to the pain of people they love. They just might not as easily see the problem. Mayan understanding of illness and health contributes to their inability to recognize abuse because it discourages women from talking about it. Believing that illness results, at least partially, from strong, upsetting emotions and worry, many women are unwilling to discuss their abuse with others. Most, however, do not hide their abuse, either. It is up to others to ask or to recognize the problem on their own.

Another reason young adult women have difficulties getting help is that their adulthood comes with the birth of the first child. Children make it difficult to leave an abusive husband. In Mayan patrilineal descent, children "belong" to their fathers; departing mothers are expected to leave their children behind. Many resist leaving them for fear that, if the husband remarries, the new stepmother may neglect or abuse her stepchildren. *Tsik* does not bind stepparents to stepchildren.

A mother who takes her children with her is less likely to get support from those who might have supported her before she had them. Housing and feeding a young woman is much easier than housing and feeding a young woman and her children. Also, if she takes her children, others may feel she is, in a sense, stealing from her husband. People are therefore less likely to help her.

A mother can arrange to "give" or "lend" her children to people whom she trusts will treat them well. But again, *tsik* does not bind the "foster" parents to the children. Furthermore, fosterage arrangements by a mother do not necessarily prevent her husband from trying to collect his children at a later date.

The mother may try to support herself and her children alone. However, small children impede a woman's attempts to perform "man's work": clearing, planting, and harvesting crops. These tasks are necessary for survival. If the children are old enough to help in the fields, life is somewhat easier. However, to live as a single mother is often to live in hunger and poverty. For some women, seeking another man is problematic, since her new husband may mistreat her or her children.

Mothers, therefore, have few resources and many fears which impede their ability to leave abusive husbands. Ideas of health, harmony, and what it means to be a "good" wife also contribute to a woman's decision to stay with an abusive husband. These ideological traps, however, can provide some women with enough psychological support to endure a husband's abuse. Friends and fictive kin may reassure her that she is a "good" wife and that she has done nothing to cause her husband's violence. Their support may allow her to position herself as morally superior to her abusive husband. The feeling of moral superiority can help her to "suffer through" her abuse. If others recognize her moral superiority, it may encourage the abusive husband to realize his violence is wrong.

Real Offenses

Women who have committed an offense, like Justina caught with her lover, also have a difficult time garnering support to leave their punishing husbands. Again, the Mayan pattern resembles the Taiwanese one (Gallin 1992) and the Bun of New Guinea (McDowell 1992): A young woman's male kin may help her husband beat her rather than come to her aid, in order to protect the alliance between the families that the marriage created (Gallin 1992). For Maya, this may be especially true if the woman comes from a relatively poor family who cannot support her return and who gain from the alliance that the marriage creates. Justina's *compadre* urged her husband to beat her to maintain male control over female sexuality. All of his responses to Justina's offense—taking her to the clinic and having her tested for sexually transmitted diseases, scaring her with the possibility of AIDS, urging her husband to beat her, and beating his own innocent wife—are forms of sexual terrorism, acts meant to control a woman's behavior, especially her sexuality, by using fear of sexuality (Sheffield 1984).

Generally, however, Mopan women's ability to gain support for leaving their husbands, or even to receive emotional support, rests on their ability to show that the punishment is excessive. Few men forgive adultery. Women sometimes do. A sexual division of support in the face of adultery is common in the village. Other offenses, like laziness and failure to respect a husband's family, are more ambiguous, and support is less likely to split along gender lines.

An abused wife may also garner support if she can show that her husband's abuse hurts her children physically or spiritually. A man carried away with his violence may strike a child, causing physical harm. He may also frighten the child badly enough to jolt all or part of its spirit/ soul loose, perhaps causing the child severe diarrhea or even death. Others consider a man who harms his children in his attempts to punish his wife to be out of control. Losing control is dangerous to society and an offense in itself.

Endurance and Respect

Generally, in the village people urge women to stay married, even to abusers. Sympathetic and supportive family members or fictive kin usually provide only temporary "escape." People generally believe that violent men will eventually see that their behavior is disrespectful and disruptive of human relationships and ultimately threatening to human survival. It is a woman's job to be patient and to guide him gently toward respectful behavior. Indeed, many women gain the strength to endure abuse from this belief.

For some, waiting, enduring, and hoping seem to pay off. Older women suffer much less abuse than younger ones. Indeed, older women seem less likely to suffer domestic abuse in many societies (Brown 1992: 10), at least partially because, in many societies, as women get older they develop many community connections. Older Mayan women tend to serve many people as *comadre*, a relationship that gives them authority and respect. This respect is verified each time a person greets them with a formal *tsik* greeting. Such authority may undermine their husband's authority to punish them.

Indeed, even though men also gain authority and respect as they age, maintaining *tsik* requires them to behave respectfully. Excessive violence and drinking endanger *tsik* and reduce the likelihood that others will ask a man to serve as *compadre*, an important source of political and economic alliances and prestige. However, few people point these facts out to their neighbors. Few people will tell a man he is too violent. A man must mind his own *tsik*. Again, every adult is responsible for his own actions.

Young Women's Revolt, New Opportunities, and Identity

The women I met in the village felt that suffering domestic violence distinguished them from white American women. This is not to say that they passively accept beatings as their lot. They do not. Rather, it is to say that they feel they suffer more domestic violence than white women. No one believed me when I talked about the extent of the problem in the United States.

Certainly Creole and Garifuna prejudices against Mayan men and women in Belize contribute to both Maya and non-Maya belief that wife abuse is integral to Mopan life. Non-Maya Belizeans think of Mayan women as "being down," suffering great oppression by Mayan men, lacking the knowledge and the courage they need to "rise themselves up." Garifuna women's relatively great abilities to escape and prevent wife abuse (Kerns 1992) certainly contribute to these beliefs. However, in Belize, as in other parts of the world, emphasizing Mopan women's oppression is part of a tendency to portray indigenous and non-Western peoples as inferior to those ethnic groups in power.

Mopan women have been taking action to "rise themselves up." Gregory (1987) uses the term "young women's revolt" to discuss the gender changes that he saw taking place in the 1970s. During his field stay in southern Belize, several women rejected the husbands their parents chose for them. Several others sought economic freedom through occupations outside their homes, namely seamstresses, nurses, and shopkeepers.

The term "revolt" is somewhat misleading, since it suggests an organized rebellion. Current gender changes in the villages occur in a context of other changes that began with the construction of roads connecting rural villages to the district capital. These roads provided easier access to economic opportunities, allowing young men to make money and gain prestige due to economic savvy. These young men "revolted" against the age-based prestige and political system and seized control over the alcaldeship. Gregory (1987) suggests a similar "revolt" may be in the making as women are beginning to seize greater control of their lives from men.

Today, the young women's revolt continues in the sense that gender relations are continuing to change and young women are moving toward changing them even further. The "revolt" consists of individual women slowly redefining what being a Mayan woman means. Many are inspired by non-Maya, such as government workers, who have lived in the United States and are educated about the women's movement there.

Arranged marriages are rare in the 1990s. Women marry in their late teens, certainly by age twenty-five; their mothers married at fourteen. Mothers and siblings sometimes encourage young women to stay home and enjoy their lives before they marry. Both mothers and sisters benefit from having older daughters/sisters who stay at home to help with household chores. Mothers sometimes use stories of domestic violence to frighten their daughters into delaying or avoiding marriage altogether.

There are still only a few seamstresses and female shopkeepers in the village. However, more economic opportunities are open to women now than in the 1970s. The Belizean government designs development projects to give women, both married and unmarried, more economic freedom. While most projects are home-based (raising chickens, making baskets), many require travel outside of the home (grinding corn) or village (selling baskets). Maya restrictions on female travel often prevent women from participating fully. Jealous husbands often see their wives' travel as "looking for another man" and retaliate with physical abuse. The tendency for such projects to focus solely on women, ignoring the importance Maya place on economic teamwork and mutual respect between married couples, upsets men. As a result unmarried and widowed women tend to participate more frequently in development projects which require them to leave the house than do married or young single women. Women, young and old, are still vulnerable sometimes to sexual and domestic violence because of their involvement in the government's strategies to "rise them up."

Older single women, widowed or never married, without husbands to "get jealous" tend to act as chairladies for women's groups. However, such a woman needs to be careful not to encourage salacious gossip. Rumors of sexual promiscuity will erode respect for her, discourage other women from associating with her, and affect her ability to serve as *comadre*.

Young women participate in women's groups by making baskets. Few get involved in marketing or acting as chairlady. One exception is the sewing project which the government designed to teach young, unmarried women how to run sewing machines. During my stay in the village, the government appointed a young woman as chair. Unfortunately, she was involved in a nationwide scandal. The young girl went into hiding, her reputation ruined. As Francesca said, "She'll never find a husband."

Many women also "job out," seeking employment outside the village. "Jobbing out" provides women another means for economic independence. Young widows and childless women who have left, or been abandoned by, their husbands most often take this route. Employment for uneducated women is often menial and low paying. Employers sometimes justify their exploitation of young women by saying that they are at least giving them some cash, and that some cash is better than none. Some young women agree, until they realize they are not making enough money to make ends meet outside of the village. Women vary in their understanding of exploitation and how much money it takes to live in a cash economy.

Some young women "job out" to help their mothers escape domestic violence. One young woman sought employment out of the village in hopes of saving enough money to return to the village and build a home for her and her mother. Her father had been abusing her mother for several years. Once, she told me, she knocked her father out with a rock, to stop him from beating her mother unconscious. She felt that if she could build a home herself, she and her mother could abandon her father.

More young women go to high school now than in the 1970s. Government workers, schoolteachers, and popular culture encourage young women to seek education. Many young women feel the experience will help them avoid marrying a jealous or violent husband. They say high school provides them a means to interact with non-Maya, which helps both boys and girls to "see how others do things." For the most part, they are referring to courtship. Girls feel that getting to know a boy before marriage helps them not to marry a violent husband. The experience of going to school also makes boys less vulnerable to violent jealousy, they think.

Education also increases opportunities for employment. Most parents who send their daughters to school consider education and marriage mutually incompatible. Going to school instead of having babies has become another means to gain adulthood.

People tolerate schoolgirls' deviation from expected social roles. A young woman attending high school can chat with young men or travel alone, to an extent, without fear of salacious gossip. A young marriageable woman in the village can do neither. People accept new gender roles for some, not all.

This tolerance rides on the young woman's ability to juggle old gender roles with new ones: not only school girls but also young women who participate in government projects and those who job out as well. They must blend traditional self-presentation with the demands of teachers, employers, and government workers who oversee development projects.

Some women do not even try to balance these demands. Instead, they reject Mayan identity and avoid activities that symbolize their ethnicity. Often their parents encourage them, especially mothers who feel that Mayan culture oppresses women. Many such women have had extensive contact with people outside of the village.

Rejecting Mayan identity is not just a psychological concern, however. Maya in southern Belize are involved in a struggle to secure resources, primarily land, from the government. As identity becomes problematic, so does their ability as a group to secure such resources. If too many people reject being Maya, the government may decrease the amount of land reserved for Maya (see Chapter 1 for more on the struggle for land rights). Sometimes, non-Maya helping Mayan women to "rise themselves up" undercuts cultural survival.

The Future

Many young women feel their new opportunities will help them avoid abusive relationships. It is difficult to say whether or not their optimism is justified. Many of these new opportunities take young women out of the village. I have little data on whether women who follow the new paths actually suffer less violence. I do, however, have some thoughts and cautions.

Not all Mayan women have the same opportunities in southern Belize. Relatively few go to high school, "job out," or participate in government development projects. Seeking employment outside the village requires a place to stay, and thus having contacts outside. Often young women stay with older brothers who have left the village. Otherwise, it is difficult to leave the village. Going to school usually requires having a sister who cannot go. It also requires having parents who are supportive and able to pay the bills. Young women who can participate in the new opportunities can delay or avoid arranged marriages. They can also, to some extent, gain control of their own sexuality and reduce the threats that gossip makes to their reputations and the threats that men make to their bodies.

Changes in gender relations are slower to reach young women who are unable to follow new opportunities. Maya are tolerant of the gender changes, but not always accepting. Acceptable and expected behavior is specific to a young woman's status. Even if the new opportunities affect gender relations in a way that reduces domestic violence, not everyone benefits. Old gender roles remain. The decrease in arranged marriages is an exception. Women's economic freedom correlates cross-culturally with low rates of domestic violence (Levinson 1989:72–76). However, in pursuing freedom, women may lose other institutionalized deterrents to severe violence.

For example, in Chamula (Rosenbaum 1993), daughters who arrange their own marriages get little help from their parents if their husbands become abusive. The parents do not feel the marriage is any of their business. Arranged marriages in Chamula build connections between people, supplying a newlywed with a support group. Marriages arranged by the couple do not.

Likewise, among Tzeltal in Chiapas, Mexico, cash payments are beginning to replace bride service (whereby the new husband works for the bride's parents for a certain period). These cash payments serve the same function, however. They are "gifts," symbols of connectedness, not purchases which negate connectedness (Siverts 1993).

In the village, arranged marriages are becoming uncommon. However, daughters and sons still seek parental approval for marriage, so that parents feel responsible for the marriage and obligated to help when something goes wrong. Newlyweds also still seek *comadres* and *compadres* as moral guides for the marriage, again obligating others to surveil the marriage.

Isolation potentiates domestic violence (Dobash and Dobash 1979; Gelles and Straus 1988, Brown 1992). In the United States, isolation stems from neolocal postmarital residence and respect for family privacy.

Although Mayan newlyweds are not isolated, this lack of isolation does not deter domestic violence. In fact, it may contribute to violence, as in Risa's case. Still, there are usually several witnesses, several voices to negotiate whether or not a woman committed an offense and, if so, what punishment might be proper. Women can garner support, especially from their female kin. This support allows some women to leave abusive husbands, at least temporarily. It can also delegitimate male violence. Many men curb their violence in response. As Brown (1992:12) says, for a wife, "there's safety in numbers."

After her first child, a woman can preserve her escape routes by making and keeping connections outside of her marriage, mostly through service. She returns home on occasion to help her mother cook for her father's work party, she works for siblings and in-laws preparing food for important occasions, and she develops friendships with her husband's female kin. As she ages, her ties to her community multiply inextricably. She earns respect, status, and support through living and serving as *comadre*. It becomes harder and harder for a man to justify violence against her. A woman's embeddedness in her community may protect her from male violence.

I do not know whether women living outside the village will be able to participate significantly in *compadrazgo*. "Jobbing out" or going to school pulls them out of the community. It is difficult for them to develop good reputations or take on *tsik* relationships. Thus, gaining economic freedom in the ways now available to Mayan women in southern Belize may isolate them, making them more vulnerable to abuse. It may also expose them to new kinds of abuse globalization has brought women elsewhere (Nash and Safa 1986, Greider 1997).

Women's economic independence and the decline in arranged marriages might change family dynamics, as in Taiwan, where couples share a greater mutual emotional commitment now than when marriages were arranged. Furthermore, the greater availability of wage employment in Taiwan has provided young women with more "private funds" than previous generations enjoyed. Both these changes have raised the status of newlywed women (Gallin 1992). Specifically, wives get more support from their husbands in confrontations with their mothers-in-law. The emotional commitment wives now have gives a more secure place in the household. These changes have decreased the violence mothers-in-law instigate (Gallin 1992).

However, a wife's income is not absolute insurance against domestic violence. Indeed, Gallin (1992) discusses a case in Taiwan where a husband and a bride's family used violence to gain control of the "private funds" she earned while single. Nor does maintaining control over cash ensure against domestic violence. Among Tzotzil Maya, women's growing access to cash through marketing weavings globally is disrupting traditional gender roles. Women are now able to bring more resources into the household than their husbands, allowing them more influence in the household. However, as wives are gaining more influence, husbands are becoming uncomfortable, increasing what Eber (1995) calls "marital conflict."

Status-inconsistency theory seems to explain this dynamic. People use violence to compensate for inconsistencies between their actual position in society and the position that society prescribes for them. In other words, in a society with a patricentric gender hierarchy, men beat their wives if their wives threaten the gender hierarchy. In Chenalho, wives threaten the gender hierarchy by earning more money than their husbands.

It is important to note that, in Chenalho, women can decrease conflict by appealing to traditional gender roles. They remind their husbands that it is a wife's duty to serve her family and her community. By participating in the weaving cooperative, wives mean to serve. They are not interested in gaining power and prestige. These women ward off violence by defining their actions as traditional community service, respectful of ideal gender roles.

The Best of Both Worlds

The future of the "young women's revolt" is unclear. Young women will probably continue to participate in development projects, continue their education, and "job out." How many will do so, and to what degree these activities will change gender relations and for whom are questions I cannot answer. It is also unclear if these changes in gender relations will decrease rates of domestic violence. As Campbell (1992:233) points out:

> it is not possible to identify simple linear causative factors of wife-battering that can easily be remedied once they are identified. As is true of most human behavior, the use of violence has complex causes that include an interplay of individual, contextual, and societal forces.

It seems, however, that there is a heavy responsibility resting on young Mopan women. Their younger sisters look to them to help redefine what it means to be a Mayan woman. Many look specifically to see how others manage to avoid abusive relationships.

The degree to which young women will be able to escape, avoid, or endure domestic violence in the future depends, at least partially, on their ability to maintain alliances and build support systems like those which traditionally arose from *compadrazgo*.

Compadrazgo has been changing in the village for a long time. Many seek *comadres/compadres* who can provide economic support rather than moral guidance. For this reason, many seek *comadres/compadres* who are non-Maya living outside of the village. As more women leave the village to seek employment, people may look to them to serve as *comadres*.

But people do not usually ask single women to serve as *comadre*. Such requests are an honor given to a couple, not to an individual. Maya understandings of marriage as a complementary union fit directly into the Mayan emphasis on human interconnections. Marriage opens one up to gain *tsik* and enhance one's embeddedness in the community. To honor people who are not involved in this basic relationship is difficult. Moreover a person should have a good reputation to serve as *comadre*. Those who deny their Mayan identity or reject traditional Mayan lifeways cannot be honored. In fact, their actions may make it difficult for parents to allow their daughters to go to school, seek jobs outside of the village, or even participate in government projects.

Several Mopan women understand this problem. They have set about redefining Mayan womanhood. Trying to balance the old with the new, they are also trying to gain respect in the community. The more women successfully forge such new identities, the more gender relations will change, and the changed gender status might affect young women who stay in the village without taking advantage of new opportunities.

There is no sure way to decrease domestic violence. However, preventing isolation, in all its forms, and increasing women's status by increasing their economic freedom and allowing them to choose their own mates are promising places to begin. These goals must be met without disrespecting tradition, especially those aspects of tradition that connect women to other members of the community.

Epilogue: Milling Data

THE VANISHING RED   (Robert Frost:1916)

He is said to have been the last Red Man
In Acton. And the Miller is said to have laughed—
If you like to call such a sound a laugh.
But he gave no one else a laughter's license.
For he turned suddenly grave as if to say,
"Whose business,—if I take it on myself,
Whose business—but why talk round the barn?—
When it's just that I hold with getting a thing done with."

You can't get back and see it as he saw it.
It's too long a story to go into now.
You'd have to have been there and lived it.
Then you wouldn't have looked on it as just a matter
Of who began it between the two races.

Some guttural exclamation of surprise
The Red Man gave in poking about the mill
Over the great big thumping shuffling mill-stone,
Disgusted the Miller physically as coming
From one who had no right to be heard from.

"Come, John," he said, "you want to see the wheel pit?"

He took him down below a cramping rafter,
And showed him, through a manhole in the floor,
The water in desperate straits like frantic fish,
Salmon and sturgeon, lashing with their tails.
Then he shut down the trap door with a ring in it
That jangled even above the general noise,
And came up stairs alone—and gave that laugh,
And said something to a man with a meal-sack
That the man with the meal-sack didn't catch—then.
Oh, yes, he showed John the wheel pit all right.

Grinding Corn and Feeding Husbands

My little plastic bucket is tucked under my arm again, and I am walking down to the mill house. Dionesia is gone, Erasma is not here. It's a different mill house than the one I visit in the village. This one is run by a man. His machine is big and shiny.

I smile, but he says nothing. I hold out my bucket and try to make a joke. "Yes, I have enough corn for two husbands." But he doesn't laugh.

Without a word he dutifully takes the bucket and dumps the corn onto the scale's pan. He weighs it, smells it to be sure it is not spoiled, and finally puts one kernel to his mouth to taste it. Then he scribbles a few notes in his account book.

Diligently, he starts the machine. He turns the crank until the engine's rhythm is steady. This machine doesn't sputter, not even at first. The machine in the village sputters all the time. Sputter and moan, sputter and moan. But this machine is well tuned, well maintained. This machine is well greased.[1]

Slowly, he adds my corn to the hopper. I can hear it scream as it hits the blades, as it is ground down into cold pale *masa*. The sound makes me shudder. So harsh. So loud.

He adds a little water to help it pass through his machine, so it doesn't scream so much. I will add water, too, later, to make it soft, pliable, easier to work with. Yes, I will add water, too.

When the *masa* is done, he puts it back into my bucket and hands it to me. It seems smaller than it was as corn. I look back up at him and nod. Is he smiling? Is that a tiny upward curl in the corner of his mouth? I smile back, but he says nothing.

The *masa* is heavy. It is enough to feed two husbands. Two different husbands. One is stoic. He hides his emotions, doesn't want to burden people with them; he doesn't even want people to know he has them. He works so hard, this husband, to be straightforward in his dealings with people. He knows a lot and people respect him for it. He is a good man.

The other is a good man, too. He likes to tell stories, especially about people he has met and things he has seen. His stories are almost like parables. They don't have morals, but they tell you much more than you might think. About people, about life. About humanity. People enjoy his stories.

Yes, maybe I will try to feed two husbands.

Throughout this book I have patted out my data to make sustenance to feed two husbands: standard ethnography and narrative ethnography. For each husband, I have transformed my data, analyzing it, struggling with the best way to present it. Like corn, data needs transformation in order to feed a husband. Academic traditions, the miller and his machine, help us to transform it.

When writing, you must use the conventions set before you. Standard ethnography and narrative ethnography each have their own conventions. Your mother-in-law, someone you have just met, someone with authority over you, will teach you how to do your work for each husband. She will teach you the conventions, the way her son likes things done. When you are done writing, your work helps support you and your husband. This system of mutual support can land you a job. It is the same for both husbands. Each may support you, if you support him.

What I am discovering now, however, as I sit here thinking about what I wrote, is what my friends in the village tried to tell me. You can't have two husbands. You can't be a part of two traditions. You might think everything is fine, that everything is balanced, that both are happy. In the end, however, you must choose. If you keep two husbands, one, maybe both, will lash you.

At least it felt like a lashing when I was trying to imagine what a conclusion would look like. I could only get so far before I realized that what I was writing for one husband went against the goals I had set out for myself with the other husband. It is difficult to keep people front and center: to provide a means for readers to develop emotional understanding, to rehumanize studies of domestic violence, and at the same time to state clear and simple facts and to develop a clear theoretical model for understanding domestic violence cross-culturally. Each time this realization came over me, it sent me back to square one, confused, humbled. How do I satisfy both in the end? I felt as though I had to decide which one to keep and which to divorce.

When I compromised the goals of the storyteller, it felt as if the academic miller became the miller in Robert Frost's poem "The Vanishing Red." Racist, dutifully seeing to it himself that the last Red Man is gone forever. The *masa* from his machine doesn't taste good to me.

It doesn't seem nutritious, either. It is as if he has ground the corn too fine or has added too much water. If the miller adds too much water, to quiet the screams, whatever is made with that *masa* just sticks to the grill and is hard to get off. The grill, the theories we use to understand human phenomena like domestic violence, can consume the data, leaving little for us to chew on. It feels as if we haven't learned anything new, and we have done a lot of damage in the meantime. The storyteller's goals are more important to me, but I felt I needed to write a conclusion that followed the tradition of standard ethnography.

Narrative Ethnography: A Sympathetic Miller

I hope that, in writing a standard ethnographic conclusion, I haven't compromised my attempt to humanize our scholarly understanding of domestic violence. I wanted this work to provide the emotional understanding that social science usually does not address. My hope is that at least one character in these narratives affects the reader the way the people I met in the village affected me. In the village, empathy was integral to my attempts to understand domestic violence and therefore, I feel, should be a part of my readers' understandings as well.

The narrative form allows me to elicit such understandings by letting me focus on people rather than abstractions. The narrative form allows room to present the ways social trends and norms affect people's lives, while those lives, in turn, affect the trends and norms. This presentation of "agency" through narrative is important to understanding not only how culture works, but how women help themselves endure, leave, or prevent spousal abuse. Each woman is different; each has access to different resources and develops different strategies to respond to her husband's violence. Presenting such variation helps avoid the impression that all battered women are alike.

The narrative form also illustrates the complexity of issues surrounding domestic violence. The emotions involved in leaving an abusive partner, the processes by which people legitimize violence, the ways men control women's sexuality, women's fears about adoption, the importance of work and respect, the complex relationships between mothers-in-law and newly married brides, how childbirth defines adult status, the limited employment and economic options for everyone in the village—all of these issues converge in women's lives. Narrative ethnography provides the best way to represent the ways these issues complicate each other, without imposing false orderliness, false simplicity. It does not make the problems seem easy to overcome.

Narrative ethnography has another benefit as well. It allows me to represent myself,[2] thereby communicating to the reader the ways I came to know what I know about Mayan domestic violence. I am a character in these narratives. Like the other characters, I also have "agency." I respond to, interpret, and act on the events around me. Likewise, those around me respond to my presence, interpret my actions, and act on the events I initiate. The reader sees how my responses, interpretations, and actions helped to mold the more distanced observations I present in the analysis sections. Perhaps in this way the narratives humanize the analysis sections.[3]

Human complexity. This is what I hope my narratives have contributed to anthropology and to domestic-violence studies. I fear that further analysis would remove the human complexity from my data. Indeed, it is this fear of losing the complexity that makes me uncomfortable with grinding the data any finer.

List of Main Characters

In alphabetical order by first name

Aledora—Erasma's oldest daughter. She is married and living in Pueblo Viejo.

Angela—Francesca's newest adoption; Cil's oldest child. She is a beautiful, bright, and wiggly seven-year-old.

Antonia—a thin woman in her thirties. A chronic gossip. Antonia is the woman who tries to sell me baskets in the Introduction.

Cil—see Graciliamo

Mr. Coc—a wealthy shopkeeper in his sixties. Mr. Coc and his wife Francesca have adopted Graciliamo, Justina, and Angela. He is a traditional-minded man who works hard raising cacao. He loves to tell folk tales.

Damiana—Francesca's aunt, Evarista's sister. She is in her seventies and wears traditional *p'ik* and *camesa*. She speaks only Mopan.

Dionesia Sho—the chairlady of the women's cooperative corn grinder. She is in her late forties and has a horsey smile. Dionesia has never married. She is Olive's mother. Dionesia wears the newer traditional dress, but less frilly and bright than most women wear. She is critical of traditional ways, especially traditional marriages and gender roles.

Erasma—a large, fun-loving woman, graceful and generous. She is the widowed mother of fourteen children. Erasma is a hard-working woman interested in trying new foods and new ways of making money. In her late fifties, she wears traditional garb.

Evangelista—Modesto's mother and Risa's mother-in-law. A severe, handsome woman concerned for her children's welfare. Although in her early fifties, she wears traditional *camesa* and *p'ik*, the dress more common for elderly women.

Evarista—Francesca's mother. This seventy-year-old woman is a midwife and a traditional healer specializing in children's diseases. She moves slowly, with precision. Evarista wears *camesa* and *p'ik* as do most elderly women.

Felicia—an attractive nineteen-year-old girl. Felicia is the primary caretaker of her brother, Innocente, and the youngest daughter of Erasma.

Fidelia Pop—a woman in her late forties who has recently died. She is Mr. Coc's sister-in-law and Cil's biological mother. She was a generous, attentive woman with many friends.

Francesca—a plump good-natured woman in her fifties. Although childless, Francesca has raised several adopted children (Graciliamo, Justina, and Angela), indulging them with gifts and praise in return for hard work. She is married to Mr. Coc. Although she never wears the old style clothing for women (*camesa* and *p'ik*), she is proud of Maya tradition.

Graciliamo (Cil)—Francesca's first adopted child. Cil is a handsome, arrogant police constable in his early thirties. Angela, Francesca's most recent adoption, is Cil's eldest child. Sylvia is his second daughter. Michaela (Mik) is his wife. Cil is one of Justina's "godparents." Graciliamo is Fidelia's natural son.

Innocente (Cente)—Erasma's youngest child. He is physically and mentally handicapped.

Juan Chiac—Cil's father; Fidelia's devoted husband. A handsome man in his early fifties.

Justina (Tina)—a young, thin, beautiful woman of eighteen. She is married to Martino. They have a bright young girl, Ronny.

Leona—a quiet, hard-working woman married to Prim. She has several children, including a daughter in high school. Leona comes from a poor family.

Martino—a large, strong young man married to Justina. Martino has a history of violence. His gentle smile and soft voice are attractive and convey his sweeter side.

Michaela (Mik)—Cil's wife. A 27-year-old, light-skinned, gentle woman. Mik's smile is a delight. She has just given birth to another girl child, Hilaria.

Modesto—a young, hard-working man who has returned to the village after working several years in Belize City. His parents arranged for him to marry Risa.

Olive Tzir—a young Maya woman critical of Mayan tradition. She is devoted to helping her community. She wears shorts and T-shirts as Creole girls do. She is Dionesia's daughter.

Prim—a successful shopkeeper in his forties. He is a friendly, amiable man.

Remalda—Risa's mother. An attractive, graceful woman in her mid-forties.

Risa—Francesca's nineteen-year-old granddaughter. Risa is shy, somewhat reserved, yet giggly. She is Remalda's daughter, and Prudencia and Amelia's sister. She has just married Modesto in a traditional arranged marriage.

Ronny (Veronica)—Justina's first-born child.

Rosa—Erasma's sister-in-law and neighbor. A talkative woman in her late fifties.

Sylvia—Cil's four-year-old. Sylvia has bright round eyes and a sweet disposition. Like most children her age, she is often sick. Mik, her mother, likes to dress her in frilly dresses.

Tomasa — Olive's friend. She was widowed at eighteen.

Tommy Cho — one of Erasma's older children. A member of the Belize Defense Force. He is unmarried.

Vernon Cayetano — a dark Creole man with a resonating voice. He serves as police constable in the village.

Notes

Introduction

1. Counts (1992:xi) mentions that some of her colleagues expressed concerns similar to Erchack's (1994). That is, anthropologists should not exploit their hosts' hospitality. She also mentions that some fear that their host community may deny them future reentry if they publish anything about domestic violence. Others fear that their informants might be punished for discussing such things with outsiders.

Interestingly, one colleague told Counts that she is trying to publish several fictionalized accounts of wife abuse she learned about while conducting extensive fieldwork in Africa. She is writing under a pseudonym. She feels that writing fiction may prevent her informants from being punished for speaking.

2. Although no one told me that women sometimes retaliate against violence with violence, Danziger (1991:93) reports that they do.

3. The term "ethnographic realism" has come to mean several different things. Marcus and Cushman (1982) use it to refer to the standard ethnographic style anthropologists have used for the past sixty or so years. For them it is an approach which tries to express an entire way of life, either through a holistic analysis of a single phenomenon or through a careful disengaged description of universal categories of experience such as kinship, economy, religion, and material culture. Ethnographic realism is a special, limited form of the realism of nineteenth-century literature. Limited, because it lacks the irony common to nineteenth-century realist fiction. These limitations, they argue, come from anthropology's scientism. Others prefer the term "ethnographic naturalism" to refer to this limited scientific form of realism (Marcus and Fischer 1986:180, fn5).

Lewis' use of "ethnographic realism" seems to be more in line with the way it is used in reference to nineteenth-century fiction. He believes that his style gives a more complete picture of the life of Mexican peasants. He also constructs his authority by being an eyewitness. Lewis' use of the term more accurately describes what I am doing, than Marcus and his colleagues' terminology.

4. John O. Stewart uses the phrase "ethnographic narratives," as in the title of his book *Drinkers, Drummers and Decent Folks: Ethnographic Narratives of Village Trinidad* (1988).

5. Kluckhohn's quote comes from an essay on the merits of life histories and other forms of "subjective data" for developing ethnographic understandings. While this quote implies that literature can provide greater understandings of the subjective factors that comprise humanity, he does not directly advocate anthropologists' use of literary devices. Indeed, his solution for dealing with the inconsistencies common to people's thoughts, feelings, and motivations and anthropologists' representation of these complexities is that, as social scientists, we need to develop our field methodology.

Chapter 2

1. This sentence in U.S. English connotes that he was getting pleasure from frequently beating his wife. In the village, however, this connotation is not accurate. This sentence glosses as "he beat me often."

2. Maya frequently use "maybe" even if they are certain. In fact, it sometimes signals great certainty, but an uncomfortable topic. Maya also use it to express what someone else thinks.

3. He got married again. "Next wife" or "next lady" sometimes refers to adulterous relationships.

4. Women involved in the women's groups make embroidery for tourists. A common pattern they use features the Mayan day names. I met no one who knew the traditional meaning of these day names. Most were only interested in whether or not tourists would buy them.

5. Risa's mother and sisters frequently asked about birth control. Her oldest sister is convinced that Juanita, a woman who died during my stay in the village, died from taking birth control pills. No other family discussed birth control with me nearly as much as this family.

6. Evangelista, like many other Maya in the village, speaks Creole like someone from town, rather than someone from the villages. I have written her words to reflect her perfect Creole accent.

7. A *p'ik* is a long traditional skirt with lace, usually worn only by old ladies. Younger women, in their forties, might wear a *p'ik* for special occasions. Evangelista is rather young for wearing a *p'ik*.

8. A *camesa* is a traditional peasant-style blouse made of white cotton. Deco-

rative embroidery adorns the neckline and sleeves. Some of the designs I saw in the village during the 1990s are the same designs Thompson catalogues in his 1938 monograph based on fieldwork he did in southern Belize in 1927.

9. Many Maya use the English word "grandmother" to mean "godmother." Francesca is the second wife of Risa's grandfather. The word here means godmother.

10. While not speaking for someone else, Maya try hard to recall exactly what was said. Maya are concerned about representing events as truthfully as possible; anything else can be said to be a lie.

11. Leaving one's husband is not exactly a divorce. She would still be tied to him until he died. Only then would she be able to marry again. Before then, however, she could possibly live with someone else.

12. The next husband here would be someone willing to live with her without being officially married. He would not be bound to her family by mutual respect.

Chapter 3

1. Although we are not married, I began calling Michael my "husband" while doing community organizing on Buffalo's east side, a predominantly African American ghetto. I continued to use the title in Belize, where people always asked if I was married.

2. Orange Walk is the capital of the northern district of the same name. It is less than two hundred miles away from the village, but a twelve-hour bus trip, and a completely different world.

3. "Likes" should not be read as enjoyment, rather as a tendency of action. This is a common phrase in Mayan use of Creole. It should read, Justina is often rough with this baby.

4. For information concerning Pomona see Mark Moberg's (1992) *Citrus, Strategy and Class.*

5. Although no one would directly confirm it, I take "talking" here to mean "having sex," as in the British "criminal conversation."

6. Francesca is saying that Justina wanted the sex that resulted in the baby, and so is responsible.

7. I began my stay in the village renting a cement house, but moved a few months later into a small thatch-roofed house. The rent was much less, but the house required more maintenance.

8. The Social Department is a division of the national government of Belize, like our Department of Welfare.

9. "Used to" does not just connote familiarity in the village but love as well (see Chapter 6: Traveling Spirits).

10. Maya often speak about death, especially murder. Murder is the ultimate

action against another person. There is no doubt in Justina's mind that Martino could kill her, and that he would clearly be to blame. The Mayan sense of self-responsibility would render impossible a self-defense plea, or a "she drove me to it" excuse. Justina is indicating this here. This idea is discussed more in Chapter 6: Traveling Spirits.

11. In the village, people, especially children, can die of spirit loss. The most common event causing loss of spirit for children is to fall in the river. Women can also lose spirit when frightened. The cure sometimes entails burning hair from the person who scared you and praying. This type of spirit loss is like *susto*, spirit loss caused by fear. I discuss another type of spirit loss, one caused by ghosts calling the spirit away, in Chapter 6.

12. Ma, or Erasma, is one of my closest friends in the village. She is Felicia's mother; see Chapter 4.

13. The tension may be the result of an avoidance relationship between young men and women of marriageable age. Andres and Justina however, seem to also be in some kind of competition.

14. One of the cayes off the coast of Belize City. It is quickly becoming a popular tourist spot (Sutherland 1998, 1986).

15. The district in southern Belize where Pomona is located. Dangriga, the capital of that district, is also called Stann Creek.

16. Immigrant Mennonites have brought Western farming techniques, livestock, and machinery to Belize. They dominate the market in the feed and medicines needed to care for such livestock.

17. I use the terms "wife" and "husband" as shorthand, to indicate that they are involved in a relationship. The cycle of violence described here need not be limited to those who are legally married, or to heterosexuals.

18. I use Rosenbaum's word, in quotations, since the reconciliation may, in some ways, be coercive. Reconciliation connotes a mutually satisfying agreement, which as Walker suggests may only be temporary.

19. Deborah Crooks has studied Maya nutrition and school achievement in southern Belize. Some of her findings can be found in *American Anthropologist* 99(3):586–601. She is also one of the graduate-school companions who appear in the Introduction of this work.

20. Eber (1995) cites MacAndrew and Edgerton (1969) as providing evidence that drunks act differently across cultures. For Maya in the village, violence is part of drunken behavior and is the reason most women fear drunks. It is, however, by no means the only behavior common to Maya who drink. Sadness and crying are also common, perhaps more common than violence.

21. I use the word "traditional" here to suggest that it is a social trait within Mayan society. I do not know how long the trait has been a part of Mayan life.

Chapter 4

1. The government began a literacy program during my stay in the village. Intended for both men and women, the literacy program was unable to serve men's needs. Men, due to their schedule of work outside the village, could only take classes at night, a time most Maya feel people should stay at home. Women's classes, however, were fairly well attended. Since Erasma could read and write pretty well, she worked as an assistant teacher. She also took classes to improve her literacy skills.

2. Maya choose *comadres* and *compadres,* to serve as co-parents to one of their children. It is a great sign of respect to ask someone to act as a co-parent.

3. Although traditionally Garifuna, Punta Rock, an electrified version of the traditional sound, is the national music of Belize.

4. Belize Defense Force, the army.

5. "Tea" in Belize means dinner.

6. Belize annually holds a series of festivals, one in each district capital. They feature parades, ethnic dances, food, gaming, and craft sales, as well as speeches by local officials.

7. Guatemala is just a few towns down the road from Pueblo Viejo, maybe seven miles.

8. *Obeah* is the Garifuna word for the work that a bush doctor does. Maya use it to refer to what anthropologists call "witchcraft."

Chapter 5

1. This scene happens after Francesca and I have returned from Orange Walk to find Martino had beaten Justina badly. Justina temporarily left Martino at that time.

2. Apolonia Cal is a pseudonym.

Chapter 6

1. *Comadres* are bound to children and their parents through *tsik*. In fact, *tsik* greetings between *comadres* and *compadres* are the most demonstrative (Danziger 1991:111, 217). However, a *comadre*'s position is more symbolic and supplementary than real and substantial. She offers small gifts and advice about life, but almost never takes in a child whose parents have died (Danziger 1991:112).

Epilogue

1. There is a rumor among Maya in Guatemala that white tourists kidnap Mayan babies, then sell the babies to people who kill them and render the fat and

use it to grease their machines. During the summer of 1993, several Maya stoned an American tourist who was admiring a small child. She was severely injured. The American government issued a travel advisory warning those planning to go to Guatemala to avoid children and to stay out of rural areas.

2. The narrator of ethnographic narratives need not be the fieldworker/ethnographer. For example, John O. Stewart (1988) published a set of excellent ethnographic narratives. While many are in the first-person singular, he narrates only one.

Likewise, narrative ethnography need not be closely based on real events. Elsie Clews Parsons' (1922) edited volume contains several ethnographic narratives. The authors fabricated most of the events they describe, yet the stories are ethnographically accurate.

3. Ironically, it might also make them a little more "scientific." Standard ethnographies often obscure the ways ethnographers come to know what they present as knowledge. The narratives in this book let readers know how I learned about Mayan domestic violence, how I responded to events in the field, and how people responded to me. Such knowledge can help readers evaluate my analysis.

Glossary

Pronunciation

Mayan vowels are pronounced phonetically as in Spanish:
"a" as in "father"
"e" as in "bait"
"i" as in "beet"
"o" as in "owe"
"u" as in "cute"
Double vowels such as "aa" symbolize the lengthened sound of the same
  vowel.

"tz" is pronounced as the last letters of "lets."
"j" is pronounced as "h" in hat.
"x" is pronounced as "sh" in ship.
" ' " is a glottal stop, indicating a sharp break between sounds.

Maya Mopan words are usually stressed on the last syllable.
The words in quotations are literal translations.

Names and Terms

alcalde (Spanish/Maya Mopan) the indigenous political leader of a village
banco (Spanish/Maya Mopan) "bench"; a small low seat carved from a
  segment of log cut lengthwise
bel in ka (Maya Mopan) "I am going"; good-bye

bel in ka ti po (Maya Mopan) "I am going to wash"

bi ki lech (Maya Mopan) How are you?

bin ka (Maya Mopan) "I'm going"; good-bye

boticex (Maya Mopan) thank you

busting (English/Maya Mopan) processing cacao or pounding hulls off rice kernels

cacao a tree or its seed pods used for making chocolate

caldo (Spanish/Maya Mopan) soup

camesa (Spanish/Maya Mopan) a traditional peasant-style blouse made of white cloth with a cross-stitch embroidered neckline and cuffs

Caribbean a Belizean brand of rum

chicarone (Spanish/Maya Mopan) deep-fried pig skin

chicha (Maya Mopan) a fermented corn drink; hard

chicha pul (Maya Mopan) "hard head"; stupid

Cobaneros (Spanish) people from Coban; (Maya Mopan) traveling salesmen usually from Guatemala

comadre (Spanish/Maya Mopan) a woman whom parents ask to morally guide their child, a "co-mother"

comal (Spanish/Maya Mopan) a grill used for making tortillas

compadre (Spanish/Maya Mopan) a man whom parents ask to morally guide their child, a "co-father"

culantro (Maya Mopan) cilantro, an herb

deyoos (Maya Mopan) hello

fu she (Creole) "for she"; hers

Garifuna the descendants of Africans aboard a slave ship marooned on St. Vincent Island and the native Arawak peoples

gibnut paca, a large rain forest rodent found throughout Central America

grandmother Maya often use this for "godmother" or *comadre*

gringo (gringa) Maya occasionally use this as a derogatory word to refer to people of Anglo-Saxon descent

in the bush (Creole) "pach kut," outside of a village, anywhere in the Toledo District

ix (Maya Mopan) "Miss"; a woman's title

ix mooch (Maya Mopan) "frog"; (Maya Mopan slang) vagina

jippyjoppa older, tough, fibrous shoots of the ku'la plant that have been boiled and dried in the sun, used to make baskets.

kichpan (Maya Mopan) beautiful, good, well-crafted

kichpan ok'ut (Maya Mopan) "good dancing"; you dance well

kichpan t'an (Maya Mopan) "beautiful speech"; formal, ritualized speech

knock (Creole) to punch, to slap hard

kuku (Maya Mopan) cacao

ku'la (Maya Mopan) the tender shoot of a rain forest plant, it tastes like a mushroom

ma (Maya Mopan) no

ma'buoy (Maya Mopan) a bright magenta pod; the bright orange pulpy matter inside is used for making soup

ma in weile (Maya Mopan) "I don't know"

mano and metate (Spanish) a two-piece tool for grinding corn and other foods

masa ground cooked corn for making tortillas and tamales

mash it down (Creole) crush it

min ka ti (Maya Mopan) "I don't like," "I don't want"

mine weile/mine weil (Maya Mopan) "I don't know"

na'chiin (Maya Mopan) grandmother; an old woman

nene (Maya Mopan) a baby

next lady/next man (Creole) a second spouse, either adulterous or a second spouse in serial monogamy

o ken (Maya Mopan) "come in"

o ken tel a banco (Maya Mopan) "come in, here is a seat"

obeah (Garifuna) the work a "bush doctor" does; manipulation of spiritual forces

pach kut (Maya Mopan) "outside the fence"; outside of the village

peccary a large animal closely related to pigs

pickney (Creole) children

p'ik (Maya Mopan) a traditional skirt decorated with lace, now worn mostly by women over sixty

potch (Maya Mopan) a meatless tamale

romero (Spanish/Maya Mopan) rosemary

shik (Maya Mopan) scat!, go away

shillings Belizean twenty-five-cent piece, approximately twelve U.S. cents

Spanish (Creole) mestizo; a Spanish-speaking descendant of Spanish colonists and native peoples; someone whose cultural origins are among nonindigenous non-African Central Americans

suk (Maya Mopan) white, a derogatory term for white people

sweet it up (Creole) to make up amorously

sweet soap (Creole) soap for bathing

ts'ah tsik (Maya Mopan) a ceremony where certain people show respect for one another often through the use of ritualized speech

tsik (Maya Mopan) respect

tumpline a sling which straps around your forehead and hangs down your back for carrying babies or anything heavy (harvest)

tzimin (Maya Mopan) horse

ve'cham   (Maya Mopan) husband

wa   (Mayan Mopan) tortilla; a round, unleavened bread, usually made of corn

watac a haa   (Maya Mopan) "here comes the rain"

watac a wix   (Maya Mopan) "here comes the urine"

yok'ol kab   (Maya Mopan) "outside the house"; the men's world

References Cited

Alcoff, Linda
1988   Cultural Feminism Versus Post-Modernism: The Identity Crisis in
            Feminist Theory. *Signs: Journal of Women in Culture and Society*
            13(7):405–436.
Alvarez, Sonia
1994   The (Trans)formations of Feminism(s) and Gender Politics in De-
            mocratizing Brazil. In *The Women's Movement in Latin America:
            Participation and Democracy*, 2d ed., ed. Jane S. Jaquette. Boulder,
            Colo.: Westview Press.
1990   *Engendering Democracy in Brazil: Women's Movements in Transi-
            tion Politics*. Princeton, N.J.: Princeton University Press.
(AAA) American Anthropological Association
1973   *Professional Ethics: Statements and Procedures of the American An-
            thropological Association*. Washington, D.C.: American Anthropo-
            logical Association.
Barry, Tom
1989   *Belize: A Country Guide*. Albuquerque, N.M.: Inter-Hemispheric
            Education Resource Center.
Behar, Ruth
1993   *Translated Woman: Crossing the Border with Esparanza's Story*.
            Boston: Beacon Press.
Behar, Ruth, and Deborah A. Gordon
1995   *Women Writing Culture*. Berkeley, Calif.: University of California
            Press.
Belize Ministry of Education
1997   *Education Statistics Digest, 1994/1995*. Belmopan, Belize: Ministry
            of Education.

Berk, Richard, Sarah Berk, Donileen Loseke, and David Rauma
1983   Mutual Combat and Other Family Violence Myths. In *The Dark Side of Families: Current Family Violence Research,* ed. D. Finkelhor. Beverly Hills, Calif.: Sage.

Berkley, Curtis
1994   *Maya Land Rights in Belize and the History of Indian Reservations.* Washington, D.C.: Indian Law Resource Center.

Beyene, Y.
1989   *From Menarche to Menopause: Reproductive Lives of Peasant Women in Two Cultures.* Albany, N.Y.: State University of New York Press.

Bible
1970   The Gospel According to Matthew. The New English Bible. Oxford University Press.

Bolland, O. Nigel
1988   *Colonialism and Resistance in Belize: Essays in Historical Sociology.* Benque Viejo del Carmen, Belize: Cubola Productions.

Bowen, Elenore [Laura Bohannan]
1954   *Return to Laughter: An Anthropological Novel.* Garden City, N.Y.: Anchor Books.

Bowker, Lee
1983   *Beating Wife Beating.* Lexington, Mass.: Lexington Books.

Brass, Paul R.
1997   *Theft of an Idol: Text and Context in the Representation of Collective Violence.* Princeton, N.J.: Princeton University Press.

Brown, Judith
1992   Introduction: Definitions, Assumptions, Themes and Issues. In *Sanctions and Sanctuary: Cultural Perspectives on the Beating of Wives,* ed. D. Counts, J. Brown, and J. Campbell. Boulder, Colo.: Westview Press.

Brown, Karen McCarthy
1991   *Mama Lola: A Vodou Priestess in Brooklyn.* Berkeley, Calif.: University of California Press.

Browne, Angela
1987   *Battered Women Who Kill.* New York: Free Press.

Bunzel, Ruth
1967   *Chichicastenango.* Seattle, Wash.: University of Washington Press.

Burgos-Debray, Elisabeth, ed.
1984   *I . . . Rigoberta Menchu: An Indian Woman in Guatemala.* London: Verso.

Campbell, Jacquelyn C.
1992   Wife-Battering: Cultural Contexts vs. Western Social Sciences. In

Sanctions and Sanctuary: Cultural Perspectives on the Beating of Wives, ed. D. Counts, J. Brown, and J. Campbell. Boulder, Colo.: Westview Press.

1985   The Beating of Wives: A Cross-Cultural Perspective. *Victimology* 10:174–185.

Campbell, J. K.

1964   *Honor, Family and Patronage.* Oxford: Clarendon.

Central Statistics Office

1990   *Abstract of Statistics 1990.* Belmopan, Belize: Ministry of Economic Development.

Chez, R. A.

1988   Women Battering. *American Journal of Obstetrics and Gynecology* 158(1):1–4.

Chez, R. A., and R. F. Jones III

1995   The Battered Woman. *American Journal of Obstetrics and Gynecology.* 173(3, part 1):677–679.

Ch'oc, Gregory

1996   Land, Value and Economic Development in Toledo: A Mayan Perspective. [http://www.belize.com/toledo/choc1.html]

Clifford, James

1988   *The Predicament of Culture: Twentieth-Century Ethnography, Literature and Art.* Cambridge, Mass.: Harvard University Press.

1986   Partial Truths. In *Writing Culture: The Poetics and Politics of Ethnography,* ed. Clifford and Marcus. Berkeley, Calif.: University of California Press.

Clifford, James, and George E. Marcus, eds.

1986   *Writing Culture: The Poetics and Politics of Ethnography.* Berkeley, Calif.: University of California Press.

Cosminsky, Sheila

1977a   The Impact of Methods of the Analysis of Illness Concepts in a Guatemalan Community. *Social Science and Medicine* 11:325–332.

1977b   Childbirth and Midwifery on a Guatemalan Finca. *Medical Anthropology* 1(3):69–103.

Cosminsky, Sheila, and Mary Scrimshaw

1980   Medical Pluralism on a Guatemalan Plantation. *Social Science and Medicine* 14B(4):267–278.

Counts, Dorothy

1992   Preface. In *Sanctions and Sanctuary,* ed. D. Counts, J. Brown, and J. Campbell. Boulder, Colo.: Westview Press.

Counts, Dorothy, Judith Brown, and Jacquelyn Campbell

1992   *Sanctions and Sanctuary: Cultural Perspectives on the Beating of Wives.* Boulder, Colo.: Westview Press.

Crapanzano, Vincent
1980   *Tuhami: Portrait of a Moroccan.* Chicago: University of Chicago Press.

Crooks, Deborah
1997   Biocultural Factors in School Achievement for Mopan Children in Belize. *American Anthropologist* 99(3):586–601.
1993   Personal communication with author.
1992   "Make They Find It Easier": A Biocultural Study of Growth and School Achievement For Mayan Children in Belize. Ph.D. diss., State University of New York at Buffalo.

Daly, Mary
1979   *Gyn/Ecology: The Metaethics of Radical Feminism.* Boston: Beacon Press.

Daniel, E. Valentine
1996   *Charred Lullabies: Chapters in the Anthropology of Violence.* Princeton, N.J.: Princeton University Press.

Danziger, Eve
1991   Semantics on the Edge: Language as a Cultural Experience in the Acquisition of Social Identity Among the Mopan Maya. Ph.D. diss., University of Pennsylvania.

Davidson, Terry
1978   *Conjugal Crime: Understanding and Changing the Wifebeating Problem.* New York: Hawthorn Books.

Davis, Henry
1997   Children Worse Off Here Than in Most Large Cities. *Buffalo News,* February 19, 1997. Sec. A, p. 1.

Deed, Martha L.
1991   Behind Closed Doors: The Secretive Sin of Domestic Violence. *Buffalo: Magazine of the Buffalo News,* November 3, 1991, pp. 6–13.

Dentan, Robert K.
1999   Untransfiguring Death: A Case Study of Rape, Drunkenness, Development and Homicide in an Apprehensive Void. *Review of Indonesian and Malaysian Affairs* 33(1):17–65.
1998   Demons: A Dilemma in the Depiction of Violence. Paper presented at Oral Historian Association annual meetings, October, Buffalo, N.Y.
1997a   "It Didn't Matter Any More What the Wailing Sounded Like": A Dilemma in the Depiction of Violence. *ACTIVE VOICES: The Online Journal of Cultural Survival* 1(2):1–4 [http://www.cs.org/AVoices/articles/LevelFour-Dentan]
1997b   The Lineaments of Ungratified Desire: How Semai Construe "Violence." Manuscript.

1995 Bad Day at Bukit Pekan. *American Anthropologist* 97(2):225–250.

Dobash, R. P., and R. E. Dobash

1992 *Women, Violence, and Social Change.* London: Routledge.

1979[1983] *Violence Against Wives: A Case Against the Patriarchy.* New York: Free Press.

Douglas, Mary

1966 *Purity and Danger.* London: Routledge & Kegan Paul.

DuBois, E., G. Kelly, E. Kennedy, C. Korsmeyer, and L. Robinson

1985 *Feminist Scholarship: Kindling in the Grove of Academe.* Urbana, Ill.: University of Illinois Press.

Dumont, Jean-Paul

1978 *The Headman and I.* Austin, Tex.: University of Texas Press.

Eber, Christine

1998 Personal communication with author.

1995 *Women and Alcohol in a Highland Maya Town: Water of Hope, Water of Sorrow.* Austin, Tex.: University of Texas Press.

Eber, Christine, and Brenda Rosenbaum

1993 "That We May Serve Beneath Your Hands and Feet": Women Weavers in Highland Chiapas, Mexico. In *Crafts in the World Market,* ed. June Nash. Albany, N.Y.: State University of New York Press.

Ellis, Cynthia

1997 Women's Development Projects in Rural Belize. Lecture November 18 at State University of New York at Buffalo.

Elmendorf, Mary Lindsay

1972 *The Mayan Woman and Change.* CIDOC Cuaderno no. 81. Cuernavaca, Mexico: Centro Intercultural de Documentación.

Erchack, Gerald

1994 Family Violence. In *Research Frontiers in Anthropology,* ed. Carol Ember and Melvin Ember. Englewood Cliffs, N.J.:Prentice-Hall.

1984 Cultural Anthropology and Wife Abuse. *Current Anthropology* 25: 331–332.

Flax, Jane

1987 Postmodernism and Gender Relations in Feminist Theory. *Signs: Journal of Women in Culture and Society* 12(3):621–643.

Flint, M.

1975 The Menopause: Reward or Punishment? *Psychosomatics* 16:161–163.

Frost, Robert

1916 The Vanishing Red. In *Mountain Interlude,* 74–75. New York: Henry Holt.

Galanti, Geri-Ann
1997   Writing Anthropology. *Anthropology Newsletter* 38(6):41.
Gallin, Rita S.
1992   Wife-Abuse in the Context of Development and Change. In *Sanctions and Sanctuary: Cultural Perspectives on the Beating of Wives,* ed. D. Counts, J. Brown, and J. Campbell. Boulder, Colo.: Westview Press.
Geertz, Clifford
1988   *Works and Lives: The Anthropologist as Author.* Stanford, Calif.: Stanford University Press.
Gelles, Richard J.
1983   Violence in the Family: A Review of Research in the Seventies. In *Family Studies Review Book,* vol. 1, ed. D. Olson and B. Miller. Beverly Hills, Calif.: Sage.
1983   An Exchange/Social Theory. In *The Dark Side of Families,* ed. D. Finkelhor, R. Gelles, and M. Straus. Beverly Hills, Calif.: Sage.
1976[1972]   *The Violent Home: A Study of Physical Aggression Between Husbands and Wives.* Beverly Hills, Calif.: Sage.
Gelles, Richard J., and Claire Pedrick-Cornell
1990   *Intimate Violence in Families.* Newbury Park, Calif.: Sage.
1983   *International Perspectives on Family Violence.* Lexington, Mass.: Lexington Books.
Gelles, Richard J., and Murray A. Straus
1988   *Intimate Violence.* New York: Simon and Schuster.
Gondolf, E. W.
1988   *Battered Women as Survivors.* Lexington, Mass.: Lexington Books.
Gonzales, Gaspar Pedro
1995   *A Mayan Life.* Rancho Palos Verdes, Calif.: Yax Te' Press.
Gould, W. T. S.
1993   *People and Education in the Third World.* Essex, England: Longman Scientific & Technical.
Greany, G. D.
1984   Is She a Battered Woman? A Guide for Emergency Response. *American Journal of Nursing* 84(6):724–727.
Gregory, James
1987   Men, Women and Modernization in a Maya Community. *Belizean Studies* 15(3):3–31.
1984   *The Mopan: Culture and Ethnicity in a Changing Belizean Community.* University of Missouri Monographs in Anthropology no. 7. Columbia, Mo.: Museum of Anthropology, Missouri University.
1975   Image of the Limited Good, or Expectation of Reciprocity? *Current Anthropology* 16(1):73–92.

1972   Pioneers on a Cultural Frontier: The Mopan Maya of British Honduras. Ph.D. diss., University of Pittsburgh.

Greider, William

1997   *One World, Ready or Not: The Manic Logic of Global Capitalism.* New York: Touchstone Books.

Griffen, J.

1982   Cultural Models for Coping With Menopause. In *Changing Perspectives on Menopause,* ed. S. Voda, M. Dinnerstein, and S. O'Donnell, 248–262. Austin, Tex.: University of Texas Press.

1977   A Cross-Cultural Investigation of Behavioral Changes at Menopause. *A Social Science Journal* 14(2):49–55.

Guiteras-Holmes, C.

1961   *Perils of the Soul.* New York: Free Press of Glencoe.

Habermas, Jurgen

1975   *Legitimation Crisis,* trans. Thomas McCarthy. Boston: Beacon Press.

Harding, Sandra

1986   *The Science Question in Feminism.* Ithaca, N.Y.: Cornell University Press.

Hastrup, Kirsten

1990   The Ethnographic Present: A Reinvention. *Cultural Anthropology* 5(1):45–61.

Haug, Daniel B.

1995   A Geographic Perspective of Cultural Demographics in Punta Gorda, Belize. Unpublished manuscript.

Hegland, Mary E.

1992   Wife Abuse and the Political System: A Middle Eastern Case Study. In *Sanctions and Sanctuary: Cultural Perspectives on the Beating of Wives,* ed. D. Counts, J. Brown and J. Campbell. Boulder, Colo.: Westview Press.

Hernández Castillo, Rosalia Aida

1997   Between Hope and Adversity: The Struggle of Organized Women in Chiapas Since the Zapatista Uprising. *Journal of Latin American Anthropology* 3(1):102–120.

Hoff, Lee Ann

1990   *Battered Women as Survivors.* London: Routledge.

Hotaling, Gerald, and Murray Straus, eds.

1980   *The Social Causes of Husband-Wife Violence.* Minneapolis, Minn.: University of Minnesota Press.

(IWGIA) International Work Group for Indigenous Affairs

1986   Belize: The Toledo Maya Homeland: A Proposal by the Toledo Maya Cultural Council. *IWGIA Newsletter* 46:17–20.

Iyer, Pico
1989   *Video Night in Kathmandu and Other Reports from the Not-So-Far-East*. New York: Vintage Books.
Jaquette, Jane S.
1994   *The Women's Movement in Latin America: Participation and Democracy,* 2d ed. Boulder, Colo.: Westview Press.
Johnson, Robert, and Camille Moreno
1994   *Belize Report for the World Conference On Women (Beijing 1995): Action for Equality, Development and Peace.* Belmopan, Belize: Ministry of Human Resources, Youth, Women, and Culture.
Keil, Charles
1966   *Urban Blues*. Chicago: University of Chicago Press.
Kerns, Virginia
1992   Preventing Violence Against Women: A Central American Case. In *Sanctions and Sanctuary: Cultural Perspectives on the Beating of Wives,* ed. D. Counts, J. Brown, and J. Campbell. Boulder, Colo.: Westview Press.
Kluckhohn, Clyde
1945   The Personal Document in Anthropological Science. In *The Use of Personal Documents in History, Anthropology and Sociology,* edited by Louis Gottschalk, Clyde Kluckhohn, and Robert Angell. New York: Social Science Research Council.
Kroeber, A. L.
1922   Introduction. In *American Indian Life by Several of Its Students,* ed. Elsie Clews Parsons. New York: Viking Press.
Kuhn, Thomas
1962   *The Structure of Scientific Revolutions*. Chicago: Chicago University Press.
Kurz, Demie
1989   Social Science Perspectives on Wife Abuse: Current Debates and Future Directions. *Gender and Society* 3(4):489–505.
1987   Responses to Battered Women: Resistance to Medicalization. *Social Problems* 34:501–513.
Landesberg, Alison
1997   America, the Holocaust, and the Mass Culture Memory: Toward a Radical Politics of Empathy. *New German Critique* no. 71 (Spring-Summer):63–68.
Lewis, Blane D.
1994   *A Poverty Profile For Belize: Final Report*. Belmopan, Belize: USAID/Belize and Central Statistics Office, Belize.
Lewis, Oscar
1959   *Five Families*. New York: Basic Books.

Lévi-Strauss, Claude
1969   *The Raw and the Cooked,* trans. John and Doreen Weightmann. New York: Harper & Row.

Levinson, David
1989   *Family Violence in Cross-Cultural Perspective.* Newbury Park, Calif.: Sage.

Lyotard, Jean-Francois
1988   *The Post-Modern Condition: A Report on Knowledge,* trans. Geoff Bennington and Brian Massumi. Minneapolis, Minn.: University of Minnesota Press.

MacAndrew, Craig, and Robert B. Edgerton
1969   *Drunken Comportment: A Social Explanation.* Chicago: Aldine Publishing Company.

Marcus, George, and Michael Fischer
1986   *Anthropology As Cultural Critique: An Experimental Moment in the Human Sciences.* Chicago: University of Chicago Press.

Marcus, George, and Dick Cushman
1982   Ethnographies As Texts. *Annual Review of Anthropology* 11:25–69.

Mathews, Holly H.
1985   "We Are Mayordomo": A Reinterpretation of Women's Roles in the Mexican Cargo System. *American Ethnologist* 17:285–301.

Maynard, Eileen
1963   Guatemalan Women: Life Under Two Types of Patriarchy. In *Many Sisters,* ed. C. Matthiason. New York: Free Press.

McDowell, Nancy
1992   Household Violence in a Yuat River Village. In *Sanctions and Sanctuary: Cultural Perspectives on the Beating of Wives,* ed. D.Counts, J. Brown, and J. Campbell. Boulder, Colo.: Westview Press.

McLeer, Susan, and Rebecca Anwar
1989   A Study of Battered Women Presenting in an Emergency Department. *American Journal of Public Health* 79:65–66.

Medina, Laurie
1997   Defining Difference, Forging Unity: The Co-Construction of Race, Ethnicity and Nation in Belize. *Ethnic and Racial Studies* 20(4):757–780.

Miller, Barbara D.
1992   Wife-Beating in India. In *Sanctions and Sanctuary: Cultural Perspectives on the Beating of Wives,* ed. D. Counts, J. Brown, and J. Campbell. Boulder, Colo.: Westview Press.

Mills, Trudy
1984   Victimization and Self-Esteem: On Equating Husband Abuse and Wife Abuse. *Victimology: An International Journal* 9(2): 254–261.

Moberg, Mark

1992 *Citrus, Strategy and Class: The Politics of Development in Southern Belize.* Iowa City, Ia.: Iowa University Press.

Mohanty, Chandra

1988 Under Western Eyes: Feminist Scholarship and Colonial Discourses. *Feminist Review* 30:61–88.

Mohrmann, Causarina, and Valerie Nelson

1993 *Land and Community Needs Assessment and Forest Production: San Antonio (Toledo) Fieldwork Findings.* Belmopan, Belize: Department of Forestry.

Moore, Henrietta

1988 *Feminism and Anthropology.* Minneapolis, Minn.: University of Minnesota Press.

Moore, Thomas

1996 Does America Have A Soul? *Mother Jones* 21(5):26–33.

Nader, Laura

1990 *Harmony Ideology: Justice and Control in a Zapotec Mountain Village.* Stanford, Calif.: Stanford University Press.

Nash, June, ed.

1993 *Crafts in the World Market: The Impact of Exchange on Middle American Artisans.* Albany, N.Y.: State University of New York Press.

1970 *In the Eyes of the Ancestors: Belief and Behavior in a Maya Community.* New Haven, Conn.: Yale University Press.

Nash, June, and Helen Safa, eds.

1986 *Women and Change in Latin America.* South Hadley, Mass.: Bergin and Garvey.

Oakes, Maude

1969 *Two Crosses of Todos Santos: Survivals of Mayan Religious Ritual.* Princeton, N.J.: Princeton University Press.

Ortner, Sherry

1995 Resistance and the Problem of Ethnographic Refusal. In *Working in The Present,* ed. Richard Fox. Santa Fe, N.M.: School of American Research Press.

Parsons, Elsie Clews

1967[1922] *American Indian Lives.* Lincoln, Neb.: University of Nebraska Press.

Pozas, Ricardo

1962 *Juan the Chamula: An Ethnological Re-creation of the Life of a Mexican Indian,* trans. Lysander Kemp. Berkeley, Calif.: University of California Press.

Rabinow, Paul
1977   *Reflections on Fieldwork in Morocco.* Berkeley, Calif.: University of
            California Press.
Randall, Margaret
1981   *Sandino's Daughters: Testimonies of Nicaraguan Women in Struggle.*
            Vancouver: New Star Books.
Redfield, Robert
1968   *The Folk Culture of the Yucatan.* Chicago: University of Chicago
            Press.
1941   The Treatment of Disease in Dzitas Yucatan. *Contributions to
            American Anthropology and History* 6:49–81.
Redfield, Robert, and Alfonso Villa Rojas
1934   *Chan Kom: A Maya Village.* Chicago: Chicago University Press.
Rosenbaum, Brenda
1993   *With Our Heads Bowed: The Dynamics of Gender in a Maya Com-
            munity.* Albany, N.Y.: Institute for Mesoamerican Studies, State
            University of New York at Albany.
Scheper-Hughes, Nancy
1992   *Death Without Weeping: The Violence of Everyday Life in Brazil.*
            Berkeley, Calif.: University of California Press.
Sexton, James D., trans., ed.
1992   *Mayan Folktales: Folklore from Lake Atitlan, Guatemala.* New
            York: Anchor Books.
Sheffield, Carole
1984   Sexual Terrorism. In *Women: A Feminist Perspective,* ed. Jo Free-
            man. Palo Alto, Calif.: Mayfield Press.
Sheridan, D. J.
1993   The Role of the Battered Woman Specialist. *Journal of Psychosocial
            Nursing and Mental Health Services* 31(11):31–37.
Sheridan, D. J. and J. C. Campbell
1989   Emergency Nursing Interventions with Battered Women. *Journal
            of Emergency Nursing* 15(1):12–17.
Shoman, Assad
1994   *Thirteen Chapters of a History of Belize.* Belize City, Belize: Ange-
            lus Press.
Siverts, Kari
1993   'I did not marry properly': The Meaning of Marriage Payments
            in Southern Mexico. In *Carved Flesh/Cast Selves: Gendered Sym-
            bols and Social Practices,* ed. Vigdis Broch-Due, Ingrid Rudie, and
            Tone Bleie. Providence: Berg.
(SPEAR) Society for the Promotion of Education and Research
1990   *SPEAR Reports 3: Profile of Belize 1989.* Belmopan, Belize: Cubola
            Press.

Stark, Evan, and Anne Flitcraft
1988   Violence Among Intimates: An Epidemiological Review. In *Hand-
              book of Domestic Violence,* ed. van Hasselt, Morrison, Bellack, and
              Hersen. New York: Plenum Press.
Stark, Evan, Anne Flitcraft, and William Frazier
1979   Medicine and Patriarchal Violence: The Social Construction of a
              "Private" Event. *International Journal of Health Services* 98:461–
              491.
Stephen, Lynn
1997   *Women and Social Movements in Latin America: Power from Below.*
              Austin, Tex.: University of Texas Press.
1994   *Hear My Testimony: The Story of Maria Tula, Human Rights Activ-
              ist of El Salvador.* Boston: Westview Press.
Stewart, John O.
1988   *Drinkers, Drummers and Decent Folks: Ethnographic Narratives
              of Village Trinidad.* Albany, N.Y.: State University of New York
              Press.
Straus, Murray, Richard Gelles, and Suzanne Steinmetz
1980   *Behind Closed Doors: Violence and the American Family.* Garden
              City, N.J.: Anchor Books.
Sutherland, Ann
1998   *The Making of Belize: Globalization in the Margins.* Westport,
              Conn.: Bergin & Garvey.
1986   *Caye Caulker: Economic Success in a Belizean Fishing Village.* West-
              view Special Studies in Social, Political and Economic Develop-
              ment. Boulder, Colo.: Westview Press.
Tedlock, Barbara
1992   *Time and the Highland Maya.* Albuquerque, N.M.: University of
              New Mexico Press.
1991   *The Beautiful and the Dangerous: Writings on the Margins of Zuni
              Lives.* New York: Viking.
Tedlock, Dennis, trans.
1985   *Popul Vuh: The Mayan Book of the Dawn of Life.* New York: Simon
              & Schuster.
Thompson, J. Eric
1930   *Ethnology of the Mayas of Southern and Central British Honduras.*
              Field Museum of Natural History, Publication 274, Anthropologi-
              cal Series 17, no. 2. Chicago: Field Museum Press.
U.S. Department of Justice
1984   *Special Report on Family Violence* (April 22).
van Maanen, John
1988   *Tales of the Field: On Ethnographic Writing.* Chicago: University
              of Chicago Press.

Vogt, Evon

1976 *Tortillas for the Gods: A Symbolic Analysis of Zinacanteco Rituals.* Cambridge, Mass.: Harvard University Press.

1969 *Zinacantan: A Maya Community in the Highlands of Chiapas.* Cambridge, Mass.: Belknap Press of Harvard University Press.

Wagley, Charles

1949 *The Social and Religious Life of a Guatemalan Village.* New York: American Anthropological Association.

Walker, Lenore

1979 *The Battered Woman.* New York: Harper and Row.

Warner, Gene

1998 Domestic Violence Taking Deadly Toll. *Buffalo News,* May 24, pp. A-1, A-12.

Watanabe, John M.

1992 *Maya Saints and Souls in a Changing World.* Austin, Tex.: University of Texas Press.

Whyte, Martin K.

1978 *The Status of Women in Preindustrial Societies.* Princeton, N.J.: Princeton University Press.

Wilk, Richard

1991 *Household Ecology: Economic Change and Domestic Life Among the Kekchi Maya of Belize.* Tucson, Ariz.: University of Arizona Press.

Wilk, Richard, and Mac Chapin

1989 Belize: Land Tenure and Ethnicity. *Cultural Survival Quarterly* 13(3):41–45.

Wilson, Carter

1974 *Crazy February: Death and Life in the Mayan Highlands of Mexico.* Berkeley, Calif.: University of California Press.

Wisdom, Charles

1940 *The Chorti Indians of Guatemala.* Chicago: University of Chicago Press.

Wolf, Margery

1992 *A Thrice Told Tale: Feminism, Postmodernism and Ethnographic Responsibility.* Stanford, Calif.: Stanford University Press.

1985 *Revolution Postponed: Women in Contemporary China.* Stanford, Calif.: Stanford University Press.

1975 *Women in Chinese Society.* Stanford, Calif.: Stanford University Press.

Index

Index of Major Characters